See the back of the book for a 1992 update.

"Author Dorothy Whitnah is a wonderful and knowledgable tour guide who manages to combine the best features of a mother, a good natured friend with a touch of Erma Bombeck, and a real pro who knows her territory and is just dying to take you on any of 84 fascinating walks, hikes, strolls and climbs within 70 miles of the Golden Gate bridge."—*San Francisco Chronicle*

IMPORTANT:
EVERYTHING IN THIS BOOK IS SUBJECT TO CHANGE WITHOUT NOTICE

This statement applies especially during weather conditions that are unusual for the Bay Area, such as droughts, floods or snowstorms. Trails, roads and whole parks may be closed; bus service may be suspended or rerouted. When in doubt, *phone ahead* to the park or transit agency. The California Highway Patrol maintains a recorded update of road conditions at (415) 557-3755.

Because fees and prices change frequently—generally upward—this book will not give exact figures for many of them. A "small" fee means $3 or under at the time this book went to press; a "moderate" fee, $10 or under.

As of January 1992 the telephone area code in Alameda and Contra Costa counties is 510. San Francisco, Marin and San Mateo counties retain area code 415.

AN OUTDOOR GUIDE
TO THE
SAN FRANCISCO
BAY AREA

*Exploring with boots, bikes
backpacks, buses
boats, books and BART*

Dorothy L. Whitnah

Wilderness Press

First edition May 1976
Second edition April 1978
Third edition April 1980
Second printing March 1982
Fourth edition April 1984
Second printing May 1987
FIFTH EDITION January 1989
Second printing April 1990
Third printing August 1992

Copyright © 1976, 1978, 1980, 1984, 1989 by Wilderness Press
Cover photos by (scenic) Robert Walker, (flowers) Roger Hawkinson
Maps by Larry Van Dyke and Hugh Dodd
Design by Thomas Winnett
Cover design by Larry Van Dyke
Library of Congress Card Catalog Number 88-40009
International Standard Book Number 0-89997-096-6
Manufactured in the United States of America
Published by Wilderness Press
    2440 Bancroft Way
    Berkeley, CA 94704
    (510) 843-8080
Write for free catalog

Library of Congress Cataloging-in-Publication Data

Whitnah, Dorothy L.
 An outdoor guide to the San Francisco Bay area.

 Includes bibliographies and index.
 1. Hiking--California--San Francisco Bay Area--Guide-
books. 2. Backpacking--California--San Francisco Bay
Area--Guide-books. 3. Outdoor recreation--California--
San Francisco Bay Area--Guide-books. 4. San Francisco
Bay Area (Calif.)--Description and travel--Guide-books.
I. Title.
GV199.42.C22S2698 1989 917.94'6   88-40009
ISBN 0-89997-096-6

Acknowledgments

I am grateful to the following persons for their help and companionship along the way:

Julia and Peter Allen
Robert and Serena Bardell
Richard A. Brown
Gerry and Jerry Cole
D. Steven Corey
Richard H. Dillon
Marjorie Drath
Gaye and Ira Eisenberg
Haskell and Linda Fain
David Forbes
Allan and Mickie Friedman
Gordon and Mary Griffiths
Gale and Marion Herrick
Richard Hilkert
Jane and Wade Hughan
Cecelia Hurwich
Esther and Harlan Kessel

Ann Kelly
Luther and Virginia Linkhart
Rose and Seymour Miller
Alma Oberst
John and Sheila O'Day
Arlen and Clare Philpott
George F. Ritchie
Madeleine S. Rose
Jeannie and Mike Sack
Shirley Sheffield
Ron Sol
Roger and Sarah Swearingen
Louise Teather
Judith Wainwright
Ann and Gregory Whipple
Jane Wilson
Lu Winnett

and my fellow-members of the Mt. Tamalpais History Project (none of whom is responsible for any errors that may have crept into that section):

Lincoln Fairley
Dewey Livingston
Fred Sandrock
Nancy Skinner

and the staff at Wilderness Press:

Barbara Jackson
Noelle Liebrenz
Jeff Schaffer
Larry Van Dyke
and Editor-in-chief Tom Winnett.

Finally, I have received help, information and advice from outing leaders, rangers and other park employees too numerous to mention, but I am nonetheless grateful.

Contents

Introduction

The Bay Area: a year-round outdoor paradise

Open Space

San Francisco is unusually fortunate among metropolitan regions in having an abundance of beautiful, varied and easily accessible outdoor recreational space. This happy situation results partly from chance. For example, the need to store enough water to provide for California's long dry season led municipalities all around the Bay to set aside, years ago, large acreages of watershed land, much of which has become available for hiking and fishing. Furthermore, until the Golden Gate Bridge was completed in 1937, Marin County could be reached from the City only by ferry, and it has retained much of its rural character. Preservation of open space has resulted also partly from design, such as the farsighted actions decades ago of the Marin Conservation League and the founders of the East Bay Regional Park District.

Despite the large-scale slurbanization of the Bay Area counties since World War II, many semiwild areas still exist near San Francisco. In fact, you can go hiking at the end of only an hour's bus ride from the City and find much less evidence of humankind than on some trails in the High Sierra. Many of these areas are likely to be preserved, since the San Francisco regional community has taken the lead in what may prove to be a nationwide—even worldwide—revolt against the doctrine of "development at any price."

People for Open Space, a San Francisco-based land-conservation organization, issued an inventory of Bay Area public lands early in 1987 and concluded that this region had the largest greenbelt of any of the country's major metropolitan centers: more than 700,000 acres of open land. Four park areas account for almost a third of this land: Henry Coe State Park, Point Reyes National Seashore, the Golden Gate National Recreation Area, and the East Bay Regional Park District. The public lands contain 61 species of rare and endangered plants and animals.

1

Climate

The Bay Area's other great recreational blessing is its equable climate, which allows residents to enjoy the outdoors the year around. Newcomers from the East sometimes complain that "California has no seasons." Although most of the state *doesn't* have four dramatically different seasons like, say, New England's, seasonal changes do occur. Basically, the Bay Area's climate consists of two phases, the wet (roughly October–March) and the dry (roughly April–September). Within these phases natural events follow a regular and noticeable progression. If a habitual birdwatcher or fisherman, for example, were placed in a time machine and deposited at chronological random in one of his favorite Bay Area haunts, he could probably guess the date to within a couple of weeks.

Significant climatic differences exist within the region because of its complex topography. Both east and west of the Bay are the Coast Ranges, which run roughly north-northwest and include several subranges, such as the Diablo Range and the Berkeley Hills. As winds come off the ocean moving eastward, they deposit successively less moisture on each range, so that each intermontane valley is a bit drier than the one to its west. Furthermore, the farther inland from the moderating influence of the ocean (and to a lesser extent the Bay), the wider are the temperature fluctuations, both daily and yearly. Hence Mt. Tamalpais is comfortable for hiking nearly all year, whereas Mt. Diablo gets unpleasantly hot and dry in summer.

The Coast Ranges contain one large gap: the Golden Gate. Through this passage flow the offshore winds and, in late spring and summer, San Francisco's celebrated fog. The fog forms when saturated air from far out in the Pacific moves over the colder water off the northern California coast: as the air cools, its moisture condenses. The prevailing westerlies blow the fog inland, and as summer progresses the increasing heat of the Central Valley helps pull it east. An always fascinating experience for hikers is to look down from one of the area's hills while fog penetrates the Golden Gate, first as wispy tendrils, then as a fleecy blanket that may soon cover even the orange tops of the bridge towers.

Because the Bay Area's climate is generally so temperate, occasional divergences from the norm can have startling results. Recently we have experienced some abnormal seasons whose effects will linger for several years.

In the winter of 1972–73 an unusually long freeze damaged and killed many plants that had been brought here from warmer regions, particularly many of the thousands of eucalyptus trees that were introduced from Australia around 1900. Damage was especially noticeable in the East Bay hills, which contain huge groves of eucalyptus. Next, in the winter of 1973–74, an unusually heavy snowfall blanketed much of the Bay Area at elevations above a thousand feet. Many native California trees, especially the broadleaf ones such as tanbark oak and madrone, are not adapted to this kind of weather, and the weight of the piled-up snow brought thousands of trees and many more thousands of branches crashing down.

These winters were followed by two seasons of extreme drought, which caused such severe fire hazard—especially among debris remaining from the preceding winters—that rangers had to close temporarily some of the parks and trails described in this book.

The winters of 1982 and 1983 were the two wettest, stormiest back-to-back winters in recorded California history and caused millions of dollars' worth of damage up and down the state. In the Bay Area, Marin and Santa Cruz counties were especially hard hit. Some roads and trails were closed for months or even years, and some were permanently rerouted.

When reading the route descriptions in this book, remember that even in years without extraordinary weather, trail conditions vary considerably from the wet season to the dry. What is in April a murmuring creek may be a dry stream bed in August and a rushing torrent in January. If I have found, or I suspect, that a particular trail is unpleasantly hot in summer or muddy in winter, I say so; but no one author can hope to anticipate all the effects of the region's varied climate on such diverse terrain.

Even though hiking in most of the Bay Area is possible and pleasant all year, a majority of hikers would probably pick early spring as their favorite season. For this region, T. S. Eliot, who called April the cruelest month, is a much less appropriate guide than Chaucer, who felt it was the ideal time to go on pilgrimages. Then, the creeks are flowing, the wildflowers are blossoming, and for a few weeks the hills and fields are a brilliant green.

You can get a recorded Bay Area weather forecast by phone. Look under "Weather" in the front of your phone book.

Recommended reading

Gilliam, Harold, *Weather of the San Francisco Bay Region.* Berkeley and Los Angeles: University of California Press, 1966.

Geology

The most conspicuous feature of the Bay Area is, of course, the Bay itself. Including its northern extension, San Pablo Bay, it is about 55 miles long and from 3 to 12 miles wide. It is by far the largest harbor on the Pacific Coast and one of the largest in the world. Father Juan Crespi, annalist of the overland expedition that discovered it in 1769, noted, "This port . . . could contain not only all the armadas of our Catholic Monarch but also all those of Europe." Yet despite its impressive size, during more than two centuries several ships of diverse nationalities sailed past it without noticing it. Probably fog hid the mile-wide entrance, the Golden Gate.

Today, two great forces operate within the Bay: the Pacific Ocean and the Sacramento–San Joaquin river system. Twice each day the ocean tide floods in through the Golden Gate and twice ebbs out of it; the volume of water that thus flows through the Gate four times each day averages about 1,250,000 acre feet—total, 5 million acre feet. (An acre-foot of water is the amount that would cover an acre to a depth of one foot.) Meanwhile, fresh water is constantly entering the Bay from the river system. Runoff from the Sierra Nevada drains into the Central Valley to form the two rivers, the Sacramento and the San Joaquin, which join in the Delta just west of Stockton and pass through Carquinez Strait to the Bay. The rivers carry huge quantities of sediment, perhaps 13,800 tons a day, most of which is deposited in the Bay. The hiker on Mt. Tamalpais or Angel Island can often, especially in spring, look down on fascinating, constantly changing water patterns as the visibly muddy river currents encounter the incoming ocean tide.

Sedimentation was even greater a few decades ago: it took the river system about 50 years to purge itself of the debris deposited by hydraulic gold mining that went on in the Sierra from the 1850s until 1884. (In that year angry farmers downstream finally succeeded in getting a court order that virtually halted hydraulic mining.) As a result of continual sedimentation, both natural and man-made, 75% of the Bay, excluding the Golden Gate area, is less than 18 feet deep, and its bottom is more of an ooze than a solid floor. The Army Engineers maintain the main channels at 50 feet; the channel through the Golden Gate, the Bay's deepest, is about 350 feet.

When the Spaniards discovered the Bay in 1769, it covered 700 square miles. Since then—and especially since the gold rush of 1849—extensive filling and diking along the shores have reduced its area to a little over 400 square miles. By the early 1960s continued filling threatened to reduce the Bay to a narrow, polluted, foul-smelling channel. At this point many citizens became alarmed and started a grassroots movement to save the Bay. Their concern resulted in the formation of the Bay Conservation and Development Commission (BCDC), a regional organization that has been remarkably successful in regulating building, filling and other activities along the shore.

The future of the Bay is far from secure, however. Pollution has drastically reduced the populations of salmon, striped bass and Dungeness crab. Developers continue to propose projects that would pave over shoreline and marshland. More ominously, the fate of San Francisco Bay is irrevocably tied to the political water struggles between northern and southern California: the more water that is diverted from the Sacramento and San Joaquin rivers to flow southward, the less will be available to cleanse the Bay.

> Saying that fresh water allowed to run through the Bay to the ocean is wasted makes about as much biological sense as saying that a whale's blood is wasted if it stays in the whale.
> —David Rains Wallace,
> San Francisco *Examiner Image,*
> December 6, 1987.

In recent years public interest in the Bay and concern over its future have produced several parks, wildlife sanctuaries and educational centers along its shores. Among the ones described in this book are China Camp State Park, Point Pinole Regional Shoreline, Coyote Point Museum and Richardson Bay Audubon Center.

A geological feature of the region that is less immediately obvious than the Bay, but vastly more ancient and probably more permanent, is the San Andreas fault zone. This zone ranges from a few feet to over a mile wide. It extends from off Cape Mendocino southeast more than 600 miles to the Salton Sea, where its surface trace disappears beneath recent sediments. Beyond this area, it extends southeast through, and is responsible for, the Gulf of California. In the Bay Area it runs through Tomales and Bolinas bays, in Marin County, and through the San Andreas and Crystal Springs reservoirs, in San Mateo County. Associated with it are two faults in the East Bay, the Calaveras and the Hayward.

Although the San Andreas Fault as we have come to know and love it was established about 30 million years ago, the rest of the Bay Area's topography was still far from having its present shape. Much of the region had become dry land, but the modern Coast Ranges were yet to form. The next 5 million years saw some volcanic activity, which increased greatly in the 10 million years after that and continued until a few million years ago. In the North Bay was formed the 700 square miles of rocks called the Sonoma Volcanics. The East Bay also experienced intermittent volcanic outpourings.

The building of most of the Bay Area's present mountains—by folding, faulting and uplifting of the layers of sedimentary and volcanic rock—occurred mostly in the past 3 million years. To the east, the Sierra Nevada was also undergoing an uplift, which enabled it to intercept much more precipitation and thus increased the amount of water that flowed into the Central Valley. (This water did not yet flow out the Golden Gate, which didn't exist, but instead went through a channel that perhaps emptied into the Russian River, whose mouth was farther south at the time.)

Only 1 million years ago did the Sacramento–San Joaquin river system find its present channel through Carquinez Strait and the Golden Gate—possibly because some movement on a fault in the Coast Ranges obstructed its previous course. At about the same time, the basin that the Bay occupies was slowly formed by the gradual downward warping of a block of the earth's crust lying between the San Andreas and the Hayward faults.

The Pleistocene epoch—the past 2 million years—also witnessed the great ice ages. Geologists have identified several major glacial periods in the Sierra Nevada, averaging about 30,000 years in duration. Although California west of the Sierra was never glaciated, it was profoundly affected by the changes in climate. During a glacial period, as ice accumulates on a continent it locks up water, and therefore sea level drops. At the peak of the ice ages, the ocean at the Golden Gate was as much as 400 feet lower than it is today, and one could have walked on dry land to the Farallon Islands. When the ice melted, sea level rose and water came flooding in through the Golden Gate to fill the Bay; this probably happened after each of the later glacial periods. The last interval between glacial periods—perhaps reaching a peak about 5000 B.C.—established the Bay in the form in which the Spaniards found it.

We have no reason to believe that the ice ages are over and the climate permanently stabilized; we very likely are, in fact, still living in the Pleistocene—despite all those optimistic geologic timetables that say it ended 12,000 years ago! Obviously a change in climate that raised or lowered sea level by even a fraction of the variations that occurred repeatedly during the last several million years would have drastic effects on the Bay Area and its inhabitants.

Organization

Save San Francisco Bay Association
P. O. Box 925
Berkeley 94701; 839-3053; 849-3044
The only organization I know of whose tax-deductible dues remain *one dollar* per year!

Recommended reading

Alt, David D., and Donald W. Hyndman, *Roadside Geology of Northern California*. Missoula: Mountain Press, 1975.

Howard, Arthur D., *Geologic History of Middle California*. Berkeley and Los Angeles: University of California Press, 1979. (California Natural History Guides)

Wahrhaftig, Clyde, *A Streetcar to Subduction, and Other Plate Tectonic Trips by Public Transport in San Francisco*. Rev. ed. Washington, DC: American Geophysical Union, 1984. Even those who consider geology the quintessentially dismal science will find this paperback introduction to the subject well worth its price. Intended for the layperson, it contains a glossary and numerous maps and diagrams, and describes trips to Angel Island, the Marin Headlands and the East Bay, as well as San Francisco.

A prime source of geological information is the California Division of Mines and Geology, 380 Civic Drive, Suite 100, Pleasant Hill 94523 (646-5920). One of its publications that will be of interest to the Bay Area hiker, driver or armchair student is: Bailey, Edgar H., ed. *Geology of Northern California*. San Francisco: 1966. Bulletin #190.

Recommended reading about the Bay

Conradson, Diane R., *Exploring Our Baylands*. 2nd ed. Point Reyes: Coastal Parks Association, 1982.

Gilliam, Harold, *San Francisco Bay*. Garden City, New York: Doubleday, 1957. The definitive history.

Jackson, Ruth A., *All Around the Bay*. San Francisco: Chronicle Books, 1987.

Flora

The Bay Area encompasses a wide variety of plant communities, including one that is found only in northern California, the coast-redwood forest. Being able to identify some of the area's plants may enhance a hiker's enjoyment, but certainly isn't necessary to it. Indeed, many hikers wander happily over the trails for years without learning to distinguish a cattail from a pussy willow.

The most dangerous plant

There is one plant, however, that even the most casual stroller should learn to recognize.

> For in all woods and by every wayside there prospers an abominable shrub or weed, called poison-oak, whose very neighbourhood is venomous to some, and whose actual touch is avoided by the most impervious.
>
> —Robert Louis Stevenson,
> *The Silverado Squatters.*

Poison oak is just as ubiquitous and abominable today as it was when Stevenson described it in 1880. For those who are susceptible, touching the plant, or even touching something else that has touched it—a dog, a knapsack or clothing—is likely to cause redness, blisters and intense itching. The incubation period is about two days.

This sneaky plant takes the form sometimes of a shrub and sometimes of a climbing vine. Its leaves are glossy green in spring and

Poison oak

gorgeous red in late summer and fall. In winter, when the stems are bare, yet still poisonous, it is recognizable by the many short, stiff, tan branchlets, averaging 4" in length and slightly upswept.

Try to avoid poison oak; and if you must walk where it abounds, wear long sleeves and long pants, and throw your clothes in a washing machine as soon as you get home. A time-honored procedure (one mentioned in previous editions of this book) was to wash any exposed skin with hot water and strong laundry soap. However, Dr. William Epstein, a dermatologist at UC San Francisco who is an authority on poison oak, advises using *cold* water and no soap, and rinsing clothes in cold water before washing them. As this book goes to press, two companies are reportedly about to start marketing poison-oak preventives: United Catalyst one called Ivy Block and Interpro, Inc. one called Multi Shield.

Trees

A few trees are so common in the region that one can expect to find some of them on almost any hike. Here they are, with—for the first and last time in this book—their Latin names.

Coast redwood (*Sequoia sempervirens*) This is the tallest and one of the longest-lived trees in the world (further described in the section "Muir Woods").

Douglas fir (*Pseudotsuga Menziesii*) This large conifer, common from California north into British Columbia, is of great importance to the Pacific Coast lumber industry. It may reach a diameter of 10 feet and a height of 300. The cones, which are 1½ to 4" long, are readily distinguishable by their three-pointed bracts protruding conspicuously from beneath the scales.

Bay tree, or California laurel (*Umbellularia californica*) This evergreen also goes under the name of pepper wood and, in Oregon, myrtle; in fact, southern Oregon has a regular tourist industry devoted to fashioning artifacts from "myrtlewood." It ranges from shrub size to a height of 75 feet. The leathery, lance-shaped leaves are notable for the pungent aroma they give off when crushed. They may be used to season food—in moderation.

Buckeye (*Aesculus californica*) This member of the horse-chestnut family is a tree 15 to 40 feet high with a rounded crown. Its bright green, palmately compound leaves, each with 5 to 7 leaflets (usually 5), appear early in spring. In May and June the buckeye produces masses of pinkish-white, candlelike flower stalks that make it one of our showiest native trees. The leaves fall off in summer, leaving the tree looking stark and dead throughout fall and winter.

Madrone, or madroño (*Arbutus Menziesii*) This beautiful evergreen may grow as tall as 125 feet. The most distinctive feature of the madrone is the smooth red or ochre trunk and limbs revealed by the peeling exterior bark. The tree has shiny green leaves. Its abundant red-orange berries attract birds in late fall.

Eucalyptus This is a tall evergreen tree with scimitar-shaped leaves and a distinctive odor. Many species of this Australian native were introduced into California in the late 19th century. The most common one in the Bay Area is *E. globulus,* or blue gum. The great freeze of 1972 appeared to have killed many of these trees in the Berkeley-Oakland hills, and the East Bay Regional Park District began cutting them down so they would not become a fire hazard when dry weather arrived. As it turned out, the eucalyptus proved hardier than expected, and in spring many supposedly dead trees began sprouting brilliant blue-green leaves from the base of their trunks. The combination of dead trees, cut trees and newly reviving trees has given the East Bay hills a rather unkempt appearance.

In February 1986 the National Park Service announced a program of removing the eucalyptus trees from Golden Gate National Recreation Area land in Marin County, on the grounds that: they are a fire hazard, especially where leaves, bark and branches have accumulated on the ground; and they have encroached into native plant communities and in some area replaced native species. This proposal unleashed a fierce controversy, which continues as this book goes to press. A group called POET (Preserve Our Eucalyptus Trees) sprang up to contest the NPS plan. They argued that the eucs provide habitat for native bird and butterfly species; that removing the trees from some areas might cause severe erosion problems; and that tree-eradication schemes ultimately involve using toxic herbicides. One eucalyptus partisan even claimed that they are thought to have existed in North America in prehistoric times, and therefore cannot be considered exotic!

Many residents of West Marin were particularly incensed by the NPS plan to log the century-old trees along Highway 1 north of Dogtown. Marin County supervisors also went on record against widespread logging.

The State Parks Department—using the same arguments as the NPS—planned to cut down many of Angel Island's blue gum trees in September 1987, but at the last minute pressure from the public and POET caused them to postpone this plan indefinitely.

People feel very strongly about eucalyptus trees—both pro and con.

Tanbark oak, or tanoak (*Lithocarpus densiflora*) This ever-green tree, 50 to 150 feet tall, is commonly found in association with the coast redwood. Its gray bark is a source of tannin for the leather industry. The conspicuous parallel veins in the leaves make this tree easy to identify. The tanbark oak is not a true oak, but a genus inter-mediate between the oak and the chestnut. It does, however, pro-duce large, handsome acorns.

Oak (genus *Quercus*) The trees listed above are usually easy to recognize. But distinguishing among the various species of oaks can be difficult—especially when you can't see the acorns. Even the experts have trouble with oaks:

> The genus [*Quercus*] tends to hybridize with ease, and species intergrade with bewildering complexity. For this reason it is often difficult to determine a specimen's exact status, particularly one of the shrubbier forms. They may be dwarfs of generally larger types, examples of true scrub forms, or hybrids of just about any small oaks present in the area.
> —Elna Bakker, *An Island Called California.*

The most common oak in the Bay Area is coast live oak (*Quercus agrifolia*), also called encina or California live oak, a spreading evergreen 20 to 75 feet tall that gave the city of Oakland its name. The leaves, shiny green on both sides but darker on the upper, are often convex and hollylike, and often have tufts of hair on the lower side, in the angles of the midrib and the veins.

Pine (genus *Pinus*) Several species are native to the Bay region, and, like oaks, they are sometimes difficult for the amateur botanist to identify. One of the most commonly found species, the Monterey pine (*Pinus radiata*), is actually native only to a few small areas in and near Monterey and Santa Cruz counties, but it flour-ishes so well in Northern California's mild climate that it has been widely planted as an ornamental and a windbreak. It grows to a height of over 100 feet and has a dense crown that provides good shade.

Chaparral

The term "chaparral" embraces the combination of species of hard-leafed, drought-resistant shrubs that form a mantle over our season-ally hot and dry hills. For many people, the evergreen growth of chaparral is *the* quintessential California plant community. The word comes from the Spanish *chaparro* ("evergreen oak"), and this derivation suggests the similarity that the first explorers noticed to the flora of their homeland. Chaparral plants are especially well adapted to dry summers and wet winters. They are highly flammable, but they regenerate quickly after a fire.

Dense chaparral is virtually impenetrable by man or any other large animal. One of the quickest ways for a hiker to get lost is to strike out cross-country through chaparral as dusk is falling, and then find himself trapped among the thickets, with no clue to how to get back to the trail.

In addition to various species of scrub oak, these are some of the most common plants of the chaparral:

Manzanita (genus *Arctostaphylos*) The Bay Area has many species of these evergreen shrubs. *How* many depends on which botany book you consult. The species range from low creepers to erect shrubs 15 feet tall. Some species sprout from the root crown after a fire; others are killed by fire but seed-sprout after burning. Most species, like the madrone, to which they are related, have dark red bark and stems, and berries that turn red when ripe. The flowers range from white to pink. Their shape—small, narrow-mouthed, upside-down urns—like that of the madrone's flowers, is characteristic of the greater part of the heath, or heather, family, to which both genera belong. Many manzanitas have light-colored leaves, the better to reflect sunlight—an advantage for a plant that needs to conserve moisture.

Ceanothus This is another genus with many species. They range from a prostrate shrub to a small tree as tall as 25 feet. The most common species in the Bay Area is blue blossom (*C. thyrsiflorus*), one of the larger ones. It is popularly called "California lilac"—a designation that is also sometimes applied to any tall ceanothus. In spring, the various species produce abundant clusters of tiny, strong-smelling flowers, from white through blue and purple. These add greatly to the hiker's enjoyment—unless he discovers he's allergic to them.

Chamise (*Adenostoma fasciculatum*) This member of the rose family is extremely common in California chaparral. It is a spreading shrub, 2 to 10 feet high, that frequently forms impenetrable thickets. Its short, linear leaves in fascicles (close, bundlelike clusters) are well suited to conserving water. Although a single one of these shrubs when considered by itself will take no prize for beauty, a dozen-acre mass of them, with thousands of plumes of small cream-white flowers waving in the breeze in May or thereabouts, is something else.

Coastal scrub

Coastal scrub is a plant community sometimes called "soft chaparral" because its shrubs are less stiff than those of the true, or "hard," chaparral. It is extensive in the easternmost Coast Ranges as well as the hills and mountains near the ocean and San Francisco Bay. Its most common constituent is coyote brush, or chaparral broom (*Baccharis pilularis* variety *consanguinea*), a shrub that is almost ubiquitous in northern California, occurring also in the true chaparral as well as in various forest communities. Another familiar name for this shrub is "fuzzy-wuzzy," alluding to the abundant soft, whitish bristles borne by the flowers of the female plants in the fall. (This is one of those species botanists call *dioecious,* meaning that all the flowers on any one plant are of a single sex. In most species, every flower has both stamens, which are male parts, and pistils, which are female parts.)

Wildflowers

One delight of springtime hiking in northern California is the great variety of wildflowers. Even the most myopic hiker usually recognizes, and appreciates, the state flower, California poppy (*Eschscholzia californica*), and the lupine (*Lupinus* spp.), which color hillsides orange and blue. Identifying the less common flowers can be a fascinating hobby. Unfortunately, however, it's a hobby that can irritate hiking companions right out of their skulls if they don't happen to share it. If you find your old buddies avoiding you during wildflower season, consider joining the California Native Plant Society and meeting some fellow enthusiasts.

A reminder: Picking wildflowers is an act of utter barbarism—as well as being illegal.

Recommended reading

Munz, Philip A., and David D. Keck, *A California Flora.* Berkeley: University of California Press, 1973.

This large, heavy, expensive book is the bible of California botanists. Anyone seriously interested in the state's flora will want it for his reference library.

Bakker, Elna S., *An Island Called California: An Ecological Introduction to Its Natural Communities.* 2nd ed. Berkeley: University of California Press, 1984.

Geary, Ida, *The Leaf Book.* Fairfax: Tamal Land Press, 1972. The author specializes in printing directly with plants. This paper-

back, which contains over 350 of her prints, is not only handsome but also useful as a field identification guide.

The Peterson Field Guide Series, published by Houghton Mifflin,
and the Audubon Society Field Guides, published by Knopf, are
extremely useful. The University of California publishes several
paperback books about plants in its California Natural History
Guide series; all are well illustrated, inexpensive and easy to carry.
The University of California Press has also published four paper-
backs on wildflowers by Philip A. Munz. Within each book, he
arranges the flowers by color, which is helpful to beginners.

Fauna

You can't always be sure of finding any particular species of animal
on a hike, because animals (unlike plants) don't stay put and their
appearances are unpredictable. I don't have much luck discovering
the creatures that nature books say one is likely to find in a particular area; on the other hand, while wandering along trails in Alameda
and Marin counties, I've encountered several I didn't expect to
find—e.g., a coatimundi, an ocelot, a margay and a reticulated
python. Needless to say, none of these is native to California.

From time to time throughout this book I mention animals I have
actually seen while hiking on a particular trail. Look for these—and
others. Even if you don't see the animals themselves, you can
usually find evidence of their presence in the form of burrows, nests,
feathers, tracks or scats. Deciphering these clues can make a
fascinating game, especially for children.

The Bay Area does provide four unique and relatively predict-
able animal adventures which are described in this book: overlooking the nesting egrets and herons of Audubon Canyon Ranch;
watching the migration of gray whales from Point Reyes; viewing the
raptors crossing the Golden Gate from Hawk Hill in the Marin
Headlands; and visiting the elephant seals at Año Nuevo.

Mammals

In many parts of the Bay Area it is almost impossible to take any
extended hike, especially in late afternoon, without seeing one or
more black-tailed deer. They will make their presence known by
suddenly fleeing through the underbrush when you unwittingly
approach. To watch these graceful animals race through a forest or
browse on a distant hillside is always a thrill, no matter how many
times you have seen them before.

Other mammals the hiker is likely to meet during daylight hours include gray squirrels, chipmunks, ground squirrels and rabbits. More unusual ones are the tule elk that have been reintroduced to Point Reyes National Seashore, the llamas that are now being used as pack animals in Point Reyes and elsewhere, and the voracious goats that are eating the surplus brush in the East Bay Regional Park District. And in 1987 a rancher in Nicasio brought in two camels to eat thistle and poison oak.

Among nocturnal mammals, the raccoon is probably the most familiar. In fact, you don't even have to go hiking to meet raccoons, because they sometimes turn up raiding garbage cans. The raccoon is a remarkably attractive and intelligent animal, but a nuisance to campers because of its prowess in ferreting out any food that isn't securely locked up. Daylight hikers who never see the animals themselves often notice their tracks near streams and picnic areas.

Nocturnal mammals less frequently seen include gray foxes and bobcats. A few mountain lions—also known as cougars or pumas—probably still inhabit some places in the Bay Area counties. In 1987 the California Department of Fish and Game lifted a 16-year moratorium on hunting mountain lions and issued 190 permits to hunters. A Mountain Lion Coalition mobilized to restore the moratorium, and a San Francisco Superior Court judge ruled that the hunt should not take place until further research was done to determine the actual populations of lions and of deer, their favorite prey.

Mountain lions (like eucalyptus—see above) arouse strong feelings pro and con.

Aquatic mammals include the harbor seal, common in bays, and the California sea lion and Steller's sea lion, common along the coast. How can you distinguish these animals? The harbor seal is 4–5 feet long and is earless. It cannot bring its back flippers up under its body. Sea lions can move their back flippers freely, and therefore can move over land much more easily than seals. Sea lions have external ears. Adult male sea lions are considerably larger than seals. The male California sea lion, which is dark brown, may reach a length of 8 feet. The male Steller's sea lion, which is lighter brown, may reach a length of 10 feet. In both species of sea lion the males are much larger than the females.

Birds

Anyone who's ever picnicked in California has seen and heard the raucous jays: Steller's (blue with crest) and scrub (blue without crest). Probably the most common soaring bird that hikers will notice is the large, black, silent turkey vulture—sometimes called, incorrectly, "buzzard." The next most common one is the red-tailed hawk, whose high-pitched squeal seems at odds with its noble appearance.

Hikers along the beach will inevitably encounter seagulls, as well as a host of other water and shore birds such as snipes, curlews and sandpipers. Cormorants frequent the offshore rocks. Brown pelicans, once a common sight on seashore strolls, have had their ranks reduced by DDT, but appear to be coming back.

The quickest way to become familiar with the region's abundant and varied birdlife is to go on field trips with the Audubon Society, which has several active local chapters (see the Appendix for addresses).

For a recorded message on where to find unusual birds in the Bay Area, phone Audubon's Rare Bird Alert (528-0288).

Recommended reading

Richmond, Jean, *Birding Northern California*. Walnut Creek: Mt. Diablo Audubon Society, 1986.

Reptiles

A rustle along the side of the trail, or a quickly glimpsed movement, usually means that the hiker has startled a small, harmless lizard. Many species are native to the Bay Area. These creatures may come quite close to anyone who sits quietly for a few minutes; they may even scamper over one's boots or knapsack.

Harmless snakes, especially garter snakes, are common. The only poisonous snakes in the area are rattlers. They appear very rarely, generally in warm weather. They want to avoid you as much as you do them, and will try to warn you away by rattling when you get close—a sound you will recognize the first time you hear it. You are unlikely to run into a rattlesnake on the trails in this book, but observe a little caution if you travel cross-country, especially in rocky areas during hot weather: don't reach for ledges you can't see, or skip carelessly through the boulders. If you should get bitten by a rattler—something that happens to about a thousand people per year in the entire United States—don't panic: rattlesnake bites are rarely fatal to human beings. Make your way to the nearest hospital with as little exertion as possible. The fatality rate is somewhat higher for dogs, so if yours gets bitten, take it to a veterinarian immediately.

Recommended reading

Taber, Tom, *Where To See Wildlife in California*. San Mateo: Oak Valley Press, 1983.

The organizations listed in the Recommended Reading for Flora also publish series of guides to Fauna:

The Peterson Field Guide Series, published by Houghton Mifflin;
The Audubon Society Field Guides, published by Knopf;
The California Natural History Guides, published by the University of California.

History

More than any other state of the Union (and most foreign countries), California has been the setting for a mixing, and occasional clashing, of diverse cultures. First the Indians settled here; then the Spanish, Mexicans, Russians and Americans; and, after the gold rush, people from every part of the world. Furthermore, the California mystique has always attracted ambitious, adventurous, strong-minded spirits. Some, like Father Serra, were motivated by religious zeal. Some, like Drake and other explorers from half a dozen countries, were motivated by a mixture of curiosity, patriotism and self-interest. Many more, like the miners and the railroad tycoons, were motivated mainly by dreams of wealth and power. And a few, like Fremont, had motives so complex and ambiguous that historians are still arguing about them.

As you wander around the Bay Area you'll encounter frequent reminders of its adventurous past. Here is a brief chronology of some events that have left their mark on the landscape. (In this chronology the term "California" refers to the territory of the present-day state. Under Spanish and Mexican rule this area was called Alta [Upper] California, as distinguished from Baja [Lower] California.)

40,000 or more years ago	Indians cross the land bridge over the Bering Strait and move south, settling in California.
A.D. 1519–21	Hernan Cortes conquers the Aztec empire, thereby bringing Mexico under Spanish domination.
1542	Juan Rodrigues Cabrillo sails up the coast of California but does not discover San Francisco Bay.
1579	Francis Drake careens his ship, the *Golden Hinde,* somewhere in northern California (probably Drakes Bay) and claims the land for Queen Elizabeth I.
1595	Sebastian Rodrigues Cermeno brings his Manila Galleon into Drakes Bay, where a storm wrecks it; he and his crew make their way back to Mexico in a launch, and they too miss San Francisco Bay.

1602–03	Sebastian Vizcaino sails up the coast of California and names various landmarks; he discovers the bay of Monterey but misses that of San Francisco.
1769	Gaspar de Portola commands an overland expedition from Baja California north to San Diego and subsequently to Monterey and the San Francisco peninsula; a scouting expedition under Jose Ortega discovers San Francisco Bay.
	Father Junipero Serra founds the first California mission, San Diego de Alcala.
1772	Pedro Fages leads an expedition north from Carmel up the east shore of San Francisco Bay as far as Carquinez Strait.
1775	Juan Manuel de Ayala brings the *San Carlos* into San Francisco Bay and surveys it.
1775–76	Juan Bautista de Anza leads a party of colonists overland from Sonora, Mexico, to San Francisco Bay.
1776	Jose Joaquin Moraga establishes the Presidio of San Francisco; Father Francisco Palou dedicates Mission San Francisco de Asis (now generally called Mission Dolores).
1777	The Spanish government establishes the first civil settlement in California, the *pueblo* of San Jose de Guadalupe (now San Jose).
1812	Russians establish a post at Fort Ross for hunting, ranching and trading.
1821	Agustin de Iturbide and his followers overthrow the Spanish rule in Mexico.
1825	California officially becomes a province of the new Republic of Mexico.
1833	The Mexican government orders the secularization of the California missions.
1841	The Russians leave Fort Ross.
	The Mexican governor of California awards John A. Sutter, a Swiss immigrant, the New Helvetia grant of nearly 50,000 acres in the area of present-day Sacramento.
	The first group of American overland immigrants, the Bartleson-Bidwell Party, reaches California.
1843–44	John Charles Fremont of the US Topographical Engineers explores Oregon and California and publishes an enthusiastic report of these regions.
1846	War breaks out between the United States and Mexico. American settlers in Sonoma, encouraged by Fremont, proclaim California the Bear Flag Republic and imprison the local Mexican officials. Commodore John D. Sloat raises the American flag at Monterey and declares California annexed to the United States.
1847	After a few skirmishes with the Mexicans, United States forces take over all of California.
1848	James Marshall discovers gold at Sutter's sawmill on the American River.
	The Mexican War is concluded by the Treaty of Guadalupe Hidalgo, which cedes California to the United States.

1849	Argonauts come from all parts of the world to take part in the gold rush; San Francisco becomes an instant cosmopolis.
1850	California is admitted to the Union.
1854	Sacramento becomes the permanent capital of the state.
1861–64	During the Civil War, California remains loyal to the Union and provides it with massive financial assistance.
1869	The Central Pacific and the Union Pacific join tracks at Promontory Point, Utah, connecting California by rail to the eastern United States.
1870	Golden Gate Park is begun.
1892	John Muir and companions found the Sierra Club.
1902	The first California state park is established, at Big Basin.
1906	Earthquake and fire destroy most of San Francisco.
1936	The San Francisco-Oakland Bay Bridge opens.
1937	The Golden Gate Bridge opens.
1941–45	World War II draws thousands of workers to the Bay Area's industries, particularly its shipyards.
1945–	California experiences unprecedented population growth and consequent urbanization.
1962	Congress establishes Point Reyes National Seashore.
1965	The Bay Conservation and Development Commission is founded.
1972	The first Bay Area Rapid Transit trains begin to run.
	Congress establishes the Golden Gate National Recreation Area.
	California voters approve an initiative establishing a commission to regulate all coastal development.
1976–77	Northern California experiences two years of drought.
1982	California voters resoundingly defeat a proposition to build a Peripheral Canal that would carry Sacramento River water south around the Delta.
1982 and 1983	California experiences killer storms, floods and landslides.
1986	The Bay Bridge celebrates its 50th birthday by getting lit up.
1987	The Golden Gate Bridge celebrates its 50th birthday with a dawn walk, and instead of the expected 40–60,000 walkers, over 800,000 show up and mill around.
	The Carquinez Bridge and the Platform Bridge near Point Reyes Station also celebrate their 50th birthdays, with more restrained ceremonies.
1988	Record crowds show up at federal hearings in Humboldt and Mendocino counties to protest the Department of Interior's proposal to allow drilling for oil off California's northern coast.

Recommended reading

Thousands of books and articles have been published on California history, and hundreds more come out every year. To pursue the subject at your leisure, just wander into your neighborhood library and start looking on the shelves under Dewey decimal number 979.

Here are a few reference books that will prove useful to the history buff:

Beck, Warren A., and Ynez D. Haase, *Historical Atlas of California*. Norman: University of Oklahoma, 1985.

Gudde, Erwin G., *California Place Names*. 3rd ed. Berkeley and Los Angeles: University of California Press, 1969. The basic authority in this field.

Hart, James D., *A Companion to California*. 2nd ed. Berkeley: University of California Press, 1987. An indispensable reference work.

Holliday, J. S., *The World Rushed In: The California Gold Rush Experience*. New York: Simon & Schuster, 1981. Not perhaps a reference book, strictly speaking, but the definitive account of the most important event in California's history.

Hoover, Mildred Brooke, Hero Eugene Rensch and Ethel Grace Rensch, *Historic Spots in California*. 3rd ed., rev. by William N. Abeloe. Stanford: Stanford University Press, 1966. A detailed county-by-county survey.

Rocq, Margaret Miller, ed., *California Local History: A Bibliography and Union List of Library Holdings*. 2nd ed. Stanford: Stanford University Press, 1970.

The Golden Gate National Recreation Area (GGNRA)

The GGNRA, created in 1972, is now the largest urban park in the world and the most-visited national park in the country—over 25 million visitors annually, or four times as many as Yosemite, the Grand Canyon and Yellowstone combined—yet a surprising number of Bay Areans apparently don't know exactly what it is. Perhaps they don't realize that every time they attend a play at Fort Mason or have a drink at the Cliff House they're visiting the GGNRA. Many don't yet appreciate the unprecedented nature of what they have in their own backyard: combined with the Point Reyes National Seashore and other public lands, the GGNRA provides a greenbelt over 40 miles long and over 140,000 acres in extent. No other metropolitan area in the world is so blessed.

The preservation of this 35,000-acre park, a unique mixture of the urban, the military, the historic and the pastoral in and near a great metropolitan area, seems almost miraculous—especially since it was established during the second half of the 20th century while the entire San Francisco Bay region was experiencing an extended development boom, when factories, office buildings and tract houses were covering marshes, farmlands and orchards.

Actually the GGNRA owes its existence mainly to the vision and tenacity of one man, the late Congressman Phillip Burton, and it is entirely fitting that the park was dedicated to him shortly after his untimely death in 1983.

The park contains an incredible diversity of attractions, the likes of which could hardly be found anywhere else in the world: an island penitentiary notorious in story and movie; examples of maritime craft from sailing schooners to the last surviving Liberty Ship; miles and miles of ocean beach; and, perhaps most important, fortifications spanning a century and a quarter—most important because it was military occupation of the Bay's headlands and islands that kept them in the public domain and available for parkland when their defense functions became obsolete. And in 1983 the GGNRA acquired over a thousand acres on Sweeney Ridge in San Mateo County, the spot from which Sergeant Ortega's scouting party in 1769 first sighted San Francisco Bay from land.

The GGNRA is unique in yet another respect: in addition to putting a park where the people are, the National Park Service has tried from the beginning to obtain a wide range of public opinion on how to plan and run it. The act that established the GGNRA also mandated the creation of a Citizen's Advisory Commission to oversee its development and that of neighboring Point Reyes National Seashore and to keep the NPS informed of the people's wishes and hopes for the two parks. The 17-member commission contains representatives from a variety of economic and ethnic groups in San Francisco, Marin and the East Bay. It meets regularly at various spots in Marin and San Francisco counties, and its meetings are open to the public. They are, in fact, a fascinating example of democracy in action at the town-meeting level, as concerned citizens rise to present their views on issues ranging from the acquisition of thousands of acres of land to the placement of the concession building in Muir Woods.

This book can mention only a few of the high spots of the magnificent GGNRA. The San Francisco and Marin descriptions appear with their respective counties. Sweeney Ridge is described in Rusmore and Spangle's *Peninsula Trails* (Wilderness Press, 1988). For more information, readers should consult park headquarters at Fort Mason and/or the ranger station at Fort Cronkhite.

Maps
The park issues an excellent free map and descriptive leaflet, available from the offices mentioned just above.

Olmsted Bros.' *Rambler's Guide to the Trails of Mt. Tamalpais and the Marin Headlands* covers the Marin section. It and Erickson's *Recreational Map: Golden Gate Recreation Area* are available from the above offices and from map stores.

Organization

Golden Gate National Park Association
Fort Mason, Building 204,
San Francisco 94123-1308; 556-2236
Designed to support the GGNRA; issues a quarterly journal *The Park;* organizes special outings for members.

Recommended reading

Liberatore, Karen, *The Complete Guide to the Golden Gate National Recreation Area*. San Francisco: Chronicle Books, 1983.

Olmsted, Nancy, *To Walk With a Quiet Mind: Hikes in the Woodlands, Parks and Beaches of the San Francisco Bay Area*. San Francisco: Sierra Club, 1975.

Getting outdoors

Choosing your outing

Many of the hikes in this book will give you a good workout, but all of them are within the capability of any middle-aged acrophobe who is in fairly good condition and is wearing adequate boots. A grade of difficulty appears at the beginning of each hike. This assessment is somewhat flexible; a climb that seems "easy" at 9 A.M., on a cool day may seem "moderately strenuous" at 1 P.M. on a hot one. It is fairly safe to predict, however, that anyone whose main exercise for the last few years has consisted in walking from the front door to the garage will be happier if he starts his hiking career with something graded "easy" rather than "strenuous." Anyone who wants a *really* easy walk should look in the Index under "Nature trails."

Some of the routes offer the opportunity for backpacking into overnight hike-in camps that are not accessible by automobile. You can visit most of these camps without backpacking by making them the lunch stop for a day-long hike.

Many routes in this book are in state and regional parks that have facilities for car camping, and I have included some information about these facilities. It is, of course, possible to backpack into car camps; but some of them are so thoroughly dedicated to the automobile that they are esthetically not very satisfying for the backpacker.

Many trails in the Bay Area are suitable for bicycling; in fact, some of them are better suited to bikes than to boots. For some suggested routes, look in the index under "Bicycle routes."

Planning your outing

Most people prefer to do the hard part (if there is a hard part) first. For example, they ascend a mountain, have lunch and then descend. This preference stems from physiology, not the Protestant ethic: it is just plain easier to climb when you and the day are both fresh.

In general, it's a good idea to *start as early as possible,* to maintain a steady but not exhausting pace for the first part of the trip, to stop for rests before you feel the need, and perhaps to dawdle toward the end.

If you're visiting a park that closes at sunset, or a beach that is flooded at high tide, be sure to check the newspaper in advance to find out when the natural event will occur.

Hiking in company—and alone

Hiking in a group

Anyone new to the area, new to hiking, newly retired, in search of companions or averse to driving may wish to join a group that sponsors regular hikes. A list of the most active groups in the Bay Area appears at the back of this book.

Of all the outdoor groups, the Sierra Club conducts the most numerous and most varied hikes. Its San Francisco Bay chapter alone plans at least one hike, and sometimes as many as four, almost every Saturday, Sunday, Wednesday and holiday of the year.

The Sierra Club schedules hikes for singles, gourmets, photographers, nature students and dogs. It also sponsors trail-maintenance days, outings combining bicycling and hiking, and bus and car camping trips—plus the more strenuous activities for which it is famous, such as backpacking, river touring, rock climbing and mountaineering.

Some of the more specialized nature organizations also conduct outings. For example, the local chapters of the Audubon Society have frequent field trips for birding, and the California Native Plant Society visits interesting and unusual plant communities.

Hiking in an organized group has many advantages: You will have the companionship of other people who share your interest in the outdoors. The leader presumably knows the trails and has scouted an interesting route. The leader or some of the other hikers may be especially knowledgeable about the history, geology, flora or fauna of the area, and will be happy to share this knowledge. An organized group can sometimes arrange entry to private land or to facilities that are off limits to the general public. An organized group can charter a bus to a hiking area some distance from the city, thereby sparing you an exhausting drive on the freeway.

Finally, and perhaps most important, hiking in a group offers safety, security and protection. During the nearly two years that the Trailside Killer was shooting hikers at random, a great many persons went out only in groups of four or more. Even if a murderer is not roaming the trails, it is comforting to know that if you should sprain an ankle, get bitten by a rattlesnake or suffer some other misadventure, there are people around to look after you and go for help.

On the other hand, hiking in a group has drawbacks. First, you are pretty much obliged to travel at the leader's pace (or at the group's consensual pace), which may be faster or slower than yours. Second, a group tends to scare off wildlife—unless, of course, it's a small, single-minded group dedicated to finding the nesting place of the marbled murrelet, or something of the sort. Finally, a group hike often becomes mainly a social event, with most of the distractions that go with such events, like flirtations, gossip and one-upmanship. Even some of the outdoor clubs with the most Spartan images contain a fair proportion of raconteurs, bon vivants and colorful eccentrics. In this kind of group you might get so involved in socializing that you wouldn't notice the landscape you're walking through.

You can drop out of a group hike along the way, but it is a cardinal rule of trail etiquette that if you do, *you must notify the leader.*

Hiking alone

When you hike alone you can go at your own speed and spend as much time as you want on your own diversions—especially the sort of diversions that make nonparticipants bored, impatient and resentful, such as fishing, sketching and lying in wait for the marbled murrelet to return to its nest. Furthermore, the solitary hiker can usually get much closer to animals than can a group or a couple who are conversing.

But the main reward of hiking alone is a heightened, almost visceral awareness of your surroundings, which you can rarely experience when distracted, however pleasantly, by the presence of another person. Colin Fletcher, solitary hiker par excellence, vividly communicates this feeling of superawareness in his books. Fletcher treks hundreds of miles through wild country; but even the day hiker in Tilden Park may experience a little of the sense of freedom and adventure Fletcher describes.

To many people, however, the idea of hiking alone seems foolhardy, depressing or just plain unthinkable. Admittedly, solitary hiking has its disadvantages: lone hikers risk a few hazards that hikers in company do not. For suggestions on minimizing such risks, see the section "Safety."

What to wear

Boots

Good boots are the day hiker's only piece of fairly expensive equipment. Some nimble persons manage to accomplish amazing pedestrian feats wearing sneakers or zoris (or even barefoot), but most hikers find Vibram-soled boots desirable for any excursion much more demanding than a walk around Ghirardelli Square.

It's a mistake to skimp on something as important to one's safety as hiking boots. Buy them at a reputable department or sporting-goods store and expect to pay plenty. Try them on over wool socks and walk around for a while—if possible, up and down ramps—until you're sure you've found a pair you can live with for years.

Many jocks, would-be jocks and pseudo-jocks have taken to wearing running shoes on practically every occasion less formal than a Royal Wedding and on practically every kind of terrain. It is important to remember, however, that running shoes don't grip the ground the way good boots do. I had occasion to ponder this axiom one day as I lay sprawled face-down in the mud on the trail above Phoenix Lake: I had said to myself, "Oh, it's just good old Phoenix Lake and I'll only be gone an hour, so I won't bother to change into my boots." SPLAT!

Socks

Most hikers prefer to wear two pairs, cotton (or polypro) inside wool or cotton inside wool-and-synthetic. If you wear sandals or sneakers to drive to the trailhead, don't forget to bring along your hiking socks. (I have forgotten more than once.)

Other clothing

Because the Bay Area's weather is so changeable, the hiker should take along a sweater, jacket or windbreaker, even if the morning promises warmth and sunshine all day. As the local Sierra Club chapter's schedule suggests, "Dress like an onion (layers that can be shed), ready for cold or hot."

Those of us who are susceptible to poison oak have learned the hard way that even on a hot day we should wear, or carry with us, long-sleeved and long-trousered garments.

What to take with you

Water

This is the most essential item. Even people who never drink water at home will want it when they go hiking. Always start out with a full canteen. Nothing, except possibly blisters, can spoil a hike more thoroughly than thirst.

Food

The old standby is a sandwich—which you may supplement with olives, pickles, radishes, celery, carrots, or cherry tomatoes. Gourmets may wince, but we *hoi polloi* find the broiled chicken from supermarket concessionaires an easy and satisfying lunch—one chicken per two persons. For dessert, nothing can beat fresh fruit. You can wash it all down with milk, vegetable juice, fruit juice, beer or wine (bearing in mind that a little wine goes a long way on a hot day). These beverages are an addition to the menu, *not* a substitute for water.

The pack

If you hike regularly, you will probably decide to get a light day-pack. These are available at sporting-goods and department stores. You can save yourself a lot of bother by stocking the pack with a permanent supply of useful items and replacing each when it gets used up. Items to keep in the pack will probably include small change for phone or bus; Kleenex; pocket knife; compass; whistle; fire starter or matches in waterproof container; bandana; stainless-steel cup; corkscrew and/or can opener; duplicate car key; gas credit card; and first-aid kit containing adhesive bandages, moleskin, pain reliever, and (perhaps) sunburn preventive, insect repellent, salt tablets and water-purification tablets.

Don't forget to take dark glasses and a map of the area.

What not to take with you

Firearms—they are illegal in most parks.

Pets—unless you know they are permitted in the area.

Transistor radios—they make for noise pollution along the trail.

Newspapers or newsmagazines—there certainly is no state law or park regulation against bringing them along. But it seems rather self-defeating to spend considerable time and effort hiking to some peaceful, sylvan spot, settle down to lunch, and then open up the newspaper to read COST OF LIVING UP AGAIN BY FIFTEEN PERCENT or BUS STRIKE LOOMS or OIL EXECUTIVE CHIDES ELITISTS—not to mention the usual ration of wars, murders, kidnappings, political scandals and natural catastrophes.

Getting to the trailhead

During most of the 1980s, residents of the Bay Area have consistently voted *transportation* as the region's number-one problem. Despite urgent appeals by state, regional and municipal authorities for greater use of public transit, Californians insist on driving, and most commuters insist on driving alone.

> The Red & White Fleet operates one commuter ferry per day between Vallejo and San Francisco, but general manager David Pence said Solano County residents seem wedded to their cars. Unless ridership increases from 150 to 200 by June, he said, Red & White plans to drop the service.
>
> "It's mind-boggling to me that business isn't booming," he said. He noted that a high-speed catamaran makes the trip in an hour and offers coffee and doughnuts in the morning and a full bar at night.
>
> "Every morning I hear those radio stations broadcasting traffic and saying there is a car overturned in Pinole and traffic is backed up to Highway 4. Why don't more people ride the ferry?"
>
> —Walt Gibbs, San Francisco *Examiner,*
> February 7, 1988.

As Mr. Pence suggests, the transit situation is currently undergoing a downward vicious spiral: as more buses, trains and ferries lose money, they cut service and/or raise fares, thereby causing even more people to drive. (In fact, a few weeks after the above interview the Red & White Fleet announced that it was planning to eliminate its Vallejo ferry service because of lack of patronage.)

Nevertheless, in the knowledge that some readers of this book *must* use public transit, and in the hope that others will want to try it, I have indicated which lines were running to the trailheads at press time. Because schedules, fares and routes are constantly changing, anyone who plans to use public transit should get up-to-date timetables.

When phoning transit agencies, it's a good idea to have something at hand to read; many of them tend to put callers on hold for several minutes. (Nowadays, in fact, it's a good idea to have something at hand by the phone to read at all times, as even your oldest and dearest friends may put you on hold in mid-sentence if they have call-waiting.)

The following abbreviations for transit agencies recur frequently in this book:

AC Transit	Alameda-Contra Costa Transit
BART	Bay Area Rapid Transit
GGT	Golden Gate Transit
Muni	San Francisco Municipal Railway
SamTrans	San Mateo County Transit
SP	Southern Pacific Transportation Company

Restaurants and other attractions along the way

This book does not intend to compete with the many guide books to the area or to trespass on the territory of our local restaurant critics. However, when I have come across an interesting museum, winery or eating place near the trailhead, I have felt that other hikers might find this information useful.

If you're planning to finish an outing with dinner at a restaurant, it's a good idea to phone ahead to find out when it's open, whether reservations are necessary, and perhaps what the prices are like. If it's a fairly elegant establishment, you may wish to take along a change of clothing, or at least footgear.

Safety

By far the most dangerous aspect of hiking is driving to the trailhead in an automobile. One can greatly reduce this danger by taking public transportation whenever possible.

Getting lost

A hiker is not likely to get lost on trails near a metropolitan area. However, if you delay your return too long and try to get back over unfamiliar trails or cross-country as darkness falls, you may possibly get lost and have to spend the night outdoors. In the Bay Area's equable climate, this experience won't be particularly hazardous, but it may be uncomfortable, especially if you have to get through the night with no fortification except a few limp carrot sticks and two ounces of chablis left over from lunch.

The easiest way to avoid this situation is to begin your return to the trailhead well in advance of sunset. If you have misjudged the time and suddenly realize that dusk is falling, it is usually wiser not to try to find a shortcut by going cross-country or over an unfamiliar trail, especially through chaparral. Instead, try to find a fire road heading for your destination, even if it's the longer route: in semidarkness, fire roads are easier to follow than trails.

Beach and swim safety

The GGNRA has issued the following advice, which is useful for all beaches and cliff areas. (Sadly enough, the brochure containing this information was made possible through donations from the family and friends of a 19-year-old man who fell to his death from a cliff— as incautious young people do every year.)

Stay on established trails. Taking shortcuts along the coastal cliffs or climbing up from beaches is dangerous and can be fatal, due to steepness and loose rocks.

Swim only at lifeguarded beaches. In the GGNRA, depending on the weather, lifeguard services are generally available in San Francisco at Aquatic Park and China Beach, and in Marin County at Stinson Beach from April through October.

Swimmers: Before entering the water, check for rip currents and longshore currents. These currents are formed when ocean waves deposit a large volume of water on the beach. The water then flows parallel to the shore (longshore current) until finding a low spot in the shore bottom, whereupon it rushes seaward, often with great force (rip current). Dirty, sandy, foamy, choppy water—or a body of water traveling seaward through an area of little or no wave activity—all indicate dangerous current conditions. If you find yourself caught in a rip current, don't panic; stay calm; swim parallel with the beach until you are out of the current, then swim toward the shore using incoming waves as an aid.

Parents: Do not allow children to play on logs along the shoreline or in the surf. They are dangerous and can cause injuries.

When fishing, know what the tide is doing. *Never turn your back on the ocean*. People have been swept off shoreline rocks by sneaker waves or trapped by changing tides.

Animals

Your chances of coming to harm from a wild animal are slight. Once in a while you might get near a rattlesnake, which will warn you off (see p. 16). Another source of possible danger is an ordinarily harmless animal, such as a squirrel or a bat, that has rabies. Any wild animal that is acting absolutely fearless may be rabid and should be avoided. Warn children not to touch any wild animal along the trail.

In the past decade, one animal has progressed from being a mere annoyance to an actual danger: the Western black-legged tick. A small percentage of these ticks—probably less than five per cent—

carry the spirochete that causes Lyme disease, named for Old Lyme, Connecticut, where it was first diagnosed in 1975. The disease has since spread to the West, but it is still so uncommon, and its symptoms are so various, that it is frequently misdiagnosed. Symptoms can include a rash and/or fever, followed by neurological and/or cardiac problems, and eventually arthritislike joint pains. Drugs are effective against Lyme disease once it is correctly diagnosed. The best way to avoid it is to avoid ticks. I quote my colleague, Jeff Schaffer:

> When you're in tick country (chaparral or tall grass), you can cut tick attachments almost to zero just by wearing rain pants—they slip right off. When a tick does get a hold, usually between your ankle and your thigh, it climbs *upward* until it reaches exposed skin. Therefore, wear long pants that cover the tops of your boots, not hiking shorts, and be sure your shirt is tucked in.

A helpful leaflet called "Facts About Lyme Disease in California" is available free from the California Department of Health Services, 2151 Berkeley Way, Berkeley 94704. It describes the symptoms of Lyme disease and gives instructions for avoiding ticks and for removing them if you get bitten. I recommend this leaflet to everyone who spends much time outdoors.

An even smaller animal than the tick has become a hazard to hikers. The parasite giardia, which causes diarrhea and great intestinal discomfort, has now become so ubiquitous in California's water supply that no stream in the Bay Area is safe to drink from, no matter how clear it looks.

The most dangerous animal

Beginning in August of 1979, at least three women hiking alone on popular trails of Mt. Tamalpais were savagely murdered. On Thanksgiving weekend of 1980 four more bodies, three of them women, were found in Point Reyes National Seashore. They were apparently victims of the same random murderer, whom the media dubbed the Trailside Killer. Hikers, joggers, birders and all other users of the outdoors were appalled, outraged and terrified by this violation of the tranquility and sanctity of Nature. Finally, after at least two more murders and one attempted murder in Santa Cruz County, a suspect was arrested who had a record of three previous convictions for violence against women. He was convicted of the two Santa Cruz County murders and subsequently went on trial for the Marin County murders. The Trailside Killings have apparently ceased; but crime and violence in the outdoors have not. Here we shall consider a few possible ways to protect ourselves against them.

When the Trailside Killer was running loose, many people—perhaps because of lingering traces of the Frontier Tradition, abetted by thirty years of television watching—immediately advised, "Get a gun!" And I confess that I briefly considered doing so, and so did some of my most pacifistic friends. However, firearms are illegal in nearly all parks, and carrying a concealed weapon is illegal nearly everywhere. Furthermore, most American middle-class civilians are so unaccustomed to using firearms that they may lack good judgment about them—either being too quick on the trigger and blazing away at an innocent stranger, or hesitating just long enough to have the weapon turned against them.

A more sensible suggestion was, "Get a dog!" However, only a fairly large dog will be much protection, and many people simply aren't able to house or care for a large dog. Furthermore, so many parks and trails prohibit dogs that a dog-owner's freedom of movement is severely limited.

An entirely sensible suggestion was, "Go with a group!" In the section above on "Hiking in company—and alone" I mention some of the many advantages of hiking in a group, and in the back of the book is a list of some of the most active hiking and nature-study organizations in the Bay Area.

For those people who want to, or have to, continue walking, jogging or hiking solo or duo, I offer the following suggestions, culled from Sierra Club journals, from friends' advice and from my own experience.

Some things you can take along that may be helpful:

1. A walking staff; this is useful in fording creeks and negotiating difficult terrain, and might deter an assailant.

2. A whistle and/or shriek-alarm; this will help you alert rescuers if you are ever lost or injured, and might frighten away an assailant.

3. MACE, or tear gas; admittedly it is not very effective against a homicidal maniac armed with a gun, but it offers some protection against the common garden variety of mugger or other assailant. Its great advantage over guns and knives, especially for women, is that you know it is not lethal and therefore you will not hesitate to use it. It is a felony to use tear gas without a license, but it is relatively easy for an adult nonfelon to obtain such a license by taking a short course of instruction. To find out more about these courses, phone your local police department.

Always leave word with a friend, relative, neighbor or ranger where you plan to go and when you plan to return.

Don't flourish expensive-looking jewelry, binoculars or photographic gear. It's wise not to leave such items in the car, either—in recent years there has been a spate of burglaries from cars parked at trailheads.

Never hitchhike unless you can choose your driver. To illustrate: I would never try to hitch a ride on the highway. However, if I wanted to go from the Five Brooks trailhead to the Bear Valley trailhead without walking five miles, or if it appeared that the #65 Golden Gate Transit bus was so crowded I'd have to stand up from Olema to San Anselmo, then I might ask a ride from a safe-looking car—preferably a family with young children, or a group of middle-aged women.

If you try to hitch rides, don't be surprised or offended when you get turned down—especially if you are a male—and don't take it personally. As a corollary, if you are driving, never pick up hitchhikers on the highway.

When you break for lunch, try to choose some place with other people around, such as a popular picnic area, beach or campground.

If you are riding Golden Gate Transit, try to avoid transferring at Marin City after dark. During the day on weekends a thriving flea market adjoins the bus stop and there are hundreds of people around, but at night the place is isolated and deserted. (A friend of mine nearly got mugged here by a group of juveniles one night.) The bus stops at downtown San Anselmo, downtown Sausalito and the toll plaza are much more frequented at night.

The rules of the trail

Hiking is one of the least organized sports, but it does have a few rules. Most of them are based on such elementary common sense that it might seem unnecessary to list them. But since one constantly finds mutilated plants, used matches, cigarette butts and beer cans along the trail, it is clear that at least some hikers haven't yet learned the fundamentals. So here is a succinct reminder.

Preventing fires

Never smoke while walking. Smoke only during rest stops, and strip or bury the cigarette when you've finished.

Make fires only in properly designated places—which are, for most of the hikes in this book, the stoves, grills and braziers provided by park services.

Preserving the environment

Leave no litter behind; take it all out. Remember that paper and orange peels, though organic and therefore technically biodegradable, may take years to biodegrade, and meanwhile they mess up the landscape.

If you have extra room in your pack, you can perform a public service by picking up other people's litter and carrying it back to a garbage can.

Don't take a shortcut up or down a hill where the trail makes switchbacks; this practice causes erosion, and damages the trail too.

Don't push, roll or throw rocks or other heavy objects down a steep hillside; this practice not only damages the trails but may possibly damage some hiker below.

Don't pick wildflowers; in general, don't pick any plant or remove any animal from its habitat. Exceptions are fish, during the season and if you have a license; ripe edible berries; and mushrooms, but only if you are very sure of the species.

Controlling dogs

Most parks require that dogs be leashed at all times. An increasing number of parks have banned dogs entirely. The reason? Many hikers unleashed their pets as soon as they were out of the ranger's sight, and the animals often followed their instinct to chase deer and other wildlife.

If you like to hike with your dog, you might consider some of the Sierra Club's canine outings.

Miscellaneous etiquette

Give horseback riders the right of way. When you see or hear them coming, step off to the side of the trail, wait for them to pass, and don't make any loud noises or sudden movements that might cause the horses to shy.

When hiking through cattle-grazing land, close gates behind you wherever signs so request.

Bicycles

The mountain bike—a sturdy, balloon-tired bicycle designed to go over rough terrain—originated and evolved in Marin County in the 1970s, and soon became popular all over the Bay Area. Unfortunately a few reckless mountain bikers, by speeding, by frightening hikers and horses, and by riding roughly over grassland and meadow, have given the sport a dubious reputation in some outdoor circles. As a result, many parks have enacted strict regulations governing *all* bicycle use. Generally, bikes are permitted on only some fire roads and not at all on trails. Some popular parks, such as Point Reyes National Seashore, Mt. Tamalpais and the East Bay Regional Park

District, issue maps showing permissible bicycle routes. More information can be obtained from bicycle clubs, a few of which are listed at the end of this book. Ray Hosler currently writes a column "Cycling" in the Monday *Outdoors* section of the San Francisco *Chronicle;* this is a good source of up-to-date information.

State park facilities and regulations

The State Park System publishes a useful list of its facilities. It is available for $2 from the Department of Parks and Recreation, Attention Publications, Box 942896, Sacramento 94296-0838. You can reserve campsites at most state parks through Mistix by phoning toll-free from California (1-800-444-7275). The toll number from outside California is 619-452-1950. You can reserve as much as eight weeks in advance and charge to Visa or MasterCard.

There is a moderate fee for camping, and small additional fees for reservations, extra vehicles, and dogs; some parks also charge a small day-use fee for parking.

In recent years the Park System has instituted a class of campgrounds called "environmental campsites." These are fairly primitive campsites separated from each other and from the regular campgrounds, most of them reached by a short hike. For information, write the Department of Parks and Recreation at the above address or phone 1-800-444-7275.

The Park System has adopted a system of trail signing that takes a little getting used to: the name of the trail appears horizontally in small letters at the top of the sign, and the destination vertically in large letters.

The State Park System has a uniform set of rules: Pets must be on leash or housed at the campsite or in a vehicle. Dogs must have a license and proof of rabies inoculation. *Dogs are not allowed on trails or in environmental campsites.*

No firearms are allowed.

Fires are allowed only in designated places, and you must bring your own fuel or buy it from the rangers; collecting wood is not allowed.

The California Riding and Hiking Trail

In 1945 the California legislature authorized an extremely ambitious program for a 3000-mile loop trail around the state. Like so many worthy recreational projects, this one was underfunded, and the loop was never completed. However, hikers will frequently encounter the distinctive yellow-topped wooden stakes with yellow bootprint and horseshoe that identify a trail as part of this system.

Proposed regional trails

Recently two major trail systems have been proposed that would link the entire Bay Area. The Association of Bay Area Governments is studying a Bay Trail—a 300-mile-long hiking and bicycling trail that would circle the Bay near the shore. And in November 1987 representatives from outdoor groups and public agencies gathered to form a Bay Area Trails Council and plan a Ridgeline Trail that might run for 350 miles or more around the hills of the Bay counties. This trail is scheduled to be completed by 1993. For more information, consult the Bay Area Trails Council, c/o People for Open Space/Greenbelt Congress, 116 New Montgomery Street, Suite 640, San Francisco 94105.

Where to get more information

Maps

This book includes a map for every hike it describes except those for which a free or inexpensive, accurate map is always available near where you start walking and those for which you don't need a map at all. An asterisk marks the start of a hike; a heavy solid line, the main route, a wide dashed line, an alternate route; a narrow dashed line, a peripheral trail; a dotted line, a side trip.

The maps in this book are here mainly to keep hikers and drivers from getting lost; they do not purport to show details of the terrain. The most detailed maps, and generally the most suitable to supplement the hikes in this book, are those in the U.S. Geological Survey's 7½-minute topographic series. The term "topo" at the head of each trail description refers to the map or maps in this series that cover the area. Their scale is 1:24,000, meaning that 1 inch represents 24,000 inches, or 2000 feet. Topo maps are available at many map and sporting-goods stores, but they are generally cheaper at the USGS offices at 555 Battery Street, San Francisco 94111 (phone 556-5627; open weekdays 8:30 A.M.–4 P.M.) and 345 Middlefield Road, Building 3, Menlo Park 94025 (phone 853-8300; open weekdays 8 A.M.–4 P.M.). The best map store in the East Bay is The Map Center, 2440 Bancroft Way, Berkeley 94704 (phone 841-MAPS; open M–F 9–5, Sat. 10–5).

Incidentally, the place names in this book conform to USGS usage where sources differ.

By far the best road maps are those published by the California State Automobile Association for its members. Some environmentalists have mixed feelings about the CSAA because in the past it has lobbied for more freeways and against public transit. However, in recent years it has muted this policy—perhaps because of protest from a vocal segment of its membership.

Miscellaneous free data

In addition to the park and transit authorities mentioned in this book, a variety of city, county and regional organizations offer an amazing amount of guidance to the enterprising hiker (or bicyclist or nature lover). Chambers of commerce and convention-and-visitor bureaus provide directions to the local industries, wineries, colleges, museums and historic sites. Park and recreation departments suggest where to picnic, camp, swim, fish and birdwatch. You can find these organizations under city and county listings in phone books.

Downtown San Francisco has two major sources of information. They're intended mainly to assist tourists, but they're also mines of useful advice for natives on what's happening and how to get to it. They are:

> The Redwood Empire Association
> 1 Market Plaza
> San Francisco 94105
> Phone: 543-8334

> The San Francisco Convention and Visitors Bureau
> Lower Level, Hallidie Plaza
> Powell and Market streets
> San Francisco 94102
> Phone: 391-2000
> Business office: 1390 Market Street
> San Francisco 94102

The pink section of our Sunday newspaper, the combined *Examiner* and *Chronicle,* familiarly called the *Exonicle,* lists nature walks and other outdoor activities.

The *Chronicle* publishes a special section called *Outdoors* every Monday. It is a gold mine of information on sports and fitness, and contains a detailed schedule for every imaginable kind of outdoor activity that is open to the public, from Backpacking to Yoga.

Backpacking guide

Winnett, Thomas, with Melanie Findling, *Backpacking Basics*. 3rd ed. Berkeley: Wilderness Press, 1988.

Recommended reading

California Coastal Commission, *California Coastal Access Guide.* Rev. ed. Berkeley: University of California Press, 1983.

Doss, Margot Patterson, *The Bay Area at Your Feet.* Rev. ed. San Francisco: Don't Call It Frisco Press, 1987. Mrs. Doss, the dean of Bay Area walkers, is well known for her regular column in the Sunday Punch section of the *Exonicle.*

Gentry, Curt, and Tom Horton, *The Dolphin Guide to San Francisco and the Bay Area.* Rev. ed. Garden City, New York: Doubleday, 1982.

Hansen, Gladys, ed., *San Francisco: The Bay and Its Cities.* New York: Hastings House, 1973. An update of the book in the American Guide Series originally compiled by the WPA.

Wayburn, Peggy, *Adventuring in the San Francisco Bay Area.* San Francisco: Sierra Club Books, 1987.

Wurman, Richard Saul, *San Francisco Access: The Complete Bay Area Guide.* Rev. ed. New York: Access Press, 1985.

Architecture guides

Gebhard, David, et al., *A Guide to Architecture in San Francisco and Northern California.* Rev. ed. Salt Lake City: Gibbs M. Smith Inc./Peregrine Smith Books, 1985.

Olmsted, Roger, and T. H. Watkins, *Here Today: San Francisco's Architectural Heritage.* San Francisco: Chronicle Books, 1978.

Waldhorn, Judith, and Sally B. Woodbridge, *Tours of San Francisco Bay Architecture.* San Francisco: 101 Productions, 1978.

Architecture guides to San Francisco alone appear in the Recommended Reading for that section.

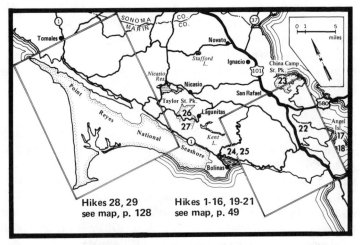

Marin County driving map

Hikes 1–29
Marin County

Marin County attained an unexpected and unwanted notoriety in 1978 as a habitat of hedonists, when NBC showed a nationwide television documentary called "I Want It All Now," suggesting that many residents spent a lot of time in such pursuits as sitting in hot tubs and being tickled by peacock feathers. The program was inspired, more or less, by Cyra McFadden's witty satire *The Serial,* which had originated in the weekly *Pacific Sun* and subsequently become a successful book; but where McFadden had used a stiletto, NBC used a sledgehammer.

The suburbia that gets the sensational publicity, however, is just one part of the county. Over 40% of Marin is private agricultural land; in fact, its dairy industry still produces 25% of the Bay Area's milk. Moreover, Marin is the site of a recreational greenbelt area that is unparalleled near any other major metropolis. It includes over a hundred thousand acres in the GGNRA, Point Reyes National Seashore, and assorted state and county parks and water-district lands. As noted in the Introduction, one reason so much open space has been preserved in Marin is that the county was relatively inaccessible from the rest of the metropolitan area until the Golden Gate Bridge was completed in 1937. Furthermore, the headlands facing the Bay have been saved from development by the happy chance that, because of their strategic value, the Army has maintained them as military reservations since the mid-19th century. The protection of Marin's open space has not been entirely due to accident, however: the county has a long tradition of militant conservationism among its residents.

One development that gained the county even more publicity than its television notoriety was its sudden inheritance of a huge sum of money. This unexpected windfall resulted from the bequest of Marin resident Beryl Buck, a childless widow who died in 1975. Her will specified that the yearly earnings from her estate were to be used "for exclusively nonprofit, charitable, religious or educational pur-

poses in providing care for the needy of Marin, and for other nonprofit, charitable, religious or educational purposes of that county."
To administer it Mrs. Buck appointed the San Francisco Foundation, a hitherto low-key institution accustomed to distributing philan-
thropic monies around the Bay Area. By the time her estate was
settled, her original bequest of a comparatively modest $7 million in
oil stock had ballooned to over $250 million, meaning that the San
Francisco Foundation now had $20 million or more to distribute
every year in what was already one of the wealthiest counties in
California.

The resulting scramble for funds would have challenged the pen
of a Moliere or a Dickens. It seemed that almost overnight half the
county's population became experts on grantsmanship as they
maneuvered for a share of the pie. Mrs. Buck's will was sufficiently
vague that a plausible argument could be made for just about any
proposal. As one critic noted, Marin County may not have many
articulate poor people, but it is full of highly eloquent and creative
writers, artists, social workers and consultants. When you see the
words "made possible by a contribution from the San Francisco
Foundation" attached to any acreage, building, or project in Marin,
you can be pretty sure that some of Mrs. Buck's bucks were at
work.

In 1984 the San Francisco Foundation, abetted by a group of
public-interest lawyers representing other Bay Area charities, peti-
tioned to break the "Marin-only" feature of Mrs. Buck's will. They
were opposed by the Marin Board of Supervisors, the Marin Council
of Agencies, and Mrs. Buck's attorney. The resulting bitter court
fight was dubbed "The Superbowl of Probate." When the trial was
over, in 1986, the San Francisco Foundation not only had to give up
its attempt to break Mrs. Buck's will, but also agreed to turn over the
giant trust to a new organization formed to distribute it, the Marin
Community Foundation. Ironically enough, over $10 million of Mrs.
Buck's estate—which, remember, was originally intended for the
"needy" of Marin—went to lawyers for both sides.

Public transit

Some Marinites have always been suspicious of what frequently
passes for progress elsewhere. As far back as 1903 a petition
prohibiting automobiles on the county's highways received hundreds
of signatures. Its circulators argued that "the physical characteristics of the county are such that it is peculiarly ill adapted to the
use of the automobile."

I quoted this petition in earlier editions of this book as an example of goofy quaintness, but in the 1980s it has turned out to be remarkably prescient. Because of the county's geography, only one major thoroughfare runs north and south through it: Highway 101; and as more and more people and businesses have moved into Marin and Sonoma counties, traffic congestion on 101 has reached maddening levels.

The Golden Gate Bridge, Highway and Transportation District has tried to encourage commuters to get out of their cars by plowing revenues from its lucrative bridge tolls into buses and ferries. Unfortunately, these services have always lost money. Commuters apparently prefer to struggle, one per car, through massive traffic jams rather than to read in comfort on the bus or enjoy their coffee in virtual luxury on the ferry. (Not quite all of them, however: reportedly, a clubby sort of cocktail hour takes place on the evening Larkspur ferry run.)

The bridge district has threatened to try to save money by drastically reducing its bus and ferry service. In 1987, in fact, it canceled its commute service to Stinson Beach, thereby ending 117 years of weekday public bus service to that town. A couple of members of the district's board have suggested that solitary drivers during commute hours should pay a $5 bridge toll. Meanwhile, the GGBHTD as a whole is under fire. An archaic fiefdom formed in the 1920s, it still contains representatives from Del Norte and Humboldt counties far to the north of the bridge. Certain powerful politicians—notably State Senator Quentin Kopp and Assembly Speaker Willie Brown—have vocally favored abolishing the district and putting the bridge under the California Department of Transportation, which administers the other toll bridges in the state.

Some outings in this book rely on the #63 GGT bus, which has traditionally run over Mt. Tamalpais to Stinson Beach on weekends and has long been the mainstay of local Sierra Club hikes. Because the current bus situation at GGT appears so unsettled, I advise phoning in advance if you are in any doubt about the schedule.

For schedules and information, the address of the Golden Gate Bridge, Highway and Transportation District is Toll Plaza, San Francisco 94129. Phone: from San Francisco 332-6600; from Marin County 453-2100; from Sonoma County 544-1323. GGT operates the Sausalito and Larkspur ferries. Within the county, Marin Transit (453-2100) provides local bus service. Additional ferry service is provided by the Angel Island-Tiburon Ferry (453-2131) and the Red & White Fleet's ferries from San Francisco to Angel Island and Tiburon (546-2815 or 800-445-8880).

Facility

The Lodging Switchboard of Coastal Marin
Box 644, Point Reyes Station 94956
Phone 663-9445 from 6 A.M. to midnight
They issue a detailed brochure with information on all kinds of
lodging, including campgrounds, hostels and inns.

Organization

Marin Audubon Society
Box 599, Mill Valley 94942-0599

Recommended reading

Howell, John Thomas, *Marin Flora,* 2nd ed. Berkeley: University of
California Press, 1970.
The late Jack Mason has written a number of histories of Marin,
published by North Shore Books of Inverness.
Teather, Louise, *Place Names of Marin.* San Francisco: Scottwall
Associates, 1986.

Mallette Dean

The Golden Gate National Recreation Area in Marin

Marin Headlands

Address and phone
Visitor Center, Building 1050, Marin Headlands, Sausalito 94965; 331-1540

Maps
Topos *Point Bonita* and *San Francisco North;* trail maps available at Visitor Center; Olmsted Bros.' *Rambler's Guide to the Trails of Mt. Tamalpais and the Marin Headlands* and Erickson's *Recreational Map: Golden Gate National Recreation Area* available for a moderate price at park visitor centers and map stores.

How to get there
By bus San Francisco Muni #76 to Fort Cronkhite on Sundays and holidays; phone 673-MUNI for schedule. (As this bus runs infrequently, it is important to have up-to-date information on its schedule.)

By car From Highway 101 northbound, take the Alexander Avenue exit (the first one after Vista Point), pass the tunnel leading back to San Francisco, and immediately turn left at the signs for Forts Barry and Cronkhite. From 101 southbound, take the Sausalito exit, curve back under the freeway and immediately turn left at the sign for the forts. You will confront a one-way, half-mile-long tunnel for which a light regulates traffic. Once through the tunnel, continue 3 miles along Bunker Road to Rodeo Lagoon, the beach and the ranger station.

A more scenic route is via Conzelman Road: From Highway 101 northbound take the Alexander Avenue exit. Immediately turn left, where the sign shows the route back to San Francisco, but instead of going back to San Francisco bear right, uphill, on Conzelman Road. From Highway 101 southbound take the Sausalito exit, turn left and then immediately turn right on Conzelman.

By bicycle Bicyclists are not allowed in the tunnel, and should use Conzelman Road instead.

History

The first human inhabitants of the headlands area were the Coast
Miwok Indians. In 1817 the Spanish established their first permanent settlement in the county, Mission San Rafael—partly for religious reasons, partly to serve as a buffer against the Russians to the
north, operating out of Fort Ross. The padres resettled Indians from
all over Marin County at the mission, and brought sick ones over
from Mission Dolores in San Francisco, which was believed to be
less salubrious. When the Mexican government secularized the missions in 1834, the Indians were either left to fend for themselves or
forced into serfdom by the colonizers. Starvation and the white
man's diseases soon killed them off.

Most of the headlands were part of Rancho Saucelito ("little
grove of willows"), a spread of almost 20,000 acres which the
Mexican government granted to William A. Richardson in 1838.
Richardson, an English seaman, arrived in Yerba Buena (now San
Francisco) on a whaler in 1822 and stayed behind after his ship left.
He subsequently married the daughter of the Presidio's Commandante and in 1835 became the first Captain of the Port of San Francisco. After receiving his land grant, he moved to Marin County.
From his headquarters at what is now Sausalito he sold beef, hides
and produce—plus spring water at 50 cents per bucket—to sailing
vessels and the young City. In Richardson's day, the valleys of
Rancho Saucelito teemed with wildlife: bears, wolves, elk and mountain lions, in addition to the black-tailed deer that are still here.

The advent of the Civil War aroused apprehension that San Francisco Bay might be invaded by warships of the Confederacy, or some
other hostile power, and Alcatraz and Angel Island were fortified to
defend the harbor. As larger guns with longer ranges were developed, it seemed desirable to fortify the Marin Headlands also, and in
1866 the Government purchased nearly 1900 acres overlooking the
Bay. Originally called Lime Point Military Reservation, it was subsequently split into three posts named for commanding officers: Fort
Baker (1897), Fort Barry (1904) and Fort Cronkhite (1937). The
forts housed batteries of ever-more-sophisticated coastal artillery
and, during World War II, antiaircraft guns. In the 1950s Nike
missiles were installed; the last one was removed in 1974. Now that,
in an era of intercontinental ballistic missiles, the forts can no longer
serve as guardians of the Golden Gate, they have become part of the
GGNRA, although some military personnel remain.

While the Army was occupying the southern headlands, the hills
and valleys to the north continued as cattle ranches. After the con-

struction of the Golden Gate Bridge and then World War II brought rapid population growth to Marin, it was inevitable that developers would seek to build on this land, so conveniently close to San Francisco. And sure enough, in 1964 an Eastern developer backed by the Gulf Oil Corporation proposed building Marincello, a "planned community" for 20,000 people on 2138 acres of the headlands. Alarmed conservationists fought the proposal for years, and in 1972 Gulf finally sold the land to The Nature Conservancy, which subsequently turned it over to the GGNRA. Some of the land proposed for Marincello was rechristened the Martha Alexander Gerbode Preserve, in honor of a leading San Francisco environmentalist.

The transition from Army preserve to public park has raised some challenges and controversies. Since the headlands are part of the GGNRA, the Citizens' Advisory Commission has had to consider various proposals for their development, use and management, and some of its meetings have featured strongly felt pleas and debates from different sections of the public. The philosophical question underlying many of them has involved the proper use of a large public open space so near a large urban area.

One brouhaha erupted in 1978 when Stewart Brand proposed that a tenth birthday party for his Whole Earth Catalog be held in Gerbode Valley. This Whole Earth Jamboree would feature an overnight camp-out of ecology- and future-minded experts plus a public festival for as many as 10,000 people a day, including New Games, refreshments and music. The proposal set up an unlikely confrontation between the usually environmentally oriented Brand and some of the hard-core conservationists on the CAC, who felt that Gerbode Valley should be maintained as a natural preserve for wildlife and not tromped on by 20,000 feet per day. A compromise of sorts was reached (partly through the efforts of the Marin County Fire Chief, who was concerned about the safety of the houses on Wolfback Ridge at the end of the dry season): the main public part of the festival was moved to the Fort Barry Rifle Range, and admission was limited to 5000 persons per day.

A more significant dispute involving the same basic issues came to a head late in 1981. The Headlands Foundation, a nonprofit group, spent a year and a half and over $300,000 of the ubiquitous Buck Fund's money to prepare a draft plan for the long-range future of the headlands. Most of their proposals agreed substantially with the NPS's General Management Plan, except for two salient points: the Headlands Foundation proposed that instead of tearing down some of the old Army buildings, as planned, the NPS should restore them and make them available for assorted cultural and educational activities; and that the administration of the headlands should be taken over by a nonprofit organization independent of the NPS, like the Fort Mason Foundation. After some loquacious public meetings the commission voted to go along with the Park Service's plan to emphasize the headlands' potential as natural open space.

Features

As a look at the topo map—or a climb to the top of a hill—will show, the headlands section of the GGNRA consists mainly of southeast-northwest trending open ridges separated by watercourses. Vigorous hikers can see quite a bit of the country in one day by going up and down the ridges on the Pacific Coast or the Miwok Trail. More leisurely hikers may wish to stroll along the protected valleys, each of which eventually leads to a sheltered beach.

Most of the "trails" in the Marin sections of the GGNRA are old Army or ranch roads. The topos show nearly all such roads, including the ones that are not official GGNRA trails; the Olmsted and Erickson maps show most of them; the park maps show mainly the official trails, the military installations and the access roads. The maps in this book do not show all the old roads leading off from the routes described.

The outings described in the following pages are just a sample of the rambles possible in the headlands. With the aid of the maps mentioned above and a pair of good Vibram-soled boots you can explore at your will. Even without a map you can't get seriously lost here, because if in doubt you can always climb to the top of one of the treeless hills and orient yourself.

Facilities

Visitor Center in Fort Cronkhite open daily 8:30 A.M.—4:30 P.M., wheelchair-accessible, provides maps and information and contains a small museum; within and nearby are water, restrooms, phones; fire rings on beach. Hang gliding is permitted in a designated section of Rodeo Valley after checking in with rangers. The Fort Barry Parade Grounds and Rifle Range can be reserved for large groups for day use.

Camping facilities

The headlands contain camps suitable for large groups, small groups, families and individuals, and bicyclists; some of the facilities are wheelchair-accessible. The availability of water and the rules regarding fires vary from camp to camp. Detailed information about the camps is obtainable from the Visitor Center (331-1540).

Battery Alexander is an old fortification south of Rodeo Lagoon now adapted to serve as a camp for groups of 25 or more.

Kirby Cove, open April through October, has three group campsites situated near the beach just west of the Golden Gate Bridge and sheltered by pines.

Bicentennial Camp for bicyclists and backpackers is spectacularly located in a nook overlooking the Golden Gate.

Haypress and Hawk backpacking camps are described in succeeding chapters.

Regulations

No trailbikes; no motorized vehicles; no smoking on trails; swimming not advised; observe caution when exploring old bunkers; stay well away from hazardous cliffs; in the back country, always close cattle gates after you; on riding-hiking trails, give equestrians the right of way.

Pet rules for the GGNRA in Marin are complex. The Park Service has issued an outline of them which you can obtain from the Visitor Center. Of the areas described in this book, pets are permitted on leash or under voice control on Rodeo Beach; they are not allowed in the natural area of Gerbode Valley.

Camping regulations

They differ for each camp. The ones that apply to all and are the most important to know in advance are:

Camping is allowed by permit only, and reservations are taken no more than 90 days in advance of use dates. Campground permits may be mailed for visitor convenience but must be confirmed by user no less than three days before use date. Sites not confirmed or used on first night will not be held.

Camping is limited to three user nights annually at each site.

All pets are prohibited except guide dogs for the blind.

Groups must have a responsible leader 18 years or older for every 10 children.

Fireworks and weapons, including sling shots, bows and arrows, are prohibited.

Cooperating organizations

A number of old Army buildings are now being used by groups whose aims are compatible with the Park Service's.

California Marine Mammal Center (open daily 10 A.M.—4 P.M.; phone 331-SEAL), located in an old Nike base, rescues sick and wounded seals and sea lions from up and down the coast and nurses them back to health so that they can be released in the ocean again.

Golden Gate Hostel (331-2777) is one of the chain of coastal hostels operated by American Youth Hostels. It is located in a large old building in Fort Barry.

Headlands Center for the Arts (331-2787), located in Fort Barry, sponsors exhibits.

Headlands Institute (332-5771) offers residential natural-science field studies and overnight conference facilities with food service.

Pacific Energy and Resource Center (open weekdays 10 A.M.— 4:30 P.M.; phone 332-8200), located near the Visitor Center, features exhibits on solar energy, energy-saving devices and renewable resources.

Point Bonita YMCA (331-9622) has overnight facilities, food service, and classrooms suitable for school groups or conferences.

Recommended reading

Killion, Tom, *Fortress Marin: An Aesthetic and Historical Description of the Coastal Fortifications of Southern Marin County.* San Rafael: Presidio Press, 1979.

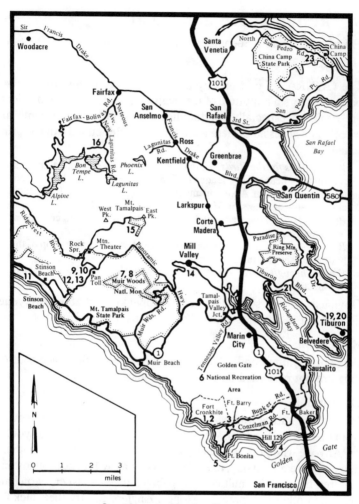

Southeast Marin County

1 Rodeo Beach and environs

How to get there   See under "Marin Headlands".

Features

The GGNRA, as part of its plan to encourage people to use their park, sponsors a multitude of free walks and nature programs. Some are designed especially for families with children, and some are wheelchair-accessible. Here are a few examples culled from a spring schedule:

> *Wednesdays for the Birds:* Watch the season evolve and greet the first returning pelicans. (The leader is Carter Faust, a retired high-school teacher and Marin Audubon member who is also one of the dedicated raptor counters on Hawk Hill—see Chapter 4.)
>
> *Pier Crabbing:* How and where to catch them and how to cook them when you do!
>
> *Blue Moon Watch:* Learn blue moon lore as we walk to the top of the battery to see the full moon rise.
>
> *Walk Through Three Generations* of batteries, including the Nike missile site.

Obviously there's something here to appeal to just about everyone. To find out in advance about the programs, phone 331-1540.

Regulations

Pets are permitted on Rodeo Beach on leash or under voice control; they are not permitted on the guided walks.

Description

Most of the nature walks begin at the Visitor Center. Where you go from there will depend on where the ranger or naturalist leads you.

Anyone who prefers to enjoy Rodeo Beach by himself or with his dog can have a field day, too. The beach is a joy for rockhounds and children because its multicolored pebbles include jasper, carnelian, agate and other semiprecious stones. Anglers can try their luck for surf perch from beach or rocks. Birders can stroll south to guano-covered Bird Island to watch cormorants and brown pelicans, and at low tide can make their way to a small beach just beyond it. (But watch out: this is one of those beaches where you can get trapped if you don't keep your eye on the incoming tide.)

You may want to finish your outing with a visit to the Pacific Energy & Resources Center and/or the California Marine Mammal Center. Children especially like to watch the pinnipeds being cared for at the Marine Mammal Center, and photographers will find lots of appealing subjects.

2   A Wolf Ridge loop

Distance   5-mile loop.
Grade   Moderate.
How to get there   See under "Marin Headlands".

Features

This loop trip of about 5 miles (8 km) is a great introduction to the
headlands, because it includes some of this terrain's most distinctive features: rolling, treeless ridges that offer ever-changing views
up and down the coast and over adjacent valleys; occasional abandoned fortifications, many of them situated on hilltops like medieval
castles; and a feeling of wildness and solitude that is almost
incredible only four miles from San Francisco as the cormorant
flies.

Another characteristic feature of the headlands is windiness.
Bring a jacket!

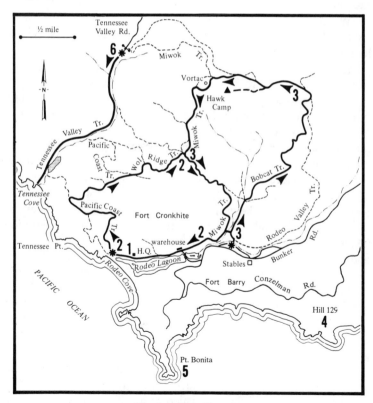

Marin Headlands

Facilities

Water, restrooms, at Visitor Center; none along the trail.

Regulations

Pets have traditionally been permitted on this route, but the rules are subject to change; better check with headquarters before bringing Fido.

Description

From the parking lot north of the Visitor Center, find the Pacific Coast Trail heading north. As you ascend gently over the exposed hill, the sound of the ocean behind you gradually recedes. The most conspicuous vegetation along this part of the trail is coyote brush (*Baccharis pilularis* variety *consanguinea*), a shrub that is extremely common along the northern California coast. An occasional introduced exotic plant (e.g., acacia, pampas grass) lends variety to the vegetative scene.

When the trail joins a paved road, go left (west) on it. At a saddle another paved road goes left toward Battery Townsley. Pause here to look back and enjoy the view: part of Rodeo Lagoon, Bird Island, a glimpse of Point Bonita lighthouse, and the City in the distance (where, as usual, Sutro Tower dominates the scene).

Continue west on the paved Pacific Coast Trail. When it makes a broad switchback, you can look northwest to see Tennessee Cove and the Muir Beach headlands with their eccentric architecture. As the trail continues gradually ascending Wolf Ridge (passing some mouldering military installations) you have views of the Golden Gate Bridge, more of the City, and eventually of the three peaks of Mt. Tamalpais. An intriguing white object that looks like a monument, on a hilltop to the east, is a prominent landmark for hikers on these headlands trails. This is a Federal Aviation Administration installation, officially called a Very High Frequency Omni-Range and Tactical Air Navigation Aid—familiarly referred to as Vortac. It is a long-distance directional homing device for commercial aircraft.

When a sign on the left shows the junction of the Pacific Coast and Wolf Ridge trails, you can stay on the road to take a side trip up to Hill 88. The top of the hill used to accommodate a missile tracking site; since the GGNRA has taken over it has occasionally served as a group campsite.

Retrace your steps to the junction, scramble off the road and begin descending on the Wolf Ridge Trail. Far below on your left is pastoral Tennessee Valley, in which you will probably see cows grazing. This valley was to be the grand entrance to the ill-fated Marincello project, which was intended to cover with tract houses and highrises much of the land that spreads before you.

The trail contours with some ups and downs around a steep cliff of layered red chert under the former missile tracking station, then runs east alongside a barbed-wire fence. When you come to a green gate, go through it (closing it behind you). This is another good spot to lunch, look for hawks and vultures, and enjoy the view before descending. (Determined hikers who want to go on for about another 4 miles can continue uphill here and return by way of the Bobcat Trail, described in the next chapter; they cannot take dogs on this trail, however.)

To return to Rodeo Valley, descend on the Miwok Trail. On your right is a hillside which is ablaze with poppies in spring; downhill on your left a willow-bordered creek, which is home to goldfinches and other birdlife (see next chapter) and eventually the remains of the old Silva ranch house. Ahead of you are the Fort Barry stables. The Silva family were among Marin's most prominent citizens of Portuguese descent. They owned ranches in western Marin, as well as the 2200-acre one here that almost became Marincello.

When you reach a trail junction, bear right and cross the meadow to the big white warehouse. The most scenic way back is on the lagoon side of Bunker Road.

Rodeo Lagoon (named for the cattle round-ups William A. Richardson held in the valley when he owned Rancho Saucelito) is never quite the same from season to season. The beach usually blocks Rodeo Creek from the sea, and the creek's fresh (albeit sometimes polluted) water backs up to form the lagoon—until a storm breaks the sand barrier and the ocean comes rushing in. Here you will invariably see birds (who don't mind the water pollution)— egrets, great blue herons and assorted ducks.

3   The Bobcat Trail and Hawk Camp

Distance   7-mile loop from Visitor Center; 5-mile loop from alternate trailhead.

Grade   Moderate; the first half is mostly uphill, but not steeply.

How to get there

Campers will start at the Visitor Center or the old warehouse (Building 1111), where they can park overnight. Day hikers can shorten the trip by parking about a mile east of the Visitor Center on an old, unsigned road that arcs off on the north side of Bunker Road.

Features

This is a wonderful hike for a spring day because of the profusion of wildflowers along the way. Birders also will find much to intrigue them. Because Gerbode Valley is a nature preserve, backpackers at Hawk Camp have a chance to see wildlife—rabbits, foxes, perhaps even a bobcat.

Facilities

At present Hawk Camp is extremely primitive and contains only a table and a chemical toilet—*no water*. The Park Service may add some other facilities.

Regulations

No pets; reservations necessary for camping.

Description

The Miwok Trail begins just east of the old warehouse, Building 1111, and in ½ mile meets the Bobcat Trail. Hikers who parked at the west end of the old arc road will find two footbridges crossing the creek among willows, and a trail that soon runs into the Rodeo Valley Trail just east of its junction with Bobcat. You may see both Brewer's and red-winged blackbirds here, and quite possibly a red-tailed hawk or a marsh hawk.

The Bobcat Trail runs above the east bank of a creek. Birders should pause to study the willows and shrubbery in the creek, which are a haunt of goldfinches. With luck and patience you may also see a northern (formerly Bullock's) oriole or a lazuli bunting, a species in which the male has upper parts of bright turquoise (the female, however, is called by Roger Tory Peterson "nondescript").

The trail ascends gently past the foundations of the old Silva ranch house. There are several introduced trees here—most conspicuously a stand of eucalyptus. The thistle, radish, mustard, and head-high fennel and poison hemlock you have been walking through are not native plants either; but the poppy and lupine on the hillside are, as is the coastal scrub (coyote brush, California sagebrush) that borders the trail. As you continue to climb gradually, you come upon more and more wildflowers: paintbrush, morning glory, monkey flower, wild cucumber, checker bloom, blue-eyed grass, yarrow, narrow-leaved mule ears, iris and, in the moister places, columbine. The view back over the lagoon, Fort Barry and the ocean becomes increasingly panoramic. Looking northwest you see a grove of eucalypti and above it a grove of pines—the site of Hawk Camp. Above all is the Vortac described in the preceding chapter.

As you near the crest of the hill, the Rodeo Valley Trail comes in from the right. The Bobcat Trail curves west, and Mt. Tam's three peaks become visible to the north. As you walk along the ridge you get views of Strawberry Point, Tiburon and Richardson Bay, then of the top of the Golden Gate Bridge and of San Francisco.

The trail to Hawk Camp is currently marked by a small sign on the left of the Bobcat Trail. The camp trail descends toward the eucalyptus grove, then ascends toward the pine grove that shelters the camp.

If you're not going to the camp, stay on the Bobcat Trail heading for the Vortac. When you are almost at the summit of the Vortac's hill, you pass a sign showing where the Miwok Trail goes north, downhill to Tennessee Valley. To pick up the Miwok Trail going south, back to Rodeo Valley, you have to go clockwise around the Vortac's fence to the road going downhill to the southwest.

This road descends, steeply in places, for about ½ mile to reach the junction with Wolf Ridge Trail at a green gate. The rest of the descent is as described in the latter part of the preceding chapter.

4 Hawk Hill

How to get there

By car From Highway 101 northbound, cross the Golden Gate Bridge and take the Alexander Avenue exit. Immediately turn left, where the sign shows the route back to San Francisco, but instead of going back to San Francisco bear right, uphill, on Conzelman Road. From Highway 101 southbound take the Sausalito exit, turn left and then immediately turn right on Conzelman.

Features

For thousands of years, raptors (birds of prey) have been flying over this spot on their southward migration. And for at least forty years, people have been coming here to enjoy the spectacular views of San Francisco and the Golden Gate. But only in the past decade have the people started coming to watch the raptors!

In the early 1970s an ornithologist at the California Academy of Sciences, noticing an unusual number of hawks flying south past his window, decided to track down their migration route. Because hawks don't like to fly over water any more than necessary, the logical place to find them seemed to be Diablo Point, from where they could make the shortest possible crossing over the Golden Gate. And that's where the flyway turned out to be; it fact, it turned out to be one of the four best hawk-watching sites in the country. The greatly increased popularity of birding during the 1980s brought hundreds of eager hawk-watchers to the hill. Their dean is a retired high-school shop teacher, Carter Faust, who has become an expert at identifying raptors.

The best season for watching the southward migration is from mid-September through mid-December. The hawks keep bankers' hours, generally flying between 9 or 10 A.M. and midafternoon. This fact perhaps helps to account for the popularity of watching hawks as opposed to so many other birds, who inconsiderately make their appearance at daybreak.

Facilities
No water; toilet; parking may get dicey on hawk-watching weekends.

Regulations
No pets; observe cautionary signs on hazardous cliffs.

Description
Conzelman Road runs uphill past Battery Spencer (construction begun in 1893) and offers a number of parking places to enjoy the superb views of Bridge, Bay and City. After 1.8 miles from Highway 101 you arrive at the 900-foot crest of the road, now called Hawk Hill but still labeled Hill 129 or Battery 129 on most maps. Here is the largest and most recent of the Headlands' batteries, and the only one not named after a soldier. Its construction started around the beginning of World War II, but before it could be completed it was already obsolete! because most people realized by 1943 that neither the Japanese nor anyone else was likely to invade San Francisco Bay by battleship. We have seen similar examples of instant military obsolescence both before and after the building of Battery 129, and no doubt will continue to see more. You can still see the huge circular area for the gun emplacement on the west side of the battery. The entire subterranean structure is awesome in size and massiveness— and no doubt was in expense, too.

A fire road to the left of the battery leads to a platform on the top, which for a short period in the 1950s housed a Nike site. This is where the birders now congregate. The hawks pass over this hill because they can catch a thermal updraft here and high-tail it across the Bay by the most direct route. Where do they go afterward? Some perhaps to South America; some only as far as Daly City.

During migration season, the Golden Gate Raptor Observatory—a subgroup of the Golden Gate National Park Association— has staff and volunteers counting the birds and banding some of them, in hopes of finding out where they will travel. Observers tallied more than 11,000 raptors during 1987, of 19 species. Red-tailed, sharp-shinned and Cooper's hawks predominated; there were also other kinds of hawks plus some golden eagles and two bald eagles.

From Hill 129 Conzelman Road continues west as a one-way route along the cliff, always overlooking the spectacular view of the Golden Gate. Eventually it loops around another large installation, Battery Wallace, completed in 1942. The battery is "camouflaged" by a grove of Monterey cypress planted over it. Since this is by far the largest grove of trees on the otherwise nearly bare hills, it must be remarkably conspicuous to any aircraft flying over the headlands. Fortunately, Japanese bombers never reached Fort Barry.

A few picnic tables are located near the battery. From here you can proceed to the lighthouse, if it's open (see next section). Or you can visit Rodeo Beach (Chapter 1). In any event, you cannot retrace your route via one-way Conzelman Road, so you must return to 101 via Bunker Road and the tunnel.

5 To the lighthouse at Point Bonita

Distance   0.8-mile round trip from parking lot.
Grade   It's a short walk, but sturdy shoes and an extra jacket are advisable.

How to get there

By car   From Hawk Hill (previous chapter) continue on Conzelman Road to its end. Or from Bunker Road turn left at Rodeo Lagoon and follow signs with the lighthouse symbol.

History

The light was first installed here in 1855—two years after the *Tennessee* missed the entrance to the Golden Gate and ran aground on what is now called Tennessee Cove, a few miles north. Originally the light was at an elevation of 324 feet, where a radar station is now. This site turned out to be fogged in too much of the time, and in 1877 the light was moved to its present location, 124 feet above the ocean. (The builders of the Point Reyes light in 1870 learned from Point Bonita's experience and located it well below the fog level, even though this site greatly increased the expense and trouble of construction.)

The Point Bonita light has a Class 2 Fresnel lens and is visible from 17 miles out to sea. Augustin Jean Fresnel, a 19th-century French physicist, developed an ingenious system of using hundreds of pieces of specially ground glass to refract light from an oil lamp inside—a technique that revolutionized beacons. The Point Bonita lens was shipped around the Horn from France. Other lighthouses in the Bay Area with Fresnel lenses are at Point Reyes and Pigeon Point.

The Point Bonita light was automated in 1981. For several years it was off-limits to the public, but in 1984 the GGNRA reopened it and began giving regular tours to it.

Facilities

Open seasonally on weekends 12:30–4 P.M.; free tours at 1 P.M. on Saturdays and Sundays; sunset walks twice a month and full-moon walks (by reservation) once a month. For schedules and moon-walk reservations phone 331-1540.

Regulations

No pets; children must be accompanied by an adult.

Description

By far the best way to visit the lighthouse is on one of the guided tours. As you walk down the steep path you can see on your left the remains of a life-saving station the Coast Guard operated here for many years. The ranger or docent will unlock the thick door to a tunnel built through the rock by Chinese laborers over a century ago. Emerging from the tunnel, you cross—in groups of no more than five at one time—a suspension bridge that looks a bit like a miniature Golden Gate Bridge. Looking down, you can see that wind and wave are eroding the pillow basalt of this narrow point, and eventually the lighthouse will be on an island.

6 Tennessee Valley and Haypress Backpack Camp

Phone

331-1540

Distance   4-mile round trip.

Grade   Easy: mostly level, suitable for bicycles, and extremely popular with joggers.

How to get there

By bus   GGT #10, #20 and #63 stop at Shoreline Highway and Tennessee Valley Road, about 1½ miles from the trailhead.

By car   From Highway 101 take the Stinson Beach exit to

Shoreline Highway (Highway 1); less than ½ mile from 101 find Tennessee Valley Road running southwest and follow it to the parking lot.

Features

The San Francisco *Bay Guardian* has dubbed this trail "The Best Nearby Country Stroll," and with good reason. For many years this lush valley was part of the Witter Ranch and hence remained an island of pastoral tranquility in the midst of rapidly suburbanizing Marin. In 1976 its 1268 acres became an extremely welcome addition to the GGNRA. Now an easy, mostly level trail leads along a cheerful creek through meadows where cattle and horses graze, to arrive at a pocket beach situated between the pounding surf and a bird-filled lagoon.

A side trail from Tennessee Valley leads to Haypress Camp— open spring and summer, and one of the easiest in the Bay Area to reach, as it is less than a mile from the parking lot on level trails. This camp offers children and beginners a golden opportunity to try the sport of backpacking.

In addition to all its delightful scenery, Tennessee Cove in 1981 was added to the National Register of Historic Places.

History

The *Tennessee* was a 210-foot steamship launched in New York in 1848. She first ran between New York and Savannah. After the gold discovery, the Pacific Mail Steamship Company bought the ship, enlarged it to hold 550 passengers, and brought it around the Horn to serve the Panama-San Francisco run. On March 5, 1853, the *Tennessee,* returning from Panama, lay off San Francisco all night in dense fog. Next morning the captain, still in fog, headed the ship toward what he thought was the Golden Gate. But the current had moved the *Tennessee* off course, and instead she ran aground on this beach. Chief Mate Richard Dowling leaped overboard and swam to shore with a hawser tied around his waist, thus enabling the crew to rig a breeches buoy and safely evacuate all the passengers—more than 550. Among them was an Adams Express Company agent who unloaded 14 chests of gold in a small boat, and Hudson's Bay Company factor Peter Skene Ogden, who successfully hid $60,000 in gold pieces under his dirty underwear and left it in the cove while he tramped to Sausalito with a group seeking help from William A. Richardson.

Efforts to salvage the vessel were unavailing, as breakers shattered it to bits. The huge cast-iron engine lay—and still lies—in the

ocean just outside the cove. After the GGNRA acquired Tennessee
Valley in 1976, NPS staff began researching the area scientifically
with the assistance of a nonprofit group of archaeologists and
historians known as the S.S. Tennessee Archaeological Project. Park
Historian James Delgado and Tennessee Project Archaeologist
Robert Bennett have led specialists and volunteers in surveying the
cove and recovering pieces of the ship and its cargo, including bolts,
nails, bottles, shards of window glass and the crosstail from the
engine. The engine itself—the earliest known American-built ocean-
going marine steam engine—has been located by electronic survey
equipment, but at present the Park Service has no plans to salvage it.

Facilities

Toilets at trailhead and near beach; no water; Haypress Camp open
May through October, contains tables, toilet, no water.

Miwok Livery, near the trailhead, offers riding classes and
guided trail rides to various parts of the GGNRA (phone 383-8048).

Regulations

No pets; no motorized vehicles; no smoking on trail; no fires; no
guns; do not approach livestock; reservations necessary for camping
(phone 331-1540).

Description

The trail begins where the red-tiled pseudo-mission-style gates to
Marincello stood in solitary and incongruous grandeur for several
years after the project was aborted; the Park Service demolished
them in 1978. (To tell the truth, I was a bit sorry to see them go: they
were so totally inappropriate to the surrounding landscape that they
had a sort of weird charm; and more important, they reminded us of
how close we came to having 400 acres of high-rise apartments, 500
of commercial development and 175 of light industry on the headlands, instead of the open meadows and hillsides we have now.)

Note the Miwok Trail running north and south from the Tennessee Valley trailhead; from strolling the various valleys in the
headlands you can get a good idea of whether you'd like to take the
Miwok (or, farther on, the Pacific Coast) Trail over the hills. The
Tennessee Valley Trail begins as a paved road, but it has footpaths
on either side for walkers who don't like paving. The route gradually
descends along a small creek bordered by eucalyptus trees.

From a junction a short ¼ mile from the trailhead, an old ranch
road leads another short ½ mile to the Haypress backpack camp.

Surrounded by bare hills with rock outcroppings, the site suggests Wuthering Heights, except for the eucalyptus trees scattered about.

The main trail continues its gradual descent where a parallel footpath offers an alternative, when it is not too muddy. In the 1840s, when this valley was part of Richardson's Rancho Saucelito, it was full of wild game. Charles Lauff, one of Richardson's guests during Christmas of 1847, describes a bear hunt in nearby Rodeo Valley, at which not only a bear but also a mountain lion were captured, and adds: "As we passed into the Elk Valley [as this valley was known before 1853] the hillside was white with bones of elk, deer and wild coyote killed from time to time for their hides." The hunting tradition continued into the 20th century in the form of a gun club on the Witter Ranch.

You pass a mission-style house (private), a barn and a corral on your left and a bike rack on your right, and continue to descend gradually along the willow-lined creek. At a fork, bear left, where a sign shows the continuation of the trail over a meadow—the most direct route, unless it looks too muddy. The graveled road, more suitable for bicycles, goes past the former gun club and subsequently rejoins the main trail. Soon after crossing a tributary creek on a culvert, you pass an intersection with the Pacific Coast Trail.

Eventually you reach the earthen weir that dams the creek to form a lagoon, generally full of ducks. From here it's a short walk to the beach guarded by steep cliffs. The Army leased this end of the valley during World War II, and some of their structures are still visible. Even if it's a windy day, you can probably find a sheltered spot to stretch out, picnic and watch the cormorants on the rugged seastacks offshore.

On a bluff a short distance above the beach is a bench dedicated to the memory of Timothy P. Murphy, July 28, 1956–June 24, 1984. Loretta Farley of the GGNRA has provided an account of how it came to be there:

The bench at Tennessee Valley was placed there in September of 1986. Mr. Murphy had climbed up the steep cliff side for a picnic and then fell to his death. It was a very tragic situation as he apparently had just completed his law degree. He was with his fiancee, who sought help from the park rangers.

The bench was donated to the park by Mr. Murphy's family in his memory. Usually, memorial plaques are not permitted in national parks, but an exception was made here due to the circumstances of the case. Today, park visitors who sit on the bench can have a pleasant and safe view of the beach.

Muir Woods National Monument

Mailing address and phone
Mill Valley 94941; 388-2595

Maps

Topo *San Rafael;* the maps mentioned in the introduction to Mt. Tamalpais (p. 68) include Muir Woods. A trail map is available from the ranger station at the entrance.

How to get there

By bus   GGT ran a weekend bus to Muir Woods and Muir Beach for several years, but canceled the service; perhaps it will be resumed in future.

By car   From Highway 101 go west on Highway 1 at the Stinson Beach exit. After 3 winding miles, where Highway 1 continues to Stinson Beach turn right on Panoramic Highway; after 1 mile, turn left on Muir Woods Road (sign) and follow it 1½ miles to the monument parking lot.

Features

Hiking in a virgin redwood forest is an experience available only in northern California. The redwoods evolved about 150 million years ago and reached their greatest distribution approximately 30 to 10 million years ago, when they were common throughout the Northern Hemisphere. The colder climates of the past one million years, including the Ice Ages, greatly restricted their range. Now two genera remain: the coast redwood (*Sequoia sempervirens*) in the fog belt along the northern California coast, and the giant sequoia (*Sequoiadendron giganteum*) on the western slope of the Sierra. The tallest trees in the world are coast redwoods that grow about 300 miles north of the Bay Area, and the biggest are giant sequoias that grow more than 100 miles southeast. (The oldest trees in the world are not redwoods, but the bristlecone pines in the White Mountains of California, near the Nevada border.) However, there are several impressive virgin redwood forests within 100 miles of San Francisco: Muir Woods in Marin County, Armstrong Redwoods in Sonoma County and Big Basin in Santa Cruz County. Some trees in these parks are over 200 feet high and more than 1000 years old.

Whether one experiences the redwood forest as calm, peaceful, awesome, eerie or ominous depends on the weather and one's mood.

The word that recurs most often in literature about these trees is "awe." Even the most hardened rationalist tends to respond with animistic feelings toward the majestic redwoods. (Perhaps this response has some basis in fact: recent research suggests that plants have not only emotions but ESP.) The awe-inspiring quality of the forest results not only from the size and age of the great trees but also from the somber shade (even on the brightest day, very little sunlight filters down to the forest floor) and the silence (the duff underfoot muffles sound). The occasional raucous croak of a jay overhead seems particularly irreverent in this setting.

Although some Californians were offended at Governor Ronald Reagan's remark about the redwood trees, "See one, you've seen them all," it would be close to the truth to say that when you've seen

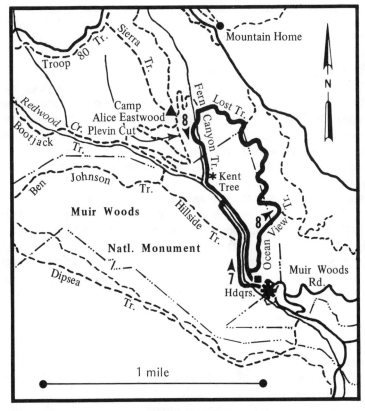

Muir Woods

one redwood-forest plant community, you've seen them all, since the dampness and shade severely limit the variety of plants that can grow under the big trees. Among these plants are sword fern, aralia and redwood sorrel. Trees that frequently associate with redwoods are bay, tanbark oak and Douglas fir.

The redwood forest is fascinating to hike in at any time of year, but it is especially enjoyable in summer, when it is cooler and less dusty than surrounding areas.

History

Muir Woods is an inspiring example of what one dedicated conservationist can do to preserve a beautiful area for following generations. This canyon full of redwoods would undoubtedly have been logged or flooded for a reservoir in the first decade of the 20th century but for one strong-minded man, William Kent. In 1905 Kent purchased 300 acres of the canyon for $45,000, intending to save it for the public, and three years later he persuaded President Theodore Roosevelt to make it a national monument named for John Muir.

Kent subsequently donated more acreage to the monument, and for many years he maintained the access roads at his own expense. He also persuaded his friend Sidney B. Cushing to run a branch line of the Mt. Tamalpais railroad, of which Cushing was then president, into the woods. The gravity cars descended from the Double Bow Knot along tracks on what is now a fire road. Kent also sold the railroad a parcel of land adjoining the monument on which to build a hotel in 1908. The first Muir Inn burned down in 1913; the second was torn down after the railroad went out of business.

The GGNRA took over the administration of Muir Woods in 1978, and has tried to cope with ever-increasing crowds of visitors—over 1½ million in 1987. During the winter of 1986–87 the sewage system collapsed, due to heavy rains plus a dramatic increase in park usage. A new system is planned, but in the meantime the visitor is greeted by an unsightly line of portable toilets near the entrance.

Facilities

Open 8 A.M. to sunset. Parking just outside the gate. Water, restrooms, snack shop, book shop and gift shop, wheelchair accessible. As noted above, until the new sewage system is completed the restrooms are somewhat primitive.

The staff gives nature walks for families; for schedule, phone 388-2595.

Regulations

No camping, smoking or picnicking; no pets.

7 Along Redwood Creek

Distance   2 miles.
Grade   Very easy.

Features

Muir Woods is one of the pre-eminent tourist attractions in the Bay
Area: on any day, and especially on weekends, charter buses unload
hundreds of travelers from every part of the world, wearing costumes
that range from saris to levis and conversing in a Babel of tongues—
but usually quietly. The awe-inspiring qualities of the forest seem to
have a subduing effect on even the most ebullient visitor.

If you are a Bay Arean entertaining friends or relatives from out
of town or out of country, you are almost obligated to take them to
Muir Woods for an hour or so. Even the very young and the very old
can enjoy the level trails on either side of Redwood Creek within a
mile of the visitor center.

Warning: the parking lot at Muir Woods on sunny weekends
frequently resembles the one at the Marina Safeway on Saturday
afternoon—an endless stream of cars circling steadily around at a
speed of ½ mile per hour while they wait for someone to pull out. Try
to go on a weekday if at all possible.

Description

From the parking lot walk north to the visitor center. Along the way,
markers—some duplicated in braille—point out common plants of
the redwood ecosystem. Near the visitor center is a cross section of a
redwood, whose rings are labeled to correlate them with various
historical events.

Now walk across the rustic bridge to the west side of Redwood
Creek, the stream that flows through the monument. If you're here in
winter, you may see salmon and steelhead fighting their way
upstream to spawn. Walking north along the creek, you soon come to
Bohemian Grove, where members of San Francisco's elite Bohemian
Club encamped in 1892. They were considering buying land here for
a permanent camp, but found the place too cold and clammy, and
decided on their present location near the Russian River instead.

At Bohemian Grove begins a ¼-mile nature trail. In 1976 this
was designated a National Recreation Trail and a tree along it,
judged to be about 200 years old, was christened the Bicentennial
Tree.

Follow the nature trail to its end, near another footbridge. Cross this bridge to return to the east side of Redwood Creek and Cathedral Grove, which contains what is perhaps the most poignant memorial plaque in the monument:

> Here in this grove of enduring Redwoods, preserved for posterity, members of the United Nations Conference on International Organization met on May 19, 1945, to honor the memory of Franklin Delano Roosevelt, thirty-first President of the United States, Chief Architect of the United Nations and Apostle of Peace for all Mankind.

Ironic as this inscription may seem from today's perspective, one cannot help being moved by the sight of continual visitors from various members of the United Nations solemnly studying it.

Walk north along the east bank of the creek ¼ mile to reach the William Kent Memorial Tree, a 273-foot Douglas fir, the tallest tree in the monument. The plaque honoring Kent is set in a 3½-ton boulder, which hikers from the Tamalpais Conservation Club brought down the mountain on the railroad and rolled by hand to its present site.

Turn back to Cathedral Grove and continue south on the east side of the creek. Soon you pass the memorial to Gifford Pinchot, Theodore Roosevelt's Chief Forester and a giant of the early-20th-century conservation movement. You can end this walk with a cup of coffee at the visitor center, where your guests from out of town can buy postcards to send to the folks back home.

8 Muir Woods without the tourists

Distance 4-mile loop.
Grade Moderate.

Features

Hikers soon learn that even in a place like Muir Woods, which attracts over a million visitors a year, anyone who is willing to walk a mile from the nearest automobile access will soon shake off 90 per cent of the crowd.

A study of the trail maps will reveal that various loops are possible from Muir Woods headquarters utilizing the Dipsea, the Ben Johnson, the Bootjack and other trails through Mt. Tamalpais State Park. Some of these are fairly strenuous hikes, especially going *up* the beautiful but rugged Bootjack Trail. Hiking was easier when the GGT #61 bus was running to Muir Woods, so that one could take the #63 to Pan Toll, hike leisurely downhill and return via the #61.

A route that will take you away from most of the tourists, yet not necessitate too much of a workout, involves the Lost Trail—so called because it was an old trail that had become completely overgrown until a Youth Conservation Corps cleared it in 1976.

Facilities

Water, toilets at Camp Eastwood.

Description

Shortly beyond the Visitor Center, at the Gifford Pinchot Tree, a trail branches off uphill to the right. At present it bears a rather forbidding sign: TO PANORAMIC HIGHWAY 3.2 KM —ALLOW 3 HOURS — STEEP AND DOES NOT LOOP. Technically speaking, this trail *doesn't* loop, but it's possible to use it as part of a loop. The Muir Woods map calls it the Panoramic Highway Trail; the Tamalpais maps and the signs in the state-park section call it the Ocean View Trail. The ocean view is at the top, beyond this loop, but this part of the trail is scenic enough, as it ascends gradually through redwoods and past a delightful waterfall.

Shortly before reaching Panoramic Highway and the Panoramic Trail, the Ocean View Trail arrives at a junction with the Lost Trail. Turn left on the Lost, which descends, steeply at times, to Fern Creek. Now you can take the picturesque Fern Canyon Trail along the creek down to the Kent Memorial and the Bootjack Trail back to headquarters. Or you can prolong your stay in the redwoods by crossing the bridge and switchbacking up to Camp Alice Eastwood, named for the botanist who may be considered the patron saint of Mount Tamalpais. Near here were the original terminus of the railroad and the first Muir Woods Inn, which burned down in 1913. During the 1930s this was the site of the base camp for the CCC men who did so much construction work on the mountain which still exists, some of which we shall encounter in subsequent chapters. In 1949 the group camp was officially dedicated to Alice Eastwood, who was present and commented that it contained her two favorite trees, the redwood and the madrone.

You can return to the valley floor by the Camp Eastwood Fire Road or by the more direct Plevin Cut, and from there via the Bootjack Trail to headquarters. (William T. "Dad" Plevin was a president of the Tamalpais Conservation Club during the 1920s.)

Mt. Tamalpais

Administration

The main hiking areas on the mountain are currently under three jurisdictions:

Mt. Tamalpais State Park
801 Panoramic Highway, Mill Valley 94941; 388-2070

Marin Municipal Water District (MMWD)
220 Nellen Avenue, Corte Madera 94925; 924-4600

Muir Woods National Monument
Mill Valley 94941; 388-2595

(As noted above, Muir Woods since 1978 has been administered by the GGNRA.)

Any extended hike on the mountain may pass through all three of the above jurisdictions, plus assorted townships, local parks, the Marin County Open Space District and the GGNRA.

Maps

Topos *San Rafael* and *Bolinas*. Mt. Tamalpais State Park and Muir Woods National Monument issue maps of their territories, available for a small price; MMWD issues a free trail map. Olmsted Bros.' multi-colored *Rambler's Guide to the Trails of Mt. Tamalpais and the Marin Headlands* contains information on facilities and place names as well as an excellent map. Erickson's *New Complete Trail Map of the Mt. Tamalpais Region* is an old standby.

How to get there

By bus   GGT #63 Stinson Beach bus on weekends and holidays goes to Mountain Home, Bootjack, Pan Toll and Stinson Beach. Other GGT routes run daily from San Francisco, Marin and Sonoma counties to Mill Valley, Ross and Fairfax; the bus stations in these towns are all within a mile of popular trailheads.

As noted above in the section on Marin transit, GGT has been threatening to cut down its bus service; it is wise to phone for up-to-date schedules.

By car   From Highway 101 go west onto Highway 1 at the Stinson Beach exit. After 3 winding miles, where Highway 1 continues to Stinson Beach, turn right on Panoramic Highway and follow signs reading MT. TAMALPAIS. After 1 mile, pass the Muir

Woods Road-Mill Valley junction. Continuing to follow MT. TAMAL-
PAIS signs, you will come successively to the parking lots for Mountain Home (on the left), Bootjack (right) and Pan Toll (left). Here are
located the state park's headquarters and several trailheads. To continue on to East Peak, turn right on Southside Road, still following
signs reading MT. TAMALPAIS, and in a mile reach a junction with
Ridgecrest Boulevard, across from which is the Rock Spring parking
lot. If you turn right on Ridgecrest, you will immediately pass the
small Mountain Theater parking lot (on the right) and after 3 miles
will arrive at the East Peak picnic area and the end of the road.

For trailheads on the mountain's north side, see Trip 16.

Features

To many Bay Areans, "hike" means Mt. Tamalpais. In fact, scores
of people are content to hike there regularly and almost never go
anywhere else. The mountain's great popularity derives from its
proximity to the metropolitan area, its magnificent views, its remarkably varied terrain and, not least, its long history of accessibility by
public transit—including, for many years, "the crookedest railroad
in the world."

Climate

Weather conditions on Mt. Tamalpais may change dramatically
from mile to mile and from minute to minute. When the rest of the
Bay Area is bathed in fog, you can sometimes climb the mountain
and emerge suddenly into brilliant sunshine. Or you may start hiking
in sunlight but soon be engulfed by fog blowing in from the ocean.

In general, the north side of the mountain is cooler, wetter,
shadier, wilder and lonelier than the south side. You can even get lost
overnight on the north side. That happened to a group of Boy Scouts
a few years ago, when they started off on what was supposed to be a
short compass exercise, somehow went astray, and ended up spending two rain-soaked nights in a makeshift camp on the shore of Kent
Lake. As their experience indicates, this is fairly rugged territory
despite its closeness to suburbia, and hikers should respect—and
appreciate—its semiwilderness character.

Geography and geology

Since the slopes of the mountain rise abruptly from the bay and
from the ocean, it has a beauty and impressiveness usually found only
in peaks much higher, and deep, steep-walled canyons separated by
sharp rocky ridges add to the general wildness and interest of the
scene.

—John Thomas Howell, *Marin Flora.*

Mt. Tamalpais actually has three peaks. The east one (2571') is the most interesting to hikers because a number of trails lead to its summit, where there is a fire-lookout tower. The middle one contains the antennae and discs of a private company's radio and microwave relay station, plus some Federal Aviation Administration (FAA) and Pacific Gas and Electric Company (PG&E) towers.

The military took over West Peak during World War II and put it off-limits to hikers. In 1951 the Air Force built a radar station here, and for another three decades the area remained off-limits. In 1982 the Air Force declared the station obsolete, and West Peak was turned over to the GGNRA—not to the Marin Municipal Water District, from whom it was originally leased. Intense controversy ensued over what to do with the peak; this is described below in the section "Preserving the Mountain." West Peak also contains two radar domes in the form of giant golf balls which have for years been prominent landmarks for hikers. These will probably remain, because they are on 3-plus acres separately leased by the FAA.

Mt. Tamalpais, like the rest of the Coast Ranges, consists mainly of rocks of the Franciscan Formation. This formation is a melange of mainly sedimentary rocks laid down from 100 to 150 million years ago: graywacke (a sandstone), shales, cherts and a small amount of limestone. It also includes some metamorphic rocks, mainly blue and green schists, and some "pillow basalt" resulting from eruptions of lava under the sea. Intruded into the Franciscan Formation are peridotite, an igneous rock, and serpentine, peridotite that has been metamorphosed by hot water under intense pressure. Serpentine is especially extensive and noticeable on Mt. Tamalpais (see Hike 12).

Flora

Mt. Tamalpais' geographical situation causes it to have a fascinating variety of vegetation and scenery. The lower flanks, being in the fog belt, remain moist enough to support redwoods, among them the famous trees of Muir Woods National Monument. The upper slopes, more exposed to sun, are covered with hard chaparral. Various species of scrub oak grow on the mountain. The most common is chaparral oak (*Quercus Wislizeni* variety *frutescens*), the scrub form of interior live oak. The most common manzanita is *Arctostaphylos Cushingiana*. Between the redwood forest and the chaparral grow oaks, firs, bays, buckeyes and madrones in various combinations. The serpentine areas support their own distinctive plant community.

Fauna

In addition to the usual Bay Area fauna, the north side of the mountain has in recent years become home to a band of feral pigs who have been enjoying luxurious Marin living in the game refuge. These pigs will eat almost anything, but—just as pigs in Europe search out truffles—their cousins on Mt. Tam especially prize the roots of the rare wild calypso orchid. Their depredations have alarmed the California Native Plant Society. The pigs have also made the mistake of raiding the lush suburban gardens of Ross and Fairfax. The MMWD rangers have begun trapping and shooting them under a special permit from the State Department of Fish and Game; the resulting pork goes to St. Anthony's Dining Room in San Francisco, which provides free meals to the needy. Park managers have installed a fence along Bolinas Ridge in the hope of keeping the pigs from spreading into Point Reyes National Seashore. Any hiker who happens to spot a pig should report it to a ranger.

History

Mt. Tamalpais may have played a prominent role in the mythology of the large Indian population that southern Marin County supported—although many of the so-called Indian legends now told about the mountain turn out, on examination, to have sprung from the imaginations of 20th-century Anglos. Most of these legends involve a sleeping maiden, probably because to some observers that is what the mountain's profile looks like when viewed from the south. The mountain is probably named for a local tribe of Miwoks, the Tamals, who had a village at its foot. Some of our current hiking trails were originally trodden by Indians.

In the 1830s, the Tamalpais area formed part of several large ranchos granted by the Mexican governors to a few settlers—British and Yankee as well as Mexican. Lumbering and dairying went on around the base of the mountain, but its ruggedness and relative inaccessibility saved it from being built over. Construction of the Mt. Tamalpais Scenic Railway in 1896 made the area a prime tourist attraction, and farsighted conservationists began a campaign to have as much of it as possible put into the public domain as a state or national park. Muir Woods became a national monument in 1908, due largely to the generosity of Congressman William Kent. The Tamalpais Conservation Club, founded in 1912, constructed hiking trails and campsites on the mountain while lobbying to establish a state park there. They achieved this aim in 1928, again with the aid of a donation from Kent. Meanwhile, the Marin Municipal Water

District, also formed in 1912, consolidated under one ownership the watershed land on the north side of the mountain and made it available for recreation.

During the 1930s men of the Civilian Conservation Corps, Franklin Roosevelt's favorite New Deal creation, did a great deal of work on the mountain, repairing trails and building bridges and other structures. Their base was at what is now Camp Alice Eastwood. Perhaps their most outstanding achievement was the Mountain Theater, described in a succeeding chapter.

Preserving the mountain

I am not in sympathy with any movement to change Mt. Tamalpais. Its greatest charm is its individuality and its rugged wildness enhanced by proximity to a large city.
—Botanist Alice Eastwood in 1914.

We note that the State Park System is encouraging concessionaires, that new housing keeps creeping up from Mill Valley, Larkspur, and Skye Ranch, that we keep having schemes to use Phoenix Lake to pay for dam resuscitation, or to log off Kent Lake, that extensions of commercial interests on the mountain are hard to reverse.

The Tamalpais Conservation Club opposes any extension of commercial interests on Mt. Tamalpais, including exten sion of already existing facilities.
—Gordon Oehser, Director and Past
President of the TCC in an open
letter to the MMWD in 1982.

One might think that a place so revered as Mt. Tamalpais by so many residents of the whole Bay Area, in such a long-established state park, would by now be secure, and that the TCC, Guardian of the Mountain, could relax after 75 years of devoted labor. But on the contrary—the TCC and other hikers' organizations, such as the Sierra Club and the California Alpine Club, still find themselves defending Tamalpais against people who want to build things on it, or set up concessions, or otherwise exploit it—and even well-meaning people who want to "develop" the mountain with "recreational facilities" so as to attract more visitors to it. The issues involved are basically the same as with the Marin headlands—the proper use of a large open space near a large metropolitan area—but much more passionately felt in the case of the mountain, which has such a long tradition as a natural environment for day hiking.

When in 1975 a bill came before the state legislature to transfer several parcels of land, including Mt. Tamalpais State Park, to the GGNRA, the TCC mustered all its forces in opposition. Although the members were in favor of the GGNRA in principle, and approved of its taking over obsolete military bases, they felt there was no need for it to take over "one of the outstanding hiking areas *in the world*" that was already in the public domain. The GGNRA's focus, as its name implies, is on recreation, whereas the TCC's is on preservation. Moreover, they feared that a bureaucracy in Washington might be less responsive than one in Sacramento. Not long before, the concessionaire at Yosemite National Park had been revealed to be encouraging large conventions in the valley and to have painted boulders for the sake of a commercial television series; the bare possibility that such things might happen to their beloved mountain galvanized them into political action. They carried the day, and Mt. Tamalpais State Park was excluded from the bill.

As noted above, another controversy ensued when the Air Force rather abruptly declared its radar station on West Peak obsolete, and turned over its 103 acres of land and 50-odd buildings to the GGNRA. Opinions on what to do with this property ran a wide gamut—from the conservationists who wanted to restore the area to its natural state, to Irate Taxpayers of Marin, one of whom asserted at an open meeting that he wanted to see "restaurants, viewpoints, concessionaires and big corporations put something useful up there." Now it appears that the buildings will eventually be removed; in fact, some volunteers have already begun this task. And the Mt. Tamalpais History Project has restored two trails that crossed West Peak in pre-war days: the Alice Eastwood from the south and the Arturo from the north.

Hiking on the mountain

Tamalpais now contains over 200 miles of trails under various jurisdictions. This book can describe only a few of the more accessible and more historic ones. The easiest and quickest way to become familiar with the trail network is to go hiking with one of the groups that schedule outings on the mountain. You can get information about them from the ranger station at Pan Toll. The most active is the Sierra Club, which schedules from one to six outings on the mountain every weekend, and frequent ones on weekdays as well; they range in difficulty from those suitable for toddlers to those suitable for mountaineers in training. The Mt. Tamalpais Interpretive Association is currently leading hikes on weekends; for information, phone 388-2070.

Bicycling on the mountain

Mountain bikes were virtually invented on the slopes of Mt. Tamalpais. As they became more and more popular in the 1980s, some rambunctious riders were causing grief to hikers and equestrians. Finally the MMWD with the cooperation of a cyclists' group issued a map of permitted routes and a code of regulations. The most important of these are: bikes are allowed only on roads, not on trails; maximum speed is 15 miles per hour; slow to 5 miles per hour at blind turns and when passing. If you plan to take any kind of bicycle on the mountain, it is essential to get this map from the MMWD, 220 Nellen Avenue, Corte Madera 94925, or from the Bicycle Trails Council of Marin, Box 13842, San Rafael 94913-3842.

Organizations

Sierra Club
San Francisco Bay Chapter
6014 College Avenue, Oakland 94618; 653-6127

Mt. Tamalpais History Project
c/o Fred Sandrock
21 South Green, Larkspur 94939

Tamalpais Conservation Club
870 Market Street, Room 562, San Francisco 94102

Facilities
Mt. Tamalpais State Park

Headquarters and ranger station at Pan Toll. Walk-in tent sites at Pan Toll on a first-come, first-served basis. Picnic facilities at Pan Toll, Bootjack and East Peak. Backpack camping at Lee Shansky Camp by reservation from Pan Toll (388-2070). Group camping at Camp Alice Eastwood, and environmental camping at Steep Ravine by reservation from Mistix (1-800-444-7275).

Marin Municipal Water District

Several picnic areas scattered about the district and adjacent municipal-park lands. Fishing for trout in the district's lakes, stocked by the Department of Fish and Game, is very popular.

Regulations
Mt. Tamalpais State Park

The usual state-park rules prevail, including *no dogs on trails*. The usual state-park fees apply for camping. Day-use areas are open from ½ hour hefore sunrise until ½ hour after sunset.

Marin Municipal Water District

The district issues a detailed list of its regulations, available from its headquarters or from the ranger station on New Lagunitas Road.

The following are the most important to know in advance:

Open from ½ hour before sunrise until ½ hour after sunset. Cars are subject to a small parking fee at Lagunitas and Bon Tempe lakes. A state fishing license is required. Swimming and boating are strictly forbidden at all times, since these lakes are reservoirs for Marin County's water supply.

Fires are not permitted during the dry season. At present, dogs are allowed on the trails if they are kept leashed. Too many hikers break this rule, and the sharp barking of dogs chasing deer punctuates too many weekend hikes on the north side of the mountain.

For bicycle regulations, see above (p. 74).

Nearby facilities

The Mountain Home Inn (810 Panoramic Highway) operated for more than 50 years as an informal German-style restaurant dispensing simple sandwiches and beer to hungry and thirsty hikers. Beginning in 1976 it went through a series of managerial changes and closings. It has now been transmogrified—one might say yuppified—into an elegant and expensive gourmet restaurant and inn.

Recommended reading

Fairley, Lincoln, *Mount Tamalpais: A History.* San Francisco: Scottwall Associates, 1987. James Heig, picture editor. This handsome, copiously illustrated book is the product of decades of hiking and research by Fairley, a founder of the Mt. Tamalpais History Project and its first president. A must for devotees of the mountain.

Martin, Don, and Kay Martin, *Mt Tam: A Hiking, Running and Nature Guide.* Illustrated by Bob Johnson. San Anselmo: Martin Press, 1986. Identifies many plants along the trails.

Wurm, Ted, and Al Graves, *The Crookedest Railroad in the World.* 3rd ed. Glendale: Trans-Anglo Books, 1983. This greatly enlarged edition is a must for both railroad buffs and Tamalpais aficionados.

9 The Dipsea Trail and Lee Shansky Camp

Distance   2 miles to the camp; 3½ miles one way to Stinson Beach;
6½ miles to Stinson Beach with side trip to the camp; return by
bus. (Perhaps I should point out here that this hike covers only a
part of the Dipsea Race route.)

Grade   Easy and mostly level to the camp; the Dipsea Trail to
Stinson has a few steep spots, but is generally easy if you hike
down and bus up.

How to get there

By bus   GGT #63 (Stinson Beach) to Pan Toll on Saturdays,
Sundays and holidays.

By car   Highways 101, 1 and Panoramic to Pan Toll (see pp.
68–69). Remember to take bus fair for the return from Stinson Beach
to Pan Toll.

Features

Except for the Boston Marathon, the Dipsea Race is the oldest
organized foot race in the U.S. The first official Dipsea Race took
place in 1905 when some members of San Francisco's Olympic Club
ran from downtown Mill Valley over a spur of Mt. Tamalpais to the
Dipsea Inn in Willow Camp, now Stinson Beach. The race has been
run nearly every year since then, except during the depths of the
Great Depression and during World War II. It has become so
popular that participation has to be limited to 1500.

For more than half a century the race was for men only.
However, in 1918-22 five Women's Dipsea Hikes took place along
the route. In 1971 the race was officially opened to women. The
Dipsea is now a handicap race, in which women and the elderly get a
head start. (In recent years, in fact, some racers have complained
that the handicapping system favors women.) Best times for young
men have been just under 50 minutes.

If someone were to give you a topographic map of the Tamalpais
area and ask you to chart a course for a 7-mile race that would
attract over a thousand runners, the Dipsea route might be the *last*
one you'd pick. In fact, the Mill Valley Jaycees, who now sponsor
the event, describe it in the entry form as "a foot race over a rugged,
narrow, unpaved, mountainous, rocky, steep and twisting course
which is not designed for running or for crowds." Perhaps this
description has a certain perverse charm for runners. And now, for
the incredibly macho—or just masochistic—there's a Double Dipsea, from Stinson Beach to Mill Valley and back, and even a

Quadruple Dipsea: from Mill Valley to Stinson Beach and back twice; total distance 28.4 miles (longer than a marathon, and over much rougher terrain).

Lazy hikers can enjoy the final, long, downhill stretch of the Dipsea Trail and its spectacular views without having to agonize through the corresponding uphill, by taking the bus back to their starting point. Lazy backpackers can walk an easy, mostly level 2 miles along fire road to the Lee Shansky Memorial Backpack Camp, one of the most accessible camps in the Bay Area. It was made possible by a donation from the Shansky family in memory of their son.

Facilities at Shansky Camp
Parking available at Pan Toll; 4 primitive campsites, one suitable for groups; toilet, tables, *no water, no fires.*

Regulations for Shansky Camp
Reservations necessary (phone 388-2070); no pets; maximum length of stay 2 nights; small fee.

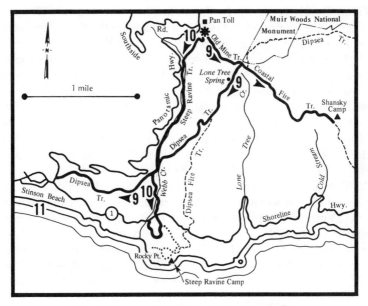

The Dipsea and Steep Ravine trails

Description

Begin at Pan Toll. After filling your canteen—especially if you're backpacking—head south from the ranger station on the paved road. Just past the sign for the Steep Ravine Trail on the right is the sign for the Old Mine Trail on the left. A Park Service sign recommends using the trail rather than the Old Mine Road, which runs parallel to it. The trail runs under Douglas firs, bay trees and coast live oaks. In a short ¼ mile a sign on the right quotes from a mining claim filed in San Rafael in 1863 for this land. Apparently nothing much came of it; but for a while a copper mine operated with modest success a few miles northeast of here, on the west slope of Bolinas Ridge.

Soon the Old Mine Trail rejoins the Old Mine Road. Continuing along it, you emerge from the forest and descend toward two signposts visible ahead—the upper one for the Dipsea Fire Trail, the lower for the Dipsea Trail proper. As you walk you can see the Tiburon peninsula, Angel Island, Mt. Diablo, Oakland and much of San Francisco—including the tops of the Transamerica and Bank of America buildings and the City's weirdest landmark, the Mt. Sutro television tower (which Herb Caen unofficially christened "The Giant Roach Holder"). In the middle distance you can also see much of the Marin headlands and can recognize the ridges separated by Frank Valley, Green Gulch and Tennessee Valley.

Now if you're going to Shansky Camp you'll continue south, briefly on the Deer Park Fire Trail and then on the Coastal Fire Trail. The latter runs along the crest of the ridge, offering views of the ocean to the west and of Panoramic Highway and beyond it Mt. Diablo to the east. As you gradually descend you can see a dark clump of trees ahead of you. When you reach it, you find that it is a dense grove of Monterey pines, a former Christmas tree farm, and the campsites are nestled under the trees.

Returning to the Dipsea junction, walk toward the ocean on the Dipsea Trail. In summer the hills are platinum-colored from the wild oats shimmering in sun and wind. An occasional stand of dark green firs or a gray rock outcropping provides contrast. The view of the hills, the Pacific and the Farallon Islands is marred only by a line of utility poles. The trail joins the Dipsea Fire Trail in ¼ mile. Soon you come to a trail that makes a short detour up a bank to a grove of trees on the right. Here is Lone Tree Spring, constructed by the TCC in 1917. The Dipsea Trail was originally called the Lone Tree Trail; it was renamed when the race became well known. The original name would hardly be appropriate today anyway, because the once lonely tree now has company.

The road descends gradually, passes under the power lines and ascends a small knoll. From here, with binoculars, you can see some of the imaginative architecture on the Muir Beach headlands to the south. Continue on the road, or on the trail that has been running alongside, until you pass under the power lines again. A sign indicates where the Dipsea Trail leaves the fire road here and veers right toward a forest.

After skirting the forest briefly, the trail descends a few stairs, then switchbacks down the slope through picturesque ferns and bay trees. Patches of tall, skinny redwoods alternate with patches of tall, skinny bays as you descend along the south side of Steep Ravine. After a brief stretch in the open, the trail goes back into the trees and down a long series of stairs which the Youth Conservation Corps constructed with old railroad ties. At one point anyone more than 5 feet tall has to stoop to squeeze under a fallen bay that is still branching toward the sun—evidence of the tenacity with which these trees reach for light and cling to life. Toward the bottom of the stairs you begin to hear Webb Creek cascading on your right and see the Steep Ravine redwoods. (Jonathan E. Webb was an early president of TCC.) Cross Webb Creek on a footbridge, turn left and walk toward the dam visible downstream.

At the dam turn right, uphill, and pass the continuation of the Steep Ravine Trail. Soon a sign indicates where the Dipsea Trail continues over some GGNRA land, a hilly, thistly, former cow pasture. The traditional Dipsea route from here to Stinson Beach was partly on or bordering private property. For the greater convenience of racers, hikers, drivers and property owners, the Park Service has rerouted the trail. You cross a dirt road and continue over the barren hills, heading almost directly toward the Seadrift sandspit visible in the distance. As you descend toward the town of Stinson Beach, you get a good view of the steep cliffs that form its backdrop, and a glimpse of some of its hillside domestic architecture.

The trail comes out on Panoramic Highway just above that road's junction with Shoreline Highway. From here it's a short walk north on Shoreline to the town, the beach, and the bus stop, which is marked by a sign at Shoreline and Calle del Mar.

10   Steep Ravine

Distance   3 miles by shortcut; more if desired; return by bus.

Grade   Moderate; much of the trail is very steep indeed, and occasionally requires descending on rough wooden ladders and slippery stone steps.

How to get there   See the preceding chapter.

Facilities

Reservations for the environmental campsites are available by phoning 1-800-444-7275. One of the cabins is wheelchair-accessible.

Features

Steep Ravine has unusually large redwoods for such a narrow canyon so near the ocean. The ravine was formed by Webb Creek, which has been eroding the mountainside for centuries in its rush to the sea. The creekside trail is at its best during early spring, when the water cascades freely and trilliums abound.

History

The first non-Indian hiker in the ravine was probably Lieutenant Felipe de Goycoechea, who explored the area in 1793. He noted that his party descended toward the ocean "by a deep ravine of pine [*sic*] trees which was traversed with difficulty." The weary lieutenant apparently felt that when you've seen one conifer, you've seen them all.

In the late 19th century artist Thaddeus Welch built a cabin in the ravine and lived there with his wife for several years. The cabin has disappeared, but many of Welch's Tamalpais paintings are in California museums.

William Kent purchased the Steep Ravine property in 1904. When you hike down the ravine you will find it hard to believe that Kent and some fellow businessmen seriously contemplated bringing a railroad down here, intending to put Stinson Beach on the map as a major beach resort. Fortunately this plan came to naught. On the day before his death in 1928 Kent formally granted Steep Ravine to the state "to have the property preserved for all time, as far as possible in its natural and wild state. . . ."

Description

From the south end of the Pan Toll parking lot find the signed STEEP RAVINE TRAIL. It switchbacks down through redwood, fir, bay and huckleberry for ½ mile to Webb Creek. From here the trail descends along the creek, crossing it from time to time on footbridges. The splashing stream almost entirely drowns out noise from nearby Panoramic Highway.

The hiker occasionally clambers over and under fallen redwoods. As one might expect in such a narrow, moist canyon, ferns abound: not only sword fern, commonly found with redwoods, but also five-finger fern, spreading wood fern, California polypody, woodwardia, and leather fern hanging from rocks and trees.

After 1½ miles of descent, the Steep Ravine Trail joins the Dipsea Trail, which comes over a footbridge from the left, and continues 50 yards downstream to a dam. From here you can cut the hike short by turning right and following the Dipsea Trail to Stinson Beach as in the preceding chapter. Or you can walk another mile to windswept Rocky Point. To do so, pick up the continuation of the Steep Ravine Trail that branches off from the Dipsea Trail about 30 yards west of the dam. Cross the highway and descend the lupine-covered slope on a rather steep trail.

At the foot of Steep Ravine the marine terrace of Rocky Point juts into the sea. This land was not included in Kent's donation to the state, and in the 1930s the Kent family built some small cabins on it. They were early works of William Wurster, who subsequently became a famous California architect, but they were extremely spartan. Looking at these small, plain buildings, one could hardly guess that their fate generated almost as much of a brouhaha as that of San Francisco's City of Paris or Fitzhugh Building. When the state took over this property in 1960, several prominent Bay Areans had long-term leases on these cabins at remarkably low rents. After years of controversy in the state legislature, the leases were finally terminated and the cabins vacated. Now Rocky Point is the site of an environmental camp, which is extremely popular although primitive.

The safest, most pleasant way to get to Stinson Beach is to retrace your steps a mile to the Dipsea Trail. The alternative is to walk a mile north on the side of Highway 1—a hairy trip, especially in weekend traffic. This is one place where I would consider hitchhiking. If the weather is good, there are usually a lot of cars just north of the Steep Ravine gate, at the parking area for the trailhead to Red Rock (suits optional) Beach.

11   Stinson Beach

Mailing address and phone

Stinson Beach Ranger Station, Stinson Beach 94970; 868-0942; weather information 868-1922.

Maps

Topo *Bolinas;* maps of the Mt. Tamalpais area also show Stinson Beach.

How to get there

By bus   GGT #63 (Stinson Beach) on weekends and holidays. The inhabitants of this traffic-clogged town will be grateful to you for coming by bus.

By car   From Highway 101 go west on Highway 1 at the Stinson Beach exit and continue following signs for Stinson Beach, which is 23 miles north of San Francisco. You can return the same way, or by Muir Woods Road, or by Panoramic Highway. All these routes are extremely scenic and extremely narrow and winding; and all are vulnerable to storm damage.

History

Stinson Beach (originally called Willow Camp) has been a seaside resort for over a century. In the 1870s Captain Alfred Easkoot rented out tents on the beach. During the '80s Nathan Stinson opened his own resort in competition with Easkoot. Around the turn of the century, as we noted in the preceding chapter, several businessmen seriously considered building a railroad over the mountain from Mill Valley down Steep Ravine to Stinson Beach and Bolinas. Among them was William Kent, who prudently bought up much of the Bolinas Lagoon sandspit, as well as Steep Ravine. If the railroad plan had succeeded, Stinson Beach and Bolinas might have become grand, fashionable resorts like those on the East Coast and in southern California. Kent, in his later days as a great conservationist, was probably just as glad that the plan fell through. The sandspit, christened Seadrift by the Kent family, is still a private development adjoining the park. The GGNRA took the rest of the beach over from the State Park System in 1977.

Facilities

Open at 9 A.M.; closing hours vary seasonally. Restrooms, picnic tables, grills. Swimming is popular here, but signs warn that you swim at your own risk because most of the year no lifeguards are on duty. Surf fishing is possible. In the town are restaurants, delis, bars, art galleries and a book store.

Regulations

No pets; no camping.

Description

The main automobile entrance to the beach's huge parking lot is clearly marked by a sign on Highway 1. The bus goes to the parking lot, too. Stinson's broad, white strand is suitable for just about any beach activity—Frisbee, volleyball and football as well as sunbathing and swimming. This beach's popularity is due partly to its sheltered position: both Bolinas headland and Point Reyes protect it to some degree from rough ocean currents and cold northwest winds. However, *no* ocean swimming in northern California is comfortably warm or truly safe, so don't expect Laguna Beach.

If you want to get away from the crowds, you can stroll along the nearly three miles of sand. To the southeast the strand ends at Mickey's Beach, where students of rock-climbing practice their skills. To the northwest is the sandspit on which exclusive Seadrift was built. For many years controversy has centered over public access to the Seadrift beach. According to state law, public ownership of tidelands extends to the mean high-water mark; but it's hard for the casual stroller to know where that is.

During the winter of 1983 a combination of heavy rains, gale winds and high tides battered Stinson Beach, destroying some houses, severely damaging others and removing much of the sand from the beach. The householders of Seadrift speedily cooperated to install over 20,000 tons of riprap along their sandspit's waterfront, thereby saving their homes—at least for the time being. The everhelpful Buck Fund contributed $50,000 toward a study of how to prevent and/or mitigate future storm damage to the beach and the town. Meanwhile, Nature has restored much of the sand . . . and the controversy over public access continues.

12 Around Rock Spring

Distance 5½-mile loop from Pan Toll, 3½-mile loop from Rock Spring.

Grade Moderate; some fording of streams may be necessary during the wet season.

How to get there

By bus GGT #63 (Stinson Beach) to Pan Toll on Saturdays, Sundays and holidays.

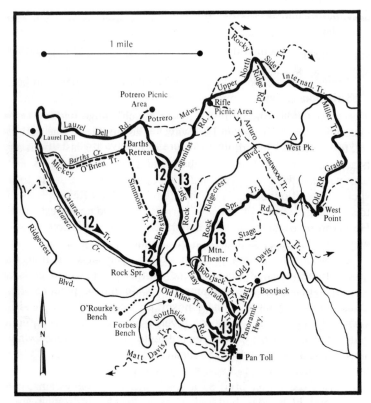

Around Rock Spring and the Mountain Theater

By car   Take Highways 101, 1 and Panoramic to Pan Toll (see p. 68–69). Or continue to the Rock Spring parking lot and thereby cut a mile from each end of the hike.

Features

One of the features that make Mt. Tamalpais so picturesque is the occurrence of large patches of serpentine. This rock, a metamorphosed peridotite, was originally part of the deep-ocean floor. Serpentine is found only in highly disrupted zones, for example, in the Coast Ranges and the Sierra Nevada. It can be almost any color; most of it on Mt. Tamalpais is greenish.

Serpentine is the official California state rock. The state mineral is, of course, gold; and most Californians know that the state flower is the California poppy, the state tree the redwood, the state bird the California quail, and the state animal the extinct California grizzly bear. But how many are aware that the state insect is the California dogface butterfly, the state marine mammal the gray whale, the state fossil the saber-toothed tiger, or the state reptile the Mojave Desert tortoise?

Armed with such knowledge, one might win a few barroom bets.

This hike provides some good views in clear weather, and it passes a number of good picnic spots. In spring, keen-eyed hikers may spot two rare orchids blooming in the woods near the trail, calypso and coralroot—unless the feral pigs have spotted them first.

Facilities

Toilets at Rock Spring, Potrero Picnic Area and Laurel Dell; water at Laurel Dell and Barths Retreat.

Description

The Old Mine Trail heading north from Pan Toll used to run steeply up the open hillside, but in 1979 the Youth Conservation Corps rerouted it. Hikers on the new route can see the old one, and signs request them to avoid erosion by staying on the new trail. To get to it, cross Panoramic Highway and find the paved OLD STAGE ROAD heading northeast. Shortly after passing the intersection of the Matt Davis Trail you turn left on the OLD MINE TRAIL, which switchbacks up through the oak-bay forest. When it comes out in the open you can look down the steep slope to see where the old trail came up from Pan Toll.

The new trail jogs east along a grassy slope, runs briefly through forest again, and then climbs the hillside to provide increasingly panoramic views. At the top of some stairs it goes clockwise around a small knoll (or you can climb the knoll). Now the trail goes slightly downhill and runs through a striking jumble of gray-green serpentine. This rock has apparently been subjected to a lot of shearing and fracturing. Just beyond the serpentine patch, at a fork (riding/hiking trail sign), stay left.

You might want to make a short detour south to the Forbes Bench, a fairly new Tamalpais landmark. Mr. John Douglas Forbes, of San Francisco and Charlottesville, Virginia, has kindly provided the following account:

> The Forbes Bench was built in 1981 to commemorate the affection for Mount Tamalpais of six generations of Forbeses but especially of John Franklin Forbes (1876-1965), my father. The location on the knoll southeast of Rock Spring is about a hundred yards from the weekly Sunday lunching place of the Cross Country Club. There, at the place on the ridge behind the knoll and toward the Mountain Theater where the woods stop and the grassy slope begins, the

walkers of that group would gather after a morning of tramping alone or in small groups. At the turn of the century, those lunches were enlivened by the reading aloud by Miss Alice Eastwood of the Sherlock Holmes stories of Conan Doyle which were appearing serially in *Colliers* magazine. . . . The bench was designed by Robert J. Walsh, landscape architect of Mill Valley, with whom I went to the Mill Valley Grammar School and Tamalpais High School. The native stone harmonizes with the living rock nearby, but it was quarried elsewhere to avoid disturbing the landscape. Permission to build was through the kindness of the California State Parks authority.

The trail descends to the Rock Spring parking lot. For almost a century there actually was a little spring under the trees here, where hikers counted on filling their canteens, but in 1972 the water district bulldozed it for fear of contamination. North of the parking lot a sign indicates the Benstein Trail. For many years this trail ran near another conspicuous outcropping of gray-green serpentine. In 1985 the MMWD, aided by a Marin Conservation Corps crew, rerouted the Benstein Trail so that it would bypass Rock Spring meadow, which was becoming badly eroded. Many hikers find the new trail, which includes six rock-and-railroad-tie stairways, even more attractive than the original. It runs through a woods of Douglas fir, madrone, coast live oak and canyon live oak—the last identifiable by its lead-colored underleaves.

After a long ½ mile the Benstein Trail joins the Rock Spring-Lagunitas Fire Road for 100 yards, and then verges off to the left at the signpost marked POTRERO (the fire road continues to Rifle Picnic Area). Take the trail, and soon reach the crest of the ridge. A few hundred feet over the crest, just before the trail curves north, a break in the dense manzanita to the left leads to a viewpoint overlooking the Pacific Ocean and the Farallon Islands.

The trail now descends through an unusual grove of giant chinquapins, recognizable by their yellow underleaves and the fallen burrs on the ground. Beyond the chinquapins a huge tanbark oak used to grow, but it was one of the casualties of a heavy snowfall in 1974, and crashed down on the trail.

As you continue to descend, you find yourself in a grove of Sargent cypress—a sign that you are now walking over a serpentine area. Serpentine is deficient in some of the elements most plants need for growth, such as calcium, whereas it contains magnesium in amounts that are toxic for many plants. Therefore vegetation on it is limited in both variety and size. Some species, like this cypress, grow only on or near serpentine areas. (In fact, two Sargent cypress trees listed by the American Forestry Association as "twin champions in the U.S." grow not far from this trail.) Other species have a serpentine form that is stunted, compared with their form when growing in ordinary soil. The trail soon comes to a **T** in a serpentine-chaparral community. Three chaparral species grow only on serpentine: a manzanita (*Arctostaphylos montana*), the scrubby leather oak (*Quercus durata*) and a ceanothus (*C. Jepsonii*) with small hollylike leaves and, in the spring, purple flowers.

Turn right here (no sign) and descend to the Laurel Dell Fire Road. Go left on it for 50 feet to find the trail heading north to Potrero Picnic Area. Potrero Meadows extend to the northeast. This flat expanse was once occupied by Rocky Ridge, which slid down the mountain fairly recently, as geologic time goes—about five thousand years ago. A similar slide here today might fill man-made Bon Tempe and Alpine lakes, with disastrous effects on Marin's water supply.

Leave Potrero Picnic Area by taking the Laurel Dell Fire Road west. Past the road to Barths Retreat on the left, you come upon a vista that encompasses Alpine Lake, the Meadow Club golf course, Fairfax and its surrounding hills, and Mt. St. Helena to the north. Unfortunately, nowadays this vista generally encompasses a considerable amount of smog too. The road continues through a serpentine area and then enters a Douglas-fir forest—a sign that you are back on normal soil, since fir won't grow on serpentine. A mile from Potrero Picnic Area you reach Laurel Dell, an extensive picnic ground shaded by lofty oak, fir and bay trees. During the spring of 1862 the young poet Edward Rowland Sill spent a month camped near here and was inspired to write *The Hermitage*, a 40-page book of poems published in 1868.

From Laurel Dell return to Rock Spring via the Cataract Trail, one of the most picturesque on Mt. Tamalpais. Just south of Laurel Dell this trail splits left from the fire road to cross Barths Creek. Now it follows Cataract Creek past waterfalls, ferns and moss-covered boulders. At one point a landslide on the right gives evidence, on a small scale, of the kind of earth movements that have taken place on the mountain. The absence of signs, and the presence of numerous unmapped trails veering off to the left, may make the route appear somewhat confusing, but as long as you stay close to the creek you will end up at Rock Spring. From here you can return to Pan Toll via the Old Mine Trail or via the Mountain Theater and the Easy Grade Trail, described in the next chapter.

Variations On a hot day the Mickey O'Brien Trail provides a shady, cool route to Laurel Dell from Barths Retreat. Professor Emil

Barth was a constant hiker on the mountain from 1886 until his death in 1927; this was his weekend campsite. The two conspicuous pine trees in the meadow here are a Monterey and a Coulter. In 1985 the TCC dedicated a memorial plaque on the Barths Retreat footbridge to Harold M. Atkinson, who had been a tireless volunteer trail worker for many of his 80 years. The trail begins at the west side of Barths Retreat and runs above the south bank of Barths Creek through fir forest and patches of huckleberry. When you emerge from the trees in a short ¾ mile, turn right to reach Laurel Dell.

Another variation is to take the Simmons Trail, which runs between Rock Spring and Barths Retreat over a serpentine ridge where the demarcation of plant communities is strikingly evident.

Side trips

For more serpentine and more views of City and ocean, walk southwest from the Rock Spring parking lot across Ridgecrest and climb the knoll. Here is another large outcropping, greasy-looking in places. Continue southwest, to the right of the windswept trees, and in a short ¼ mile come to O'Rourke's Bench, dedicated to "Dad" O'Rourke, one of the founders of the Mountain Theater. The TCC newsletter commented in April 1927: "In February, a stone seat on one of the knolls west of Rock Springs was dedicated to Dad O'Rourke in honor of his 76th birthday. We are sure that this is not a hint to Dad to stop his hiking, but rather a fitting testimonial to the love and interest that Dad has always had for old Tamalpais."

The Cataract Trail *down* from Laurel Dell is very steep, but it is one of the most spectacularly beautiful trails in the Bay Area, particularly in spring, when the creek flows freely, the flowers bloom and the maples are leafing.

13   A Mountain Theater loop

Distance   6½-mile loop from Pan Toll, 4½-mile loop from the
   Mountain Theater.
Grade   Moderate.

How to get there

   By bus   GGT #63 (Stinson Beach) to Pan Toll on Saturdays, Sundays and holidays.

   By car   Highways 101, 1 and Panoramic to Pan Toll (see pp. 68–69); or continue driving to the Mountain Theater's small parking lot and thereby cut a mile from each end of the hike.

Thomas Winnett

At Limantour Beach

Rock City, Mt. Diablo

Jeffrey P. Schaffer

The Old Pine Trail in Point Reyes

Luther Linkhart

Looking toward Marin County

Gull on Stinson Beach at sunset

Near the visitors center in Muir Woods

Thomas Winnett

Napa Valley, High Sierra from Bald Mtn. in Sugarloaf Park

Jeffrey P. Schaffer

The Golden Gate Promenade

Inside the Berkeley BART Station

Author on the Steep Ravine Trail on Mt. Tamalpais

Richard A. Brown

Canoeing near Limantour Beach

Dorothy Whitnah

The boathouse at Lake Chabot

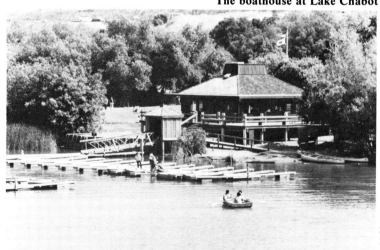

Luther Linkhart

Dorothy Whitnah

Jack London's ill-fated Wolf House

History

The Mountain Theater is one of Tamalpais' most prominent land-marks. Three early devotees of the mountain—Garnet Holme, John Catlin and "Dad" O'Rourke—conceived and promoted the idea of staging performances in this natural amphitheater. With the aid of the mountain's various hiking clubs they produced the first one, *Abraham and Isaac*, in 1913. In 1915 William Kent donated the six-acre site of the theater to the newly formed Mountain Play Association on condition that it be named for his good friend Sidney B. Cushing, President of the Mt. Tamalpais and Muir Woods Railroad, for these reasons:

> He built trails that others might enjoy them. He built the mountain railroad more with the idea of its public benefit than with the idea of private profit. His soul was broad and liberal; he wished to share his joys with all men. He is the man who first taught me the lesson that this mountain is too good a thing to be reserved in the hands of a few and that it should not be a place from which the great public may be excluded.

Since 1913 the Mountain Play has been an annual May event, with three interruptions: a hoof-and-mouth epidemic in 1924; World War II in 1942-45; and the prospect of excessive traffic congestion in 1973. For a while it seemed that the play might be another casualty of the internal-combustion engine, but in 1974 the Mountain Play Association revived the tradition, encouraging playgoers to park elsewhere and make their way to the theater by bus or on foot. In 1983 the Mountain Play Association installed a plaque near the northwest corner of the theater to celebrate 70 years of plays and commemorate Kent, Cushing and their friend Alfred Pinther.

Features

For year-round hikers the Mountain Theater is a grand place to loaf or lunch. Some of the most popular Tamalpais trails lead through it. The route described here makes a loop from the theater around the north side of the mountain, so you can enjoy a variety of scenery.

Facilities

Water and restrooms at the Mountain Theater and at West Point; beverages at West Point; toilets and tables at Rifle Picnic Area.

Description

From the Pan Toll parking lot, cross Panoramic Highway and turn right on the paved OLD STAGE ROAD. After passing the Matt Davis and Old Mine trails, turn left on the EASY GRADE TRAIL. After crossing a draw, the trail turns left and soon crosses the riding/hiking trail to Rock Spring. The Easy Grade Trail continues uphill gently, as befits its name, under firs, tanbark oaks and bays, offering occasional panoramic views. In less than a mile it arrives at the lower edge of the Mountain Theater (water, restrooms).

The theater is the pre-eminent legacy of the CCC to the mountain. The Mountain Play for its first two decades was staged in a purely natural amphitheater without any facilities, while the audience sat on the grass. The Mountain Play Association engaged a San Francisco landscape architect, Emerson Knight, to plan a more elaborate theater. By 1930 he had prepared a plan that would suggest a classic Greek theater yet utilize only native rock and vegetation. As funds were short during the Depression, progress was gradual. The CCC worked on the project from 1934 until 1939. The major challenge to the builders was the stone seating for 6000 people in 40 rows. Knight's plan called for about 5000 stones each weighing from 600 to 4000 pounds; they were to be buried so deeply that only a small fraction would remain above ground. The workers accomplished this feat by using a host of derricks, cranes and tripods. In 1983 the National Association of CCC Alumni dedicated a plaque and an oak tree to the theater builders, and in 1985 the CCC alumni held a reunion here.

Aspiring actors and actresses can enjoy the thrill of declaiming their favorite passages from *Macbeth* or *Medea,* or belting out their favorite numbers from *Oklahoma,* to a more or less attentive audience of squirrels and bluejays in the great amphitheater. They might also want to poke about the stage and see how cleverly the performers' entrances and exits are camouflaged with native shrubs. At the southwest corner of the theater a plaque commemorates Dan Totheroh, author of several Mountain Plays including the all-time favorite, *Tamalpa.* Less histrionic hikers can lounge on the theater's seats and drink in the spectacular view. It is an extraordinary experience to sit in the silent theater and contemplate the Bay and its bustling cities 2000 feet below.

After declaiming, singing, lunching, contemplating or whatever the theater has inspired you to do, climb to its top and turn right on the Rock Spring-West Point Trail, which runs northeast from the top row of seats. (The trail passes a large rock dedicated to Austin Ramon Pohli; this young man was the general manager of the first Mountain Play, and shortly after its production he died in a climbing accident in Yosemite.) Most of this trail goes through chaparral that permits views of the panorama below, but occasionally it ducks into a little forested canyon to cross a stream. After 1½ miles it reaches

West Point Inn. Formerly a station on the Mt. Tamalpais railroad, this building is now managed by the West Point Inn Association. Hikers may use its veranda and may purchase coffee, tea and lemonade. (Restrooms are behind the main building.) The veranda is a pleasant place to enjoy a snack, and you may see hummingbirds, also enjoying a snack, at the feeders hanging from the roof. The pine trees around West Point—like all the pine trees on Mt. Tamalpais—are not native, but were planted here by the water district.

Go clockwise around the inn and take the road behind it running northeast, part of the old railroad grade. Proceed on it for ½ mile and after passing a stream and emerging from a ravine climb the left bank on the Miller Trail. This trail ascends steeply through chaparral for ¼ mile to Ridgecrest Boulevard. Catch your breath while you admire the view of the San Francisco peninsula; then cross the road and admire a new view, to the north. You can see Lagunitas and Bon Tempe lakes beneath you, the Meadow Club golf course, part of Fairfax, Tomales Bay and Mt. St. Helena.

Now go west on the INTERNATIONAL TRAIL (sign), named for the varied ethnic backgrounds of the four men who constructed it. The change in ambience from the dryer south side of the mountain is immediately apparent as the trail descends under live oaks, tanbark oaks and bays, plus California nutmegs, which increase in number and height as you proceed downhill. This conifer, which may at first glance look a little like a Douglas fir or a redwood, has needles so sharp they can draw blood if you carelessly grab a branch.

After ½ mile you reach a junction with the Upper North Side Trail; bear left on it and immediately cross the Rocky Ridge Fire Road. Now you are on an exposed ridge of serpentine, which is covered with various chaparral species (see the preceding chapter) and some Sargent cypresses. Soon the trail reenters forest, crosses a creek, and ½ mile from the ridge arrives at Rifle Picnic Area (toilets, tables). This was formerly Rifle Camp, and according to a TCC newsletter from 1926, it "was named after an old rifle which was dug up by a dog named Schneider that belonged to Dick Maurer, President of the Down and Out Club. The Club is composed of a few old-timers who are also members of the TCC."

The most direct route back to the Mountain Theater is the Rock Spring-Lagunitas Fire Road heading south. Where the road forks just after leaving the camp, bear left or take the shortcut trail straight across the meadow. It's about a mile back to the theater. From there you can retrace your steps to Pan Toll, or you can take the Bootjack Trail to Bootjack Camp and either the Old Stage Road or the Matt Davis Trail to Pan Toll.

14   The Old Railroad Grade

Distance   8¼ miles; shortcuts and detours exist, and variations on
the route are described at the end of the chapter.
Grade   See Features below.

How to get there

By bus   GGT #10 to Mill Valley.

By ferry and bus   GGT ferry to Sausalito connecting with #10
bus to Mill Valley. This route approximates the time-honored
journey of generations of San Franciscans on holiday, the difference
being that after debarking from the ferry they took the Northwestern
Pacific's electric train to Mill Valley. The entire round trip from San
Francisco to the summit and back cost $1.90 in 1913.

By car   From Highway 101 northbound take the Highway 1
(Stinson Beach) exit. Where Highway 1 turns left at a signal, continue north on Almonte Boulevard. Then bear right on Miller Avenue
and follow it to Throckmorton, where the bus depot is.

From Highway 101 southbound, exit on East Blithedale and
follow it to Throckmorton.

Features

The Old Railroad Grade is certainly the least strenuous route to the
top of the mountain: you know in advance that if you stay on it the
gradient will never exceed 7 per cent. The problem is that 8¼ miles
of walking up an old railroad grade is a bit much for everyone except
dedicated train buffs. Another problem is that once you reach the
summit, you have to find a way back down, and the bus does not currently run there. In the first edition of this book I suggested descending by the Temelpa Trail, which runs almost straight down the east
face of the mountain. However, this solution will appeal to only the
young and/or extremely vigorous. I myself plan never to ascend or
descend the Temelpa Trail again in this life.

The Description below follows the Old Railroad Grade up its
entire route and indicates possible shortcuts. At the end of the
chapter I suggest some easier Variations.

In 1972 a Boy Scout troop put up mileposts along the route which
were helpful to hikers, but some of the lower ones have since
disappeared.

History

The complete history of the railroad is recounted in *The Crookedest
Railroad in the World,* by Ted Wurm and Al Graves. Trans-Anglo

Books of Glendale issued a greatly enlarged third edition of this classic in 1983.

The Mill Valley & Mt. Tamalpais Railway corporation was formed in January 1896 by a group of optimistic Mill Valley businessmen, and construction began in February. One of the prime movers in the group, and president of the railroad for many years, was Sidney B. Cushing. Although William Kent subsequently claimed in dedicating the Mountain Theater that his good friend "built the . . . railroad more with the idea of its public benefit than with the idea of private profit," still Cushing might have hoped that the trains would encourage people to visit his Blithedale resort hotel in Corte Madera Canyon. His father had originally founded this resort as a sanatorium and named it for Hawthorne's novel *The Blithedale Romance.*

It is rather ironic that this railroad—which we now regard so nostalgically as the product of a more easygoing, unpolluted era— faced strong opposition, during construction, from both its laborers and the nearby property owners: the laborers objected to their wages ($1.75 for a 10-hour day), while the property owners "rebelled against the use of steam locomotives and the ruination of their most scenic driveway, Corte Madera Avenue, by the dirty, smoking

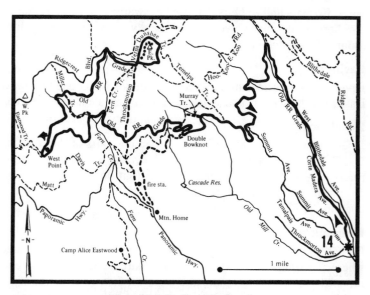

The Old Railroad Grade

engines" (Wurm and Graves, p. 15). The railroad executives managed to outmaneuver their opponents, however, and on August 22,
1896, the first passenger train made its run to the summit. (Eight
months for construction—compare BART!)

In 1907 the company built a branch line from the Double Bow-
Knot down to Muir Woods. The gravity cars coasted down the tracks
at 10 to 12 miles per hour and were hauled back up by engine. From
time to time the company talked of running a line to Stinson Beach
and Bolinas, but these plans never came to fruition.

The Mt. Tamalpais & Muir Woods Railway, as it was renamed in
1913, and its associated taverns—at the summit, West Point and
Muir Woods—became world famous and captivated both natives
and tourists for three decades. The railroad finally expired in 1930,
done in by a fire that swept over the southern slopes of the mountain
in 1929, plus the Great Depression and competition from the
automobile.

It is tempting to imagine that the automobile—which has dominated, and sometimes infuriated, Californians in the 20th century
much as the railroad did in the 19th—may someday be as much an
object of nostalgia as its predecessor. Perhaps, in the not-too-distant
future, Sunday hikers will reverently trudge up a cracked, overgrown Panoramic Highway, comparing lore on the vanished Mus-
tangs, Cougars and Rabbits that used to swarm over it, while cursing
the hordes of solar-powered anti-gravity devices spewing litter
around the mountain.

Facilities

Beverages and restrooms at West Point Inn; water and restrooms at
East Peak; snack bar and visitor center at East Peak on weekends.

Regulations

After the storms of 1982–83 had washed out parts of the road, the
Old Railroad Grade was off-limits to bicycles for a while. Now the
roads have been repaired and bicycles (but not motorcycles) are
once again allowed. It is essential for cyclists to follow the rules out-
lined in the MMWD map mentioned on p. 74.

Description

From the bus depot walk 1 block northeast to Corte Madera Avenue,
where the trains began their run. This street follows a redwood-
forested creek; nestled under the trees are houses in a variety of
architectural styles—one of the charms of Mill Valley. Walking along
this pleasantly shaded avenue, one can understand why the resi-

dents in 1896 objected to the railroad. (This part of Corte Madera is narrow, and it lacks sidewalks, but at least automobile traffic is one-way—oncoming—as far as King Street.)

In less than a mile, Corte Madera Avenue crosses the creek and runs into West Blithedale. Continue on it, or on an obvious trail that runs sporadically along the left bank. Just past Lee Street (on the right) and a small bridge, where the paving veers slightly left, go through a red gate onto a fire road. This is the continuation of the Old Railroad Grade, which gently ascends above the east bank of the creek.

After about two miles the grade makes a hairpin turn in the densely forested canyon (where the Corte Madera Trail branches off to the right) and continues winding up the hillside to the junction of Summit Avenue and Fern Canyon Road. Along the way you emerge from forest to overlook the Corte Madera arroyo and the mansion called "Garden of Allah," officially the Ralston L. White Memorial Retreat, designed by Willis Polk in 1913.

The Old Railroad Grade continues on what is now paved Fern Canyon Road and comes to a fire gate. Go through the gate, past an elegant and well-fenced mansion on the left. If you are a true rail-road buff, you will stay on the road and walk up the Double Bow-Knot, one of the most unusual features of this line, "where the tracks paralleled themselves five times on a broad shoulder of Tamalpais, in order to gain elevation for the final charge to the summit" (Wurm and Graves, p. 62). If you're not a true buff, you may be inclined to take the shortcut Murray Trail, which starts soon after milepost 4 and runs uphill along a creek to emerge on the Hoo-Koo-E-Koo Road. Turn left here to rejoin the Old Railroad Grade at the top of the Double Bow-Knot, and immediately turn sharp right at the riding/hiking-trail sign. Now the road proceeds mainly through chaparral, with increasingly extensive views to the south and east. You soon look down on the Double Bow-Knot and the Hoo-Koo-E-Koo Trail.

Soon after milepost 5 you arrive at the junction of the Throck-morton (Hogback) Trail—a possible shortcut to the summit for the very energetic. Tamalpais historian Lincoln Fairley thinks it was probably this trail that in 1901 nearly cut short Pablo Casals' career as a cellist at age 24: Casals and some companions had climbed the mountain and were descending when a boulder came hurtling down upon him and smashed his left, or fingering, hand. Doctors predicted he might never regain its full use, but fortunately it healed after a few months.

The Old Railroad Grade proceeds through chaparral and dips into a small, ferny canyon, then a larger one, where the east fork of Fern Creek cascades down. The Fern Creek Trail here provides a steep shortcut to Ridgecrest Boulevard near the East Peak parking lot—thereby cutting 2½ miles off the route. At milepost 6 another shortcut, the Miller Trail, runs up the right bank of Fern Creek's west fork; this cuts off 1½ miles.

If you ignore shortcuts and stay on the railroad grade, ¾ mile past milepost 6 you arrive at rustic West Point Inn, the one hostelry that survives from the railroad's glory days. The company built the inn in 1904 to provide a stopover place for passengers connecting with the stage to Stinson Beach and Bolinas (via the Old Stage Road, which you can still hike on). West Point Inn became popular with hikers, and the TCC in 1916 designated it the club's mountain head-quarters. When the railroad went out of business in 1930 the MMWD took over the property and leased it to concessionaires. When it then failed financially, the water district considered destroy-ing it, until a group of hikers banded together to form the West Point Club, now the West Point Inn Association, to maintain the buildings. Hikers may use its veranda (and the restrooms behind the main building) and may purchase liquid refreshments. Pause here, as did the old engines, and stoke up with West Point lemonade.

Circle clockwise around West Point, passing the Old Stage Road and the Rock Spring Trail, and head north on the final 2 miles of rail-road grade. Most of it runs through chaparral, with panoramic views to the south and east. When you reach paved Ridgecrest Boulevard, turn right on it to arrive at the summit parking lot and picnic area, where the Tamalpais Tavern flourished in the days of the railroad's glory (see the next chapter).

Variations

1. One way to hike the Old Railroad Grade in a civilized (some would say effete) manner is to take the bus to Bootjack or Pan Toll and make your way to West Point, where you can pause for refresh-ments. From here you can proceed downhill to the Double Bow-Knot and from the lower bow head west on the old branchline grade to Mountain Home, where you can pick up the descending bus. Total distance: 5 or 6 miles.

2. For a longer hike, you can follow the Old Railroad Grade from West Point all 6¾ miles down to the Mill Valley bus depot. If you're doing this for the first time, remember to turn left where Fern Canyon Road meets Summit Avenue: Summit does go to downtown Mill Valley, but much more abruptly than the Old Railroad Grade.

15   Around East Peak

Distance   ½ mile.
Grade   Easy.
How to get there

By car   See pp. 68–69.

By foot   A study of the trail maps reveals various possibilities: The Old Railroad Grade is described in the preceding chapter.

An even earlier route dating from 1884, originally constructed for wagons, is the Eldridge Grade Fire Road, which meanders up the north slope of the mountain.

Several more direct routes exist: the Throckmorton Trail, the Temelpa Trail, the Indian Fire Trail and the East Peak Fire Trail; they are all very steep and rugged.

History

According to Lincoln Fairley's history of the mountain, the first written account of a climb to the summit is that of William H. Brewer, who was mapping for the California Geological Survey in 1862. He wrote: "It was most grand, more like some views of the Alps than anything I have seen before—those glimpses of the landscape beneath through foggy curtains." A visitor register kept on the summit from 1880 to 1884 has the signatures of 850 persons who made the climb.

The railroad company built the first Summit Tavern near the present picnic area in 1896, the same year the train itself started running. The tavern flourished along with the railroad, and provided refreshments to the throngs of tourists who came from all over the world to take the "wiggle train" to the top of the mountain. Novelist Gertrude Atherton spent an entire winter there, wrapped in her fur coat, writing *The Ivory Tower*. The tavern was the site of memorable celebrations of Mountain Plays, Thanksgiving, Christmas, and especially New Year's Eve; it had a reputation for ignoring the Prohibition laws. When the building burned down in 1923, another was constructed in its place. This one survived the demise of the railroad and was taken over by the MMWD, which leased it to the Army during World War II. The Army and subsequent vandalism left the place a mess, and in 1950 the water district burned it down. Parts of its foundations are still visible.

Facilities

Water, restrooms, picnic tables; snack bar and visitor center on weekends.

Description

If the visitor center is open, start there, to look at the exhibits and pick up a leaflet describing the view from the summit. Next find the Verna Dunshee Trail near the picnic area and take it in either direction around the summit. Mrs. Dunshee was a long-time Marin conservationist and a president of the TCC.

On a really clear day—the sort that nowadays we seem to get only once or twice a year—you can see the Sierra Nevada glistening in the east. On an ordinary day you can see Mt. St. Helena to the north, Mt. Diablo to the east and Mt. Hamilton to the south; to the west stretches an endless sheen of ocean. Nearer at hand lie the works of man—most noticeably, the Marin cities, San Francisco, the East Bay cities and the bridges. In the foggy season, you may find yourself looking down on a sea of cotton, perhaps punctured by a bridge tower, the Transamerica pyramid or ungainly Sutro Tower.

Viewing this scene from the vantage point of the mountaintop, one is tempted to wish for a time machine. We might set the controls first for 1928, when the City's buildings were all light-colored and in scale with one another, when a fleet of ferries plied the Bay and the bridges were only a gleam in a few engineers' eyes. Then perhaps back to 1850, when just off the waterfront of boom town San Francisco floated hundreds of ships abandoned by crews hastening to the gold fields. And then back to 1750, before the arrival of the Spaniards, when the Bay covered 700 square miles instead of its present dwindling 400, and the only signs of man were a few Indian villages. If we were feeling truly brave or optimistic, we might even set the time machine's controls for the future.

You might want to finish off with a climb to the watch tower. In 1901 the San Francisco *Examiner* installed a lookout station, called the Marine Exchange, at the top of the peak to chart the progress of ships entering the Golden Gate. This station was abandoned in 1919 because wireless had made it obsolete. In 1921 the Tamalpais Forest District placed the first fire lookout in the building. During 1935 and 1936 the CCC built a new building here for the fire lookout. As there was no road to the summit, the men had to rig an overhead cable running up from the railway roadbed to carry the huge stones. These were quarried at West Peak and trucked to the cable. The new lookout was dedicated to Edwin B. Gardner, the first warden of the Tamalpais Forest District. The lookout is occupied 24 hours a day during fire season.

16   The North Side

Address and phone

Most of the area is under the jurisdiction of the Marin Municipal Water District (MMWD), 220 Nellen Avenue, Corte Madera 94925; 924-4600.

Maps

Topos *San Rafael* and *Bolinas;* the Olmsted Bros., Erickson, and MMWD maps mentioned on p. 68.

How to get there

The main route to lakes Lagunitas and Bon Tempe and their many trailheads is as follows:

Take Highway 101 and Sir Francis Drake Boulevard to Fairfax. From Drake turn left onto Broadway, go one block west on Broadway, and turn left onto Bolinas Road. Follow it 1½ miles to the white gate on the left with signs CREST FARM, LAGUNITAS, BON TEMPE. Go through this gate and after a short, winding ½ mile arrive at the MMWD entrance kiosk and ranger station.

Two other popular trailheads and picnic areas are at local parks only a mile from bus routes:

Natalie Coffin Greene (Ross City) Park and Phoenix Lake:

By bus   GGT #20 to Ross. The stop is at Sir Francis Drake Boulevard and Lagunitas Road. Note the Bufano bear at the police and fire station just across from the bus stop. Walk up Lagunitas to its end in the park. Along the way you will have a chance to see how the upper crust lives, as you pass discreetly elegant mansions and the Lagunitas Country Club.

By car   From Highway 101 take Sir Francis Drake Boulevard to Ross, turn left on Lagunitas Road and follow it to the park. Note the sign at the entrance telling when the gate will be closed. Parking can be a real problem here.

Deer Park (County) in Fairfax:

By bus   GGT #23 from San Anselmo to Fairfax daily; GGT #65 from San Rafael to Fairfax on weekends and holidays. Walk south on Bolinas Road, turn left on Porteous Avenue and follow it to the end, in Deer Park, 1 mile from the bus stop.

By car   From Highway 101 take Sir Francis Drake Boulevard to Fairfax and drive the mile that bus riders walk.

Features

As noted in the Introduction to Mt. Tamalpais, the north side of the mountain is generally cooler, wetter, shadier, wilder and lonelier than the south side. It is possible to spend a whole day roaming some of the north-side trails without running into another soul (not in the immediate vicinity of the lakes, however). The trails here are not as meticulously signed as are those in the state-park areas of the mountain, so an up-to-date trail map is a virtual necessity.

Facilities

The picnic grounds at Lake Lagunitas, Natalie Coffin Greene Park and Deer Park all have water, toilets and tables; they also have grills or stoves, but use of these may be prohibited during periods of fire hazard. Fishing is popular in the lakes, which are stocked by the Department of Fish and Game.

Regulations

The MMWD issues a detailed list of its regulations, available from its headquarters or from the ranger station. The following are the most important to know in advance: entrance gate to Lagunitas and Bon Tempe open 8 A.M.–sunset; small parking fee; dogs allowed on leash only; swimming and boating forbidden; state fishing license required. Bicyclists should get a copy of the district's map and leaflet (p. 74).

Description

A delightful introduction to the north side of Tamalpais is a walk around one or more of the three most popular lakes: Phoenix, Lagunitas and Bon Tempe. The trip around either Phoenix or Lagunitas takes about an hour; Bon Tempe takes a bit longer. Trails connect the three lakes with one another and with much larger Alpine Lake. The entire family can spend a happy afternoon picnicking, strolling and perhaps fishing in Marin's own Lake District.

More ambitious hikers will find that the Lake District provides trailheads for climbs up the mountain, either in chaparral (e.g., the Rocky Ridge Fire Road) or in forest (e.g., the Colier Springs Trail). With the aid of their trusty map they can explore at leisure such exotic spots as the Hidden Lake, the Foul Pool, the Hogan Tree, the Serpentine Knoll and—best of all—the Azalea Meadow.

Angel Island State Park

Mailing address and phone
Box 318, Tiburon 94920; 435-1915

Maps
Topo *San Francisco North;* trail map available from vending machine near dock.

How to get there
By private boat   Sail to Ayala Cove, the principal harbor.
By ferry   On weekends and holidays throughout the year, and daily during summer, ferries go to the island from Pier 43½, San Francisco's Fisherman's Wharf (Red & White Fleet, 546-2815), and from the Main Street dock in Tiburon (Tiburon-Angel Island Ferry, 435-2131). The ferries will transport up to 25 bicycles. Schedules and fees vary, so call the ferry of your choice to get up-to-date information.

Features
Angel Island, which covers about one square mile, is the largest island in the Bay. It is one of the few spots in California where a pedestrian can wander almost totally secure in the knowledge that he will not see, hear, smell or be run over by motor vehicles. (The park service does operate a few necessary pickup trucks, but these scarcely detract from the generally motor-free ambience.) This feature is only the beginning of Angel Island's charms: it also has unique views of the Bay, a variety of recreational facilities, and a remarkable history.

The island is also the site of some of the State Park System's first environmental campsites, constructed in 1981. Camping on an almost deserted island in the middle of one of the world's busiest harbors, where as night falls you can watch the lights of a great metropolis sparkling, is obviously a unique experience; hence these camps have become very popular and one should reserve well in advance.

History
For such a (nowadays) tranquil spot, Angel Island has had an unusually checkered career. This one square mile has reflected in

microcosm much of the past 1½ centuries of U.S. history—including some of its darker aspects. The story of U.S. acquisition begins, in fact, with a disputed land claim. In 1839, while Mexico still ruled California, Governor Juan B. Alvarado granted the island to Antonio Mario Osio, who ran cattle on it. After the Yankee conquest, the U.S. Army sought to take over the island for military use, while Osio wanted his claim affirmed. The case finally went to the U.S. Supreme Court, which in 1860 ruled against Osio—who thereupon moved permanently to Mexico.

In subsequent years the island served as a prison for rebellious Indians, a dueling ground, a quarantine station, an immigration detention center, a staging area for soldiers during three wars and, briefly, a Nike base. Now that it's a park, nothing much more violent occurs than an occasional game of touch football on the lawn in front of headquarters, but as you walk along the old Army road that circles the island you will encounter frequent reminders of its eventful past.

Facilities

Ayala Cove has water, restrooms, picnic tables, grills and a snack bar. The park sells charcoal briquets. Some tables are on other parts of the island. Picnic facilities for groups are available at the East Garrison by advance reservation. There is a large beach for sunbathing at Ayala Cove, another at the East Garrison, and a few smaller beaches elsewhere. Swimming is forbidden, since the park has no lifeguard facilities. (In any case, swimming in chilly, polluted San Francisco Bay is an activity with limited appeal.) Fishing is permitted—and popular. For campsite reservations, phone 1-800-444-7275.

If you come on the Tiburon ferry, you can rent bikes at Ken's Bike Shop, 94 Main Street; phone 435-1683.

Regulations

The entrance fee is included in the ferry charge. *No dogs are allowed*—and this is one park where the staff can enforce that rule! No skateboards allowed.

Recommended reading

Evans, Elliott A. P., and David W. Heron, "Isla de los Angeles: Unique State Park in San Francisco Bay." *California History,* March 1987, pp. 25–39. *California History* is the journal of the California Historical Society and is available in many libraries.

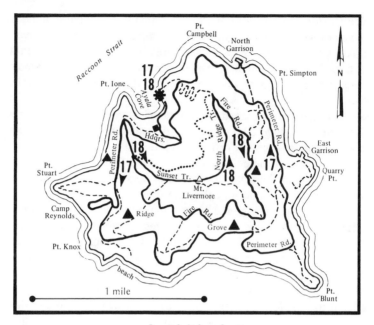

Angel Island

17 Around Angel Island

Distance 5-mile loop plus about 1 mile of optional side trips.
Grade Easy; you can wear sneakers.

Features

There are two ways to explore the island: by going around it or by
climbing to the top of it. The trip around the island on old Army
roads takes in most of the historic sites, and if you travel counterclockwise you will encounter them in roughly chronological order.
This level route is popular with bicyclists and it passes near the
environmental campsites. The trip to the summit can be about 3
miles long or as much longer as you want, and is especially good for
views and for studying the island's natural history. Actually, if you
arrive fairly early in the day you can hike both routes.

Description

Disembark at Ayala Cove—named for Lt. Juan Manuel de Ayala,
the first European to drop anchor in San Francisco Bay (unless, of
course, Sir Francis Drake deserves this honor). Ayala brought the

San Carlos into this cove in 1775 and named the island in honor of "Nuestra Señora de los Angeles." The ship remained here for over a month while the crew explored the area and exchanged hospitality with the Indian inhabitants. (The inhabitants might not have been so hospitable if they could have foreseen the ultimate results of Ayala's visit.)

From the cove, proceed toward the wide green lawn and impressive white building. This is now park headquarters, but for many years it was the bachelor officers' quarters of a U.S. quarantine station that operated here from 1892 to 1949. During that period the area was called "Hospital Cove." The headquarters building now contains exhibits and a model of the island.

As you approach headquarters you will notice many strange, nonnative plants. The island was forested when Richard Henry Dana first visited it in 1835. The Forty Niners subsequently used it as a source of lumber, and when Dana returned in 1859 he noted that it was "clean shorn of trees." To fill the void, the residents of the island over the years imported all sorts of exotic flora. Conspicuous around the headquarters area are blackwood acacia, Canary Island palm, and echium (also called "tower of jewels" or "pride of Madeira"), which produces masses of blue-purple flower spikes in spring. Other trees introduced to the island include eucalyptus, Monterey pine and Monterey cypress.

As noted in the section on trees in the Introduction to this book, the State Park System was prepared to start logging the island's eucalyptus in the fall of 1987. At the last minute, the Marin Conservation League and the group called POET (Preserve Our Eucalyptus Trees) in effect shouted "Woodsman—spare that tree!" and mobilized enough public pressure to postpone the cutting—at least for the time being.

Take the road that goes uphill on the left of headquarters, and in less than ¼ mile reach Perimeter Road. Turn right on it and begin going counterclockwise around the island, passing the Sunset Trail on the left. From the west side of the island you will have fine views of Tiburon, the old Northwestern Pacific Railroad terminus, the Corinthian Yacht Club and Belvedere. (With binoculars, you can watch the denizens of Tiburon's waterfront restaurants savoring their pre-lunch martinis.)

In a few minutes you come to some of the abandoned buildings of the West Garrison, or Camp Reynolds, the first Army installation on the island, named for an officer killed at the battle of Gettysburg. Established in 1863, it operated continuously until 1946. You can see that Camp Reynolds and its nearby batteries are situated so as to command, with Alcatraz and Fort Point, the approach to San Francisco through the Golden Gate. The men who garrisoned these forts feared that Confederate raiders might come sneaking in, or that some European power—notably England, France or Russia, all of which had formerly entertained territorial designs on the West Coast—might take advantage of the U.S. preoccupation with the Civil War to seize California, and possibly Oregon too. If in retrospect this apprehension seems a trifle paranoid, let's not forget that only forty-some years ago many residents of the Pacific Coast feared being bombed by Japanese airplanes or shelled by Japanese submarines.

A path leads down to the main part of the camp. A retired couple, Bob and Mary Noyes, took the lead in restoring one of the original Civil War-era buildings, Quarters 11, and inspired volunteers to start restoring others. Already the repainted buildings along the parade grounds look vastly spiffier than they did a few years ago. On summer weekends docents offer tours of Quarters 11 and the nearby area.

At the Bay end of the parade grounds are the remains of a wharf, near a large, sturdy building that was built in 1908 of bricks brought around the Horn as ballast in sailing ships. Along the way you pass some more introduced flora: French broom and century plant.

Near the brick building are water, toilets, picnic tables, and a small beach. From this vantage point you get an unusual view of the Golden Gate Bridge. Toward the southern part of the island you can see an old bell that warned off ships during fogs, before the invention of more sophisticated equipment.

Returning to Perimeter Road, in a few minutes you overlook a massive gun emplacement, Battery Ledyard, which dates from 1900. From here there is a spectacular view of San Francisco and the Golden Gate. A side road to the right of the main road leads downhill for ¼ mile to a moderately steep trail that gives access to small, sheltered Perles Beach. A bit farther on, a side road to the left leads to the Ridge environmental campsites.

The main road continues eastward, above what were once the Alcatraz Gardens, cultivated by men from that island when it was still being used as an Army prison. (Alcatraz didn't become a federal penitentiary for errant civilians until 1934.) Shortly beyond an old rock quarry (water), you arrive at the Alcatraz View Point, which offers a spectacular view not only of the old prison but also of San Francisco (straight up Van Ness Avenue), both bridges, and Oakland. Looking toward Point Blunt, on the southeast corner of Angel Island, you may see cormorants and seals in the rocks just offshore; in fact, you may hear the seals barking.

Continuing along Perimeter Road you pass a big landslide and the trail on the left leading to the Grove environmental campsites. At a four-way junction turn right and soon find yourself at an old Nike missile site—now just as obsolete as Battery Ledyard, but not as picturesque.

Below you is Point Blunt, which during the 19th century was a favorite dueling ground for San Franciscans. The most famous duel fought here was undoubtedly that between U.S. Commissioner George Pen Johnston and State Senator William I. Ferguson in August 1858. These two erstwhile friends fell out over a rather complicated legal case involving an escaped slave, Archy Lee, whom Commissioner Johnston had just declared free. Ferguson, a Southerner, objected to this ruling, tempers ran high, and a duel was arranged on Point Blunt. Each man wounded the other; Johnston recovered, but Ferguson died three weeks later.

The ironic part of this story is that Johnston, while in the California legislature, had authored the state's antidueling law, under which he was tried after Ferguson's death. He was acquitted, on the ground that Ferguson had refused proper medical attention for his wound.

Now the road goes downhill, with the University of California campanile in view straight ahead across the Bay, and then it forks; go left here. The right-hand road leads to the Point Blunt Coast Guard Station, which is off limits. The road curves north, past acacias, to Quarry Point (site of an old sandstone quarry) and then to the East Garrison. This garrison was established in 1899 for soldiers returning from the Philippines; to modern tastes, its architecture seems more institutional and less attractive than the older buildings at Camp Reynolds. Part of the East Garrison is inhabited by park personnel.

Continuing north, you soon overlook Point Simpton. Beginning in 1909 this was the site of an immigration station called "the Ellis Island of the West." The immigrants here, most of whom were Asian, encountered just as rude a welcome as their European counterparts did in New York—maybe even ruder. The park has established in one of the old barracks a museum that relates the history of the immigration station. This museum is definitely worth the short detour from Perimeter Road. Currently it is open from 11 A.M. to 4 P.M. on summer weekends and holidays, or by appointment for group tours; eventually it will probably have longer hours. In front of the museum is a black granite memorial to the Asian immigrants, donated by the late "Trader Vic" Bergeron.

Incidentally, the most famous deportation hearing to take place on Angel Island, in 1939, involved not an Asian but an Australian— Harry R. Bridges, who had successfully organized the longshoremen's union on the West Coast. Accused of being a Communist, Bridges after nine weeks of hearings won his case, and six years later became a U.S. citizen.

Back on Perimeter Road, as you round Point Campbell, the northernmost part of the island, you can see through the toyon the oil tanks of Richmond and the humpbacked Richmond-San Rafael Bridge. Next, Tiburon comes into view again across Raccoon Strait. Soon a sign shows where the North Ridge Trail leads downhill, mainly on stairs, to Ayala Cove. This shortcut is quicker than returning by the road.

18 To the top of Mt. Livermore

Distance 5-mile loop; more or less if desired.
Grade Moderate, except for the 700-foot climb to the summit.

Features

The 360-degree view from the summit of Angel Island, unequaled at any time, is especially exciting on a breezy day when the Bay is full of boats of all sizes, from dinghys to yachts, including sloops, yawls and even Chinese junks. If watching them tempts you to take up sailing, remember that not only are boats expensive, but they also require vast amounts of attention. Their owners seem to spend every other weekend cleaning, scraping, sanding, varnishing, painting, polishing and mending. It's much more relaxing to go hiking and look at *other* people's boats.

Facilities

Water, toilets, tables at the summit.

Description

From Ayala Cove take Perimeter Road counterclockwise, as described in the preceding chapter, to the Sunset Trail. This fairly steep trail offers panoramic views of Tiburon, Belvedere and the Golden Gate as it switchbacks up. Soon you can also look down on the old buildings of Camp Reynolds.

The trail crosses a fire road and continues uphill, now with views of the City. You will note as you climb that the higher parts of the island contain fewer exotic plants than the lower parts. In fact, the upper west side consists mainly of standard California coastal scrub, although the aggressive broom has invaded here and there. A wild-flower society seeded the island from the air with native plants in the 1920s, and anyone who hikes here in spring will reap the visual results of that sowing: along the Sunset Trail are buttercups, blue-eyed grass, paintbrush, zigadene, pansies, lupine, various members of the genus *Brodiaea* and the sunflower family, and many more.

A mile from its beginning the Sunset Trail arrives at the 781' summit of Mt. Caroline Livermore (formerly Mt. Ida, but renamed in honor of a prominent Marin County conservationist). One can spend hours here taking in the sights: not only the sailboats and an occasional tanker, freighter or liner, but also the principal land-marks of the Bay Area and the changing tidal patterns. This is an appealing spot for a leisurely lunch.

Leave the summit by the North Ridge Trail, which runs north-ward through Monterey pine, coast live oak, madrone and ceano-thus. After ¾ mile the North Ridge Trail runs into the fire road. If you want to cut the hike short here, just continue down steep North Ridge and turn left on Perimeter Road to reach Ayala Cove.

To continue hiking, turn right on the fire road. It circles the island fairly levelly, generally a couple of hundred feet above Perimeter Road. It has the same superb views, but more trees and fewer buildings—also fewer fellow hikers and bicyclists. As the trail meanders around the island, it offers ever-changing views of the City, the Golden Gate and the Tiburon peninsula. In the spring you may see yellow lupine on the grassy slopes, and perhaps flocks of mourning-cloak butterflies. After you reach the Sunset Trail inter-section you can retrace your steps down to Perimeter Road and cut through the picnic ground to Ayala Cove. Or if you just missed a ferry you can continue another mile on the fire road—thereby com-pleting the circle—and descend by way of the North Ridge Trail.

19 Tiburon

Maps

Topos *San Francisco North* and *San Quentin*, or any road map that includes the Tiburon peninsula.

How to get there

By ferry The Red & White Fleet runs ferries from Pier 43½ on San Francisco's Fisherman's Wharf to Tiburon on weekends and holidays all year, and daily during summer. They also run a commute service from the Ferry Building on weekdays. Phone 546-2815 for schedules and fares. The ferry carries bicycles. (You can rent bikes at Ken's Bike Shop, 94 Main Street; 435-1683.)

By bus GGT #10 daily from San Francisco to Tiburon; get off at Main Street, the end of the line.

By car From Highway 101 take the Tiburon-Belvedere exit (Highway 131) and drive east on Tiburon Boulevard to its end at Main Street.

Features

Tiburon exhibits on a small scale the forces of development that have changed the Bay Area's landscape so dramatically since World War II. (The Santa Clara Valley exhibits them on a large scale.) For the first half of the 20th century, Tiburon (whose name means "shark" in Spanish) was a little town notable mainly for being the terminus of the Northwestern Pacific Railroad. In the late 1940s, with-it Berkeley students used to take their dates here—by way of the San Rafael auto ferry—to wander around the semisecret village and end the afternoon lounging on the deck of Sam's Anchor Cafe. In those days, plain little St. Hilary's Church dominated the bare hills on the north side of town.

It was probably inevitable that developers would cover those hills with houses. Meanwhile, in the 1950s a canny paint-company tycoon, the late Fred Zelinsky, bought up much of downtown and refurbished it. A community "paint up" in 1955 paved the way for the refurbishing.

Probably the most desirable land in town was the 38 acres of old railroad yard that had originally formed the terminus of the Northwestern Pacific Railroad. Southern Pacific became sole owner of this railroad in 1929 and ran trains here until 1967. When the trains stopped running, SP wanted to dispose of this prime piece of real estate. (Incidentally, the railroad had originally *paid* for this land—it was not part of a federal grant.) There followed years of negotiating and wrangling among the citizens of Tiburon and Belvedere, various would-be developers, and SP. Eventually the Innisfree Companies, a Sausalito-based developer, bought the land and commissioned the San Francisco architectural firm of Fisher-Friedman Associates to design Point Tiburon, a project to include 155 condos plus a mix of shops and restaurants. The town struck a hard bargain with SP and the developers, who promised to provide extensive highway improvements, traffic signals, a flood-control system, public tennis courts, a shoreline park, a marsh wildlife refuge and preservation of the old Northwestern Pacific depot.

In April 1986 the citizens of Tiburon elected a supposedly "slow growth" majority to the town council and also passed a two-year building moratorium. One of their chief concerns was that more development would lead to an ever-worsening traffic jam on Tiburon Boulevard and Highway 101. After the election, six developers promptly sued the town. When it appeared that the resulting litigation would cost hundreds of thousands of dollars and bankrupt the Tiburon treasury—and after months of labyrinthine infighting—the town caved in to the developers.

Tiburon contains three main centers of visitor interest: Downtown and environs—now including Point Tiburon; Old St. Hilary's church and wildflower preserve; and Richardson Bay Audubon Center. The latter two are described in succeeding chapters.

Downtown and environs

It is always fun to stroll along Main Street, which now sports fancy shops and a number of restaurants in addition to the venerable Sam's. (Incidentally, the oldest buildings on Main Street date from the 1880s; the earlier dates on some facades are purely fanciful.) At #72 you can taste wine in the century-old house of the Tiburon Vintners. Now Main Street turns into Ark Row, Mr. Zelinsky's creation. Ark Row commemorates the time when the area now occupied by the parking lot and the Boardwalk Shopping Center was under water. In those days many people lived here in houseboats, or arks. Now that the land has been filled in, the arks have metamorphosed into chic boutiques and gift shops. Some unauthentic new arks have also made their way onto the scene!

Main Street runs into Beach Road. If you walk south on Beach you will immediately encounter a stunning view of San Francisco across Belvedere Cove and the Bay. A few yards further along Beach is the China Cabin, a restoration project of the Belvedere-Tiburon Landmarks Society. It is open to the public 1–4 P.M. Wednesdays and Sundays, April through October. The Society describes it as follows:

> Too beautiful to burn, the Social Saloon of the S.S. *China* was removed from the ship in 1886 and survives today because it was purchased intact by J. T. Keefe, Port Captain of the Corinthian Yacht Club. Barged to Belvedere Cove, it became known as the China Cabin and was used as a residence until 1978 when it was slated for demolition under the City of Belvedere waterfront open space plan. The Landmarks Society intervened to save the structure comprising the

saloon and two adjacent staterooms of the ship's surgeon and chief
engineer. . . . The National Trust for Historic Preservation recognizes the national importance of the China Cabin as the only 19th
century ship's passenger accommodation known to exist in the world.

Architecture buffs can continue past the San Francisco Yacht
Club (private) and up the hill of posh Belvedere. More leisurely
strollers may want to turn back and follow Beach to Tiburon
Boulevard and the Boardwalk shopping center designed by John
Lord King. Built on fill, it has foundation beams that can be adjusted
to allow for differential settling of the building!

Or you may want to cross Tiburon Boulevard and explore Point
Tiburon—possibly tour a model luxury condo, if one is open. The
development won an award in 1987 for site planning from the
Pacific Coast Builders' Conference. The Chronicle's crusty architecture critic, Allan Temko, takes a dimmer view: "Affluent Tiburon is
getting what it deserves, architecturally and otherwise, in the 155-
condo compound—a kind of yuppie millionaires' row—that should
have been a great waterfront park." (San Franciso *Chronicle,*
February 11, 1985)

In any event, the developers have provided a marvelously scenic
walkway along the waterfront: Shoreline Park. They have also
preserved the old depot (1884)—now the Peter Donahue Building,
named for the original owner of the San Francisco and North Pacific
Railroad. A little farther along is Elephant Rock and pier, from
which only anglers 16 years old or less may fish.

20 Old St. Hilary's Historic Preserve

How to get there

The church is located on Esperanza Street just above Mar West
Street. There is another, *new* St. Hilary's a bit north of the old one,
which sometimes confuses newcomers to Tiburon.

By ferry From the dock, walk east along Shoreline Park,
passing the Peter Donahue Building; turn left on Mar West and right
on Esperanza.

By bus GGT #10 to the west end of Mar West, or to Main
Street and follow the above directions.

By car Although the surrounding hillsides are now built up,
Old St. Hilary's is still a prominent part of the view, and if you drove
in on Tiburon Boulevard you passed the historical marker pointing to
it from the west end of Mar West Street.

Description

This church, built in 1888, is a pleasant, unassuming example of Carpenter's Gothic. It is named for the patron saint of Hilarita Reed, the daughter of John Reed, who built the first sawmill in Marin County. The Tiburon peninsula was originally part of Reed's Rancho Corte de Madera del Presidio ("Cut Wood for the Presidio"). Hilarita married Dr. Benjamin Lyford from Vermont, who was what we might nowadays call a health nut. He hoped to establish in Tiburon a Utopian community called "Hygeia," where drinking and smoking would be unknown. This plan did not come to fruition—as a glance at present-day Main Street will show. However, a circular stone tower that the doctor built, intended as an outpost of his envisioned city, still overlooks Lyford Cove from Paradise Drive.

Old St. Hilary's, which was used for Roman Catholic services until 1954, is now owned by the county and maintained by the Belvedere-Tiburon Landmarks Society (Box 134, Tiburon 94920; phone 435-1853). It is currently open to the public 1–4 P.M. on Wednesdays and Sundays, April through October. Surrounding the church is the John Thomas Howell Botanical Garden, named for the man who is the curator emeritus of botany at the California Academy of Sciences and the author of *Marin Flora*. The garden is famous for its flowers. In fact, the Landmarks Society brochure claims: "Nowhere else in California can so many kinds of wildflowers be found in so small a space as on the few acres surrounding the old church. Many are extremely rare and two, the black jewel flower and Tiburon paintbrush, are found nowhere else in the world."

From the rock seats in front of Old St. Hilary's you can enjoy a view of the posh peninsula of Belvedere and the San Francisco and Corinthian yacht clubs' harbors. Walking clockwise around the church, you overlook and overhear the swimming pool and tennis courts of the Tiburon Peninsula Club. On the hillside behind the church, look for the boulder with plaque designating the Caroline S. Livermore Vista Point (named for the same conservationist as the peak on Angel Island). From here you can see part of San Francisco, the Golden Gate Bridge towers, the hills of the Marin headlands and—to the west—Mt. Tamalpais.

You can complete the circuit by walking down a path that leads to the northeast corner of the church; this is Dakin Lane, named for another family of conservationists who are commemorated by a plaque along the way.

21   Richardson Bay Audubon Center

Address and phone

376 Greenwood Beach Road, Tiburon 94920; 388-2524

How to get there

By ferry   From the dock, proceed northwest on Tiburon Boulevard 2 blocks to Cove Road and pick up the paved bicycle/jogging path that runs for 2 level miles to Richardson Bay Park; another half mile along Greenwood Beach Road brings you to the center.

By bus   GGT #10 from San Francisco to the first stop after the Cove Shopping Center. A nice one-way 3-mile walk is possible by taking the bus to the center and then following the bike path to the bus terminus.

By car   From Highway 101 take the Tiburon-Belvedere (Highway 131) exit and drive east on Tiburon Boulevard for about a mile. Turn right at Greenwood Cove Drive (which soon becomes Greenwood Beach Road) and proceed ¼ mile, to where you see a distinctive yellow Victorian mansion on the right.

Features

The center, formerly called the Richardson Bay Wildlife Sanctuary, comprises 11 acres of land and 900 acres of water, preserved in the mid-1950s through the efforts of conservationists and local residents who rejected the idea of a marina-type development on this part of Richardson Bay. The area is closed to boats from October through March so that thousands of ducks migrating from Alaska and Canada can find a safe harbor in which to winter.

As noted above, one of the most striking features of the center is its handsome Victorian house, which has been lovingly restored.

Facilities

Open Wednesday through Sunday 9 A.M.–5 P.M., except holidays; water, restrooms; the Book Nest, a bookstore; nature trail; extensive educational program, including nature walks every Sunday; Lyford House open 1–4 P.M. Sundays from October to May, and at other times for groups by appointment. It can also be rented for weddings and other festivities.

Regulations

Small fee except for Audubon Society members; no pets; no picnicking.

Description

Descriptive leaflets are available at the entrance. Visitors will find a
variety of things to do here, depending on their ages and inclinations
and on what sorts of programs are taking place. A delightful introduction to the center is via the self-guided nature trail, which begins
just beyond the Whittell Education Center and climbs the hill for a
view over the Bay. The accompanying booklet is well worth its small
price at the bookstore.

If you visit on a Sunday afternoon when the Lyford House is
open, you will be able to tour this wonderful Victorian mansion. It
was built around 1876 by Dr. Lyford and his wife Hilarita (mentioned in the preceding chapter) and originally stood on Strawberry
Point, southwest of the sanctuary. When it was threatened with
demolition, the Marin Conservation League succeeded in having it
barged across Richardson Bay to this land, which had been donated
for use as a wildlife sanctuary by the late Rose Verrall. The house
has been restored and redecorated in authentic style and is the site of
art and nature exhibits.

22   Ring Mountain Preserve

Mailing addresses and phone

3152 Paradise Drive, #101, Tiburon 94920; 435-6465. (Note that
this office is several miles from the actual preserve.)
c/o The Nature Conservancy
785 Market Street, San Francisco 94103; 777-0487

Maps

Topo *San Quentin;* map posted at entrance.

How to get there

From Highway 101 northbound or southbound, exit on Paradise
Drive in Corte Madera and follow it 1¾ miles to the preserve
entrance gate on the right. A much more indirect route is to take
Paradise Drive north from Tiburon for 7 winding miles.

Features

Ring Mountain is a fascinating piece of original California that has
almost miraculously been preserved in a nearly pristine state while
housing developments have sprung up around it. The top of the ridge
is serpentine rock, which, as we saw in Chapter 12, supports its own
distinctive flora. Ring Mountain is home to seven rare endemics, one
of which—the Tiburon mariposa lily (*Calochortus tiburonensis*)—

grows nowhere else in the world. The mountain's lower slopes are covered with native California bunchgrasses, which have disappeared from almost everywhere else in the state. Intermittent stream channels running down the slopes provide enough moisture for stands of bay and live oak trees, which offer habitat for deer, foxes and other wildlife. Recently a rare daddy longlegs and a rare moth have also been discovered here—but the casual hiker is unlikely to meet them.

History

Native Americans obviously inhabited this site, as evidenced by a bedrock mortar and some fascinating circular petroglyphs on one of the rock formations, perhaps chipped as long as 2000 years ago. In 1834 the Mexican government granted the entire Tiburon peninsula to John Reed as Rancho Corte de Madera del Presidio ("Cut Wood for the Presidio"). Reed and his family ran cattle on the land, and the Ring Mountain acreage remained relatively unchanged, the property of his descendants, until the 1980s. (It received its name, however, from a Marin County supervisor, George E. Ring, who lived nearby from 1879 until 1913.)

As developers covered the surrounding hillsides with houses, plant-lovers and geologists became concerned about the fate of Ring Mountain. After several years of negotiations among the owners and various other concerned parties, The Nature Conservancy purchased 377 acres here and is preserving it for all to enjoy.

Facilities

Open free during daylight hours; to find out when nature walks will be given, phone 435-6465 or 777-0487.

Regulations

Dogs and bicycles permitted on fire roads only; dogs must be on leash at all times.

To the top of the mountain

Distance   2 miles round trip.
Grade   Easy: although this is called a mountain, it's only 602' high; but boots or sturdy shoes are advisable.

Description

If you just want to enjoy the spectacular view, or if you're interested in the different kinds of schist that attract geologists from all over the world, any time of the year is good for a visit. But if you're interested mainly in the flowers, spring is of course the ideal time to come here. Different flowers appear serially from March through June, and at different elevations. A brochure posted at the entrance indicates the growing seasons for the rare species.

After studying the entrance poster, proceed up the Phyllis Ellman Trail, named for a Marin County naturalist who is very active in the efforts to save the mountain. As you climb, look for the seasonal flowers. The most seductive is the Tiburon mariposa lily, which is found only on Ring Mountain and was not even discovered until 1971. It blooms in early June, on the upper slopes of the mountain. The preserve's brochure describes the flowers as "tan, cinnamon and yellow." I might have used the words "violet" or "lavender" somewhere in the description. At any rate, it's a delicate bloom that blends in unobtrusively with its background.

If you continue all the way up to the ridgetop, you might want to wander over to the remains of an old Army anti-aircraft installation that was here for a while during the 1950s. The Conservancy has plans to restore this site to its original contour and vegetation. The sensational view from the top of the ridge includes much of Marin, the San Rafael-Richmond Bridge, the Berkeley Hills, the Bay Bridge and some of San Francisco.

You may want to return to the entrance by different trails in the hope of seeing different flowers.

23   China Camp State Park

Mailing address and phone
Route 1, Box 244, San Rafael 94901; 456-0766

Maps
Topos *San Rafael, San Quentin* and *Petaluma Point;* brochure with map available at campground ranger station.

How to get there
From Highway 101 northbound, take the Central San Rafael exit and immediately turn right on Second Street, which becomes Point San Pedro Road. The Historic Village is about 6 miles from 101.

From 101 southbound in north San Rafael, go northeast on North San Pedro Road (passing Frank Lloyd Wright's Marin County Civic Center, known irreverently to the locals as "Big Pink") and follow it to the park.

Features
These 1500 acres of Bay shore, marshland, meadowland and oak forest became a state park in 1977. The most eye-catching feature of

the park is the remnant of a century-old Chinese fishing village, at first glance an unlikely apparition to find on the shore of San Pablo Bay.

History

The Chinese who had come to California to mine gold in the 1850s and to build the railroads in the 1860s found themselves competing with other nationalities for jobs in the depressed 1870s. Anti-Chinese sentiment culminated in the Exclusion Act of 1882 forbidding further immigration from China. To find a refuge and an occupation, they settled at various spots around the Bay and successfully took up shrimping on a large scale. After the earthquake and fire of 1906 the original settlers were joined by refugees from San Francisco's Chinatown.

In 1910 the state introduced sea bass into San Pablo Bay and forbade their taking by net. As the Chinese could not keep the bass out of their shrimp trap-nets, they were immediately in violation of the law. Within a few years most of the 26 Chinese shrimping villages that had dotted the Bay shore had disappeared. But the Quan family stayed on at China Camp, utilizing a new method of trapping shrimp that would allow the bass to escape the nets. They successfully operated their shrimp business for many years, and also opened a store, a cafe and a boat rental. Bay pollution has vastly reduced the

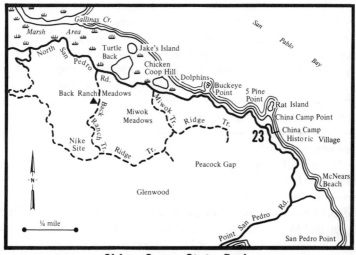

China Camp State Park

shrimp catch, but one member of the Quan family remains at China
Camp and runs the boat concession.

Facilities

Historic Village open 8 A.M.–7 P.M.; contains water, toilets, picnic
tables, phone; small museum, snack bar and bait shop open on
weekends.

Other picnic sites are located on some of the points overlooking
the Bay.

Fishing is popular from various spots along the Bay.

Back Ranch Meadows Camp contains 30 primitive sites; this is
called a walk-in campground, but many of the sites are only a very
short walk from the parking lot (e.g., 30 yards). Campground hours
and ranger-station hours vary seasonally. Campsites can be reserved
in advance by calling Mistix; unreserved sites are available on a
first-come, first-served basis.

Regulations

The usual for state parks; *no open fires*.

Description

The park is spread out over a lot of different kinds of territory. The
part that most people visit first is the Historic Village near the southeast boundary. If when you first arrive you get a *dejá vu* feeling that
you have seen this ramshackle place before, you may be right: China
Camp served as location for a 1954 movie, *Blood Alley*, starring
John Wayne and Lauren Bacall; the director wanted a setting that
would pass for a remote Asian fishing village.

It is *very* difficult to visualize thousands of people living in this
small cove, as they did before 1910; some sources say 3000, some
say as many as 10,000, but probably nobody knows for sure. Many
of the inhabitants lived in stilt cabins over the Bay which long ago
disappeared under the water. Refugees from the 1906 earthquake
camped out in tents on the hillside. Nowadays the almost-ghost-
town of China Camp offers the visitor opportunities for sunbathing,
photographing, fishing and just hanging loose.

There's a lot more to the park than just the village, however.
Birders and botanists will want to explore the marshland. Jake's
Island, at the north end of the park, is accessible through the marsh
except during high tide. On the south side of the road, the Back
Ranch and Miwok trails leading to the Ridge Trail are a bit steep and
gravelly; but the meadows offer a pleasant spot to look for wildflowers.

Audubon Canyon Ranch

Address and phone

4900 Shoreline Highway, Stinson Beach 94970; 868-9244

Maps

Topo *Bolinas;* trail maps available at headquarters.

How to get there

By bus GGT #63 (Stinson Beach) currently runs one morning trip to the ranch and one afternoon return trip on weekends and holidays during its open season; phone for schedule. (The bus doesn't come in to the ranch; you have to wait for it on the highway.)

By car From Highway 101 take narrow, winding Highway 1 west to Stinson Beach and continue northwest for 3¼ miles.

Features

Even people who ordinarily consider ornithology a bore—or who don't know what it is—are fascinated by the sight of egrets and great blue herons feeding their young in the treetop nests of Audubon Canyon. This unique sanctuary offers the big birds a protected nesting site in a redwood grove, near an ample source of food— Bolinas Lagoon.

The continued existence of the rookery is something of a miracle, because beleaguered conservationists have had to defend it during the last few years against threats of logging, subdividing, highway widening and marina building, and against the great oil spill of 1971. Somehow a dedicated group of volunteers, with the Marin chapter of the Audubon Society as its nucleus, managed to raise enough money to purchase not only Audubon Canyon itself, but adjoining Volunteer Canyon (named for the workers who kept the oil out of Bolinas Lagoon) and Kent Island in the lagoon. The ranch is now co-sponsored by the Marin, Golden Gate, Sequoia and Madrone Audubon societies.

In 1975 disaster struck the egrets when raccoons raided many of their nests. Before the raccoons were captured, they had dispatched most of the egret eggs and chicks. Raccoons—possibly abetted by possums and great horned owls—struck again in the spring of 1983 and destroyed almost the entire first laying of both egrets and herons. Fortunately the raid occurred early in the nesting season, and the birds rebuilt more than a hundred nests and began laying new eggs.

The birds fared well in 1987: 18 pairs of herons raised 45 young—the highest reproductive rate in 20 years—and 113 pairs of egrets raised about 185 young. Apparently no predators made the scene.

The herons begin nesting in February, the egrets in March. The most interesting time to visit the ranch is between mid-April and mid-June, when the nestlings have hatched and are squawking for food. Audubon Canyon is an excellent place to bring children, as well as visitors to the Bay Area, who probably have never seen anything like it.

Facilities

From mid-March through mid-July open 10 A.M.–4 P.M. weekends and holidays, and open to school (and other) groups by appointment Tuesday through Friday. Free, but donations welcome.

Parking, water, restrooms, museum, bookstore—all wheelchair-accessible. Large picnic area behind the museum. On the south side of the picnic lawn near the stream is the Bird Hide, a discreet wooden structure designed by Clifford Conly, Jr. "Hide" as used here is the British equivalent of our "blind" as in "duck blind"—a secret place from which to watch birds.

Extensive natural-history programs, outings and workshops for adults and families.

Loaner binoculars sometimes available at registration center for those who don't own them or forgot to bring them.

Regulations

Pets not allowed; no picnicking on trails.

24 To the overlook

Distance   1-mile loop.
Grade   Short but steep.

Features

The recommended route, especially when foot traffic is heavy, is to take the Rawlings Trail up, and the Alice Kent Trail down.

Description

Begin by registering at headquarters, a handsome ranch house that dates from 1875, and picking up a leaflet with trail map. Next, you may want to go back to the big former barn that houses the bookstore and museum; or you can postpone this until after you've seen the birds.

The main trail to the bird overlook begins just north of the ranch house. It soon makes a U at the Clem Miller Overlook, named for the late congressman who worked so hard to establish Point Reyes National Seashore. You can rest on a bench here and observe herons, egrets and other birds fishing in Bolinas Lagoon.

Now climb a steep but short half mile to the side trail that goes right, to the Henderson Overlook, where informal wood seating has been installed for birdwatching. Here you are slightly above the nests, which are in the tops of second-growth redwoods. The grove is a scene of constant activity as the parents fly to and from the lagoon to fetch food for their demanding nestlings. The graceful flight of the adults contrasts sharply with the raucous, undignified behavior of their young. The keen observer will note that both egrets and herons practice sexual equality: males and females of each species bear the same plumage, incubate the eggs and feed the young.

When you can tear yourself away from the birds, you can take the Kent Trail back to the picnic area and barn/museum; or you can continue uphill on the Griffin Trail, described below.

25   The Griffin Loop Trail
25½   The North Loop Trail

Distance   Each is a 3-mile loop.
Grade   Each is moderately strenuous, involving an ascent of 800'.

Features

Both routes begin with a climb up the steep Griffin Trail, which forks after a mile. From here the Griffin loops right and the North Loop runs in a sort of mirror image to the left. Both routes include both redwood canyon and open hillside, and lots of different wildflowers.

Facilities

None except those at the headquarters area.

Regulations

Trails open mid-March through mid-July; no pets; no picnicking on trails.

Description

From the overlook, the Griffin Trail climbs fairly steeply, under the shade of bay, oak and buckeye trees. In early spring the path is bordered by lots of iris and zigadene lilies; later in the season, by blooming yerba santa, woolly sunflower, hedge nettle, pitcher sage, nightshade and sticky monkey flower. After about a mile, the North Loop Trail forks off to the left; it is described below. The Griffin Trail levels off under redwoods and begins to descend toward the head of the canyon. Here a creek splashes down past ferns, aralia and horsetail, and a rustic bench invites the hiker to rest.

The trail continues by contouring along the south side of the canyon, under redwoods and bays. You may find some scarlet columbine flowering here. In ½ mile you emerge from the forest and, after a brief ascent through chaparral, overlook Bolinas Lagoon. Soon the Bourne Trail comes in from the left. The Bourne family owned the canyon during the late 19th century and in 1875 constructed the house that is now headquarters.

From here on, your route is all downhill and in the open, with views of Stinson Beach, Bolinas and, in the distance, the Point Reyes peninsula. As you descend the grassy hillside you may see and hear finches, sparrows, blackbirds, hawks and quail; over 90 species of land birds have been identified on the ranch, of which about 60 are permanent residents. The trail curves around under coast live oaks to return to the ranch buildings.

25½   The North Loop Trail

Turning left off the Griffin Trail, you enter a ferny redwood grove. The trees still show charring from the great fire that swept over West Marin in 1945. Soon you cross a creek on a footbridge and climb along its north bank on a narrow trail. After some ups and downs, the trail emerges into a meadow with a swing entitled the Chase Lookout. Three people at once can swing leisurely and enjoy the striking view of Bolinas Lagoon and the Seadrift sandspit.

After venturing briefly back into redwoods, you come out into the open again and start downhill on a broad trail bordered by coyote bush and coffeeberry. Actually this trail is the remains of an old logging road dating back to the 1850s, when Bolinas was a lumbering center and schooners pulled into the lagoon to load the logs from Bolinas Ridge bound for booming San Francisco. (The lagoon obviously had deeper channels then.)

As you descend toward the lagoon you have a good view, especially with binoculars, of the herons, egrets and other birdlife feeding there. At the bottom of the ridge the trail crosses Garden Club Canyon. It then ascends briefly to the Clem Miller Overlook and back down to headquarters.

Samuel P. Taylor State Park

Mailing address and phone
Box 251, Lagunitas 94938; 488-9897

Maps
Topo *San Geronimo;* trail map available at headquarters for a small price.

How to get there
By bus GGT #65 on weekends and holidays.
By car From Highway 101 take Sir Francis Drake Boulevard 14 miles west to Lagunitas; the main park entrance is about 2 miles farther on.

Features
Samuel Penfield Taylor, a Forty-Niner from New York State, made his stake in the gold rush and subsequently purchased 100 acres on Lagunitas Creek, where in 1856 he established the first paper mill west of the Mississippi. (Although it is Lagunitas on the topo, a lot of West Marinites still call this Papermill Creek.) Taylor's mill produced most of the newsprint for San Francisco's newspapers and much of the paper used for official documents in Sacramento. As the mill flourished, the settlement of Taylorville grew up around it, and after the North Pacific Coast Railroad came through Taylor's property, the area became a popular resort. It contained a campground and a three-story hotel, which occupied the site of the present picnic ground—rather hard to visualize today!

> In West Marin one gets the sense of a place little changed since the first settlers arrived; the major difference seems to be an increase in visitors and commerce. But in reality, much of West Marin saw much more activity than now. Point Reyes and Bolinas Ridge once supported five times the number of dairies and ranches as they do now, protected as parks by the federal government.
>
> Samuel P. Taylor State Park was practically an industrial park before the turn of the century. In the area between Lagunitas and Tocaloma there were three factories, two hotels and a restaurant-resort, a school, four dairies, a Chinese village, a number of stores . . . in all, a striking difference from the quietude to be found there today.
>
> —Dewey Livingston, *Point Reyes Light,* March 31, 1988.

Taylor made the mistake of selling his riparian rights for $10,000, and the resulting diversion of water from the stream worked a hardship on the mill. Taylor died in 1886; the mill was foreclosed after the panic of 1893; and in 1915 the whole settlement burned down. The Marin Conservation League acquired the property in 1945, and subsequently turned it over to the state. The present park of 2700 acres contains remarkably varied terrain: second-growth redwood groves along the creek, and open hills on the north side of Drake Boulevard. Just inside the park boundary is Barnabe Peak (1466'), described below.

Taylor Park was hard hit by the storms of winter 1982 and 1983. Normally cheerful little Lagunitas Creek turned into a raging, muddy torrent, ripping trees from its banks and dashing them downstream. The storms also caused numerous floods and mudslides along the hillsides. Some of the campground and many of the trails suffered considerable damage.

Facilities

Over a hundred picnic sites; 59 campsites with grills (no electrical outlets), reservable through Mistix; one is suitable for the disabled. The park also has walk-in campsites for backpackers and bicyclists. A group picnic area and an equestrian camp may be reserved by phoning 456-1286. A bicycle trail runs along the old railroad grade.

Regulations

The usual for state parks.

Fishing for steelhead trout and silver salmon used to be popular here; in fact, the park brochure states that "the largest silver salmon ever caught in California (22 pounds) was caught in January 1959 in Papermill Creek." Since then, however, storm damage, low stream flow and man-made destruction of habitat have greatly reduced the fish population. The California Department of Fish and Game and a group of volunteers are trying to restore the fishery. Meanwhile, fishing *is not permitted* in Lagunitas (Papermill) Creek.

26 To the Old Mill Site

Distance 2-mile round trip.
Grade Easy.

Features

The walk to the Old Mill Site offers a good introduction to the park for picnickers and campers.

Description

You can walk north from the campground on the Ox Trail, or on a trail that starts from campsite 17 and runs along the creek, or on the service road/bike path. This is actually the old roadbed for the narrow-gauge North Pacific Coast Railroad. The first train on this line ran from Sausalito to Tomales in 1875; subsequently track extended up to the Russian River and east as far as Cazadero. Over a thousand Chinese laborers were hired, at $1 a day, to build this railroad. Many of them had taken part a few years earlier in building the transcontinental railroad across the Sierra. The North Pacific Coast Railroad was chronically short of funds and was constantly plagued by fires, storms, accidents and managerial incompetence. Northwestern Pacific took over the troubled line in 1907. The completion of Sir Francis Drake Boulevard in 1930 finally drove the railroad out of business.

The Old Dam Site and the Old Mill Site are marked by historical plaques. You can return by a route not taken, and perhaps try one of the other easy trails around the picnic area, or continue on the bike path. (Just beyond the gate indicating the continuation of the bike path, toward the creek, are a couple of secret picnic tables!)

27 Climbing Barnabe Peak

Distance   6-mile loop.
Grade   Strenuous; an ascent of 1300′.

Features

Barnabe Peak is named for John C. Fremont's white mule, who spent his last days as a pet of Samuel P. Taylor's family and is buried somewhere in the area. This trip offers a day-long (preferably not a hot day) workout with some spectacular views. Good boots and *a full canteen* are strongly recommended.

The route described here involves a lengthy but fairly moderate ascent and a steep descent. You can, if you prefer, go directly to the top via the Barnabe Trail.

Description

From the main picnic area, cross Lagunitas Creek and turn left on the bike trail/old railroad grade. The trail runs along the creek under redwoods, bay, hazel and maple—the latter colorful in fall—and crosses both creek and highway on a bicycle/pedestrian bridge where the old railroad trestle used to be. The trail continues level along the north bank of the creek, joining the riding/hiking trail.

After 0.6 mile from the junction, turn left on the clearly signed Ridge Trail and begin a steady ascent. When you emerge from the bay forest, you begin to have increasingly panoramic views of West Marin. At a sign indicating that you are 1.2 miles from the summit, the Ridge Trail—which has so far been a fire road—sprouts a footpath running parallel to it. The footpath may be better for flowers in spring—wild hollyhock, blue-eyed grass, poppy, Indian paintbrush, suncups, creamcups and buttercups—but the road offers more scenic views to the east, over the town of Lagunitas and a lot of *private property*.

The final mile to the peak is still an ascent, but not as steep; you can walk slowly and enjoy the view: to the west, Bolinas Ridge, partly bare Mt. Wittenberg and Inverness Ridge; to the south and east, Kent Lake, the San Geronimo Valley and Mt. Tam's golf balls. The Barnabe Peak fire lookout is one of two in Marin County, the other being on Mt. Tam. During the dry season the Barnabe lookout is continuously staffed by two watchers.

Return via the Barnabe Trail, which descends steeply for just over a mile to join the riding/hiking trail. Here, if you wish, you can take a side trip to visit Taylor's grave site, visible downhill to the right behind a picket fence. Otherwise, turn left on the riding/hiking trail, then right, following signs to the Madrone Picnic Area. From Madrone you can cross Sir Francis Drake and make your way back to the main picnic area on the trail that runs along the creek.

28 Point Reyes National Seashore

Mailing address and phones

Point Reyes 94956

Bear Valley headquarters—weekends 8 A.M.–5 P.M., weekdays 9 A.M.–5 P.M.—663-1092.

Drakes Beach—weekends and holidays 10 A.M.–4:30 P.M.—669-1250.

Lighthouse—Thursday through Monday 10 A.M.–5 P.M. (but closed when very foggy or windy)—669-1534.

Maps

Topos *Tomales, Drakes Bay, Inverness, Double Point* and *Bolinas;* free trail map available at headquarters; USGS *Point Reyes National Seashore and Vicinity* (scale 1:48,000); Erickson's *Map of Point Reyes National Seashore, Tomales Bay & Taylor State Parks;* Molenaar's *Pictorial Landform Map: Point Reyes National Seashore and the San Andreas Fault* (Berkeley: Wilderness Press, 1982) also contains information about trails, facilities and natural history.

How to get there

By bus GGT #65 from San Rafael to Bear Valley headquarters on weekends and holidays.

By car There are three main routes to Bear Valley headquarters:

The quickest is from Highway 101 west on Sir Francis Drake Boulevard (which subsequently becomes Sir Francis Drake Highway) through Samuel P. Taylor State Park to Olema, where signs point the way to park headquarters ½ mile west.

A slower, more scenic route from San Francisco or southern Marin is via winding Highway 1 north to Olema.

Another scenic route is by Highway 101 and Lucas Valley Road through Nicasio to Point Reyes Station and south to Olema.

Once at Bear Valley you can pick up a map showing how to get to other trailheads, the beaches and the lighthouse.

South of Bear Valley are two major trailheads without ranger stations:

Five Brooks is just off Highway 1, 3½ miles south of Olema.

Palomarin is 4½ miles north of Bolinas, at the end of Mesa Road.

The village of Bolinas is reclusive to the point of xenophobia, and some of its citizens have made a habit of tearing down the road signs for it on Highway 1. Coming north, turn left on the Olema-Bolinas Road 4½ miles north of Stinson Beach. Coming south, turn right on Horseshoe Hill Road 8 miles south of Olema; it runs into the Olema-Bolinas Road. Before you get to the town itself, turn right on Mesa Road, about 2 miles from Highway 1, and follow it to its end.

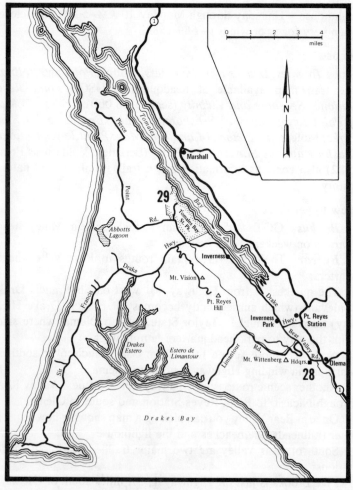

The Point Reyes Peninsula

Thomas Winnett

Limantour Beach

Features

The 65,000+ acres of the Point Reyes National Seashore constitute the largest and wildest section of the unique greenbelt stretching north from the San Francisco metropolitan area. In fact, 32,000 acres of the National Seashore are officially designated as wilderness or potential wilderness (no permanent structures or major roads, no motorized vehicles allowed except for emergencies). In 1985 the designated wilderness area of the National Seashore was officially dedicated to Congressman Phillip Burton, who had died in 1983. Burton, U.S. Representative from San Francisco since 1964, was responsible for more than doubling the wilderness acreage in the entire national-park system. Congress chose Point Reyes to commemorate Burton because it was the wilderness area closest to his home.

Another 18,000 acres are zoned for ranching on long-term lease.

The storms of 1982 and 1983 hit parts of the National Seashore especially hard. The Bear Valley Trail was overwhelmed by mud and debris and had to be closed for months. The Limantour Road suffered major landslides and was closed during more than a year for major reconstruction.

Facilities

Picnicking

At present the only food concession in the park is at Drakes Beach, open Friday through Tuesday 11 A.M.–4:30 P.M., "weather permitting." However, several towns near the park have grocery stores, restaurants and delicatessens where you can purchase food for picnicking.

Next to the parking lot near headquarters is a picnic ground with tables and grills. All the backpacking camps have picnic tables and grills; so does Drakes Beach.

Swimming

The best swimming in the area is at Tomales Bay State Park (see the next chapter). It is possible to swim at Drakes and Limantour beaches, though neither has lifeguard service—and the water at both is cold. Drakes has a bathhouse.

Camping

The only overnight camping in the park is at hike-in camps for backpackers. Headquarters will provide visitors with a free list of nearby car-camping facilities. The four hike-in camps present a golden opportunity to the novice backpacker or the family that wants to spend a weekend outdoors without driving far. All the camps contain water, toilets, picnic tables, grills and hitchrails. The camps are described briefly on the park handout. Incidentally, you don't have to backpack to visit these camps: each is close enough to some trailhead so that you can make it the destination for a picnic lunch on a one-day hike.

Hostel

Within the park, near Limantour Road, is the Point Reyes Hostel (Box 247, Point Reyes Station 94956; 663-8811). The hostel is open to the public according to the regulations of the International Youth Hostel Association. For up-to-date information phone the above number or the San Francisco number of American Youth Hostels' Golden Gate Council: 863-1444, weekdays 1–6 P.M.

Educational programs

The rangers offer a variety of nature walks and other programs; inquire at the visitor centers.

The Point Reyes National Seashore Association (successor to the Coastal Parks Association) in cooperation with the National Seashore sponsors programs of the Point Reyes Field Seminars, covering a wide variety of subjects in natural history, education and the arts; phone 663-1200.

Regulations

No dogs (except seeing-eye dogs) or other pets are permitted on trails, in campgrounds or on Drakes Beach or McClures Beach; they are permitted on a few designated beaches.

Wood fires are prohibited in campgrounds. Use only charcoal, gas stoves or canned heat.

No fireworks, firearms or weapons of any kind are permitted.

Motorcycles are not permitted on trails.

Bicycles are not permitted in the wilderness area. For a map showing permissible bike routes, consult the Bear Valley Visitor Center.

Observe warning signs on cliffs and beaches: The powerful surf and unpredictable undertow make the ocean beaches too dangerous for wading or swimming. Furthermore, great white sharks frequent the waters off Tomales Point and have been known to attack skin divers. If you plan to beachcomb, check the tide tables in advance. Sleeping on beaches is prohibited and dangerous, because the tides may come up to the cliffs.

Camping regulations

Campers must register at Bear Valley headquarters and get a permit; campsites may be reserved as long as 60 days in advance (663-1092). Camping is limited to one night in each campground, or two nights for groups at Wildcat; the camps are close enough together that you can easily hike from one to another during a day. Quiet hours are from sunset to sunrise.

Nearby facilities and attractions

You can rent bicycles at Point Reyes Bikes, 11431 Highway 1, Point Reyes Station (663-1768). You can rent horses at Bear Valley Stables (663-1570) and Five Brooks Stables (663-8287).

In recent years, bed-and-breakfastry has become a leading growth industry of West Marin. To find out about these places, phone The Inns of Point Reyes, 663-1420.

Recommended reading

Arnot, Phil, *Point Reyes: Secret Places and Magic Moments*. San Carlos: Wide World Publishing/Tetra, 1987.
Whitnah, Dorothy L., *Point Reyes National Seashore*. 2nd ed. Berkeley: Wilderness Press, 1985.

Description

The logical place to begin is at the Bear Valley Visitor Center. This structure in the form of a giant barn was designed by the architectural firm of Bull, Field, Volkmann and Stockwell under the administration of the Coastal Parks Association, which upon the center's completion donated it to the NPS. The idea of an interpretive center for the Seashore was in the NPS's plan for several years, but funding was not available for it until the late William Field bequeathed up to $750,000 specifically for such a center, conditional upon matching funds being obtained. Those who have been reading the Marin section of this book attentively will immediately guess where the Coastal Parks Association sought, and found, the matching funds. The 7000-square-foot center contains an auditorium, a library, plant and animal specimens, and historical exhibits. It is designed to introduce visitors to the main features of the Seashore.

There are plenty of interesting short walks near the Visitor Center: to Kule Loklo, the Miwok Indian village; to the Morgan Horse Farm; along the Earthquake Trail, which is wheelchair-accessible; and along the Woodpecker Nature Trail. The Bear Valley Trail, 4½ miles to the ocean, has long been one of the most popular trails in the Bay Area. It used to be a favorite of bicyclists, but since 1984 the NPS has forbidden bicycles in wilderness areas, and the final ¾ mile of the Bear Valley Trail is now off-limits.

The other two visitor centers are located in spots of unique historic and scenic interest:

1. Drakes Beach is where Francis Drake probably careened the *Golden Hinde* in 1579, although controversy has raged over this subject for decades. In any event, it's a beautiful beach, and if you walk along it a mile or so east toward the estero you can find a monument erected by the Drake Navigators' Guild.

2. The lighthouse is generally open to visitors Thursday through Monday from 10 A.M. to 5 P.M., weather permitting. The cliffs above the lighthouse are among the best places in northern California to watch gray whales migrating in winter. Whale watching has become so popular, in fact, that in recent years the Park Service has run a free shuttle bus from the Drakes Beach parking lot to the lighthouse parking lot to ease the monumental traffic congestion on Drake Highway.

29 Tomales Bay State Park

Mailing address and phone

Star Route, Inverness, 94937; 669-1140

Maps

Topos *Tomales* and *Drakes Bay;* trail map available at headquarters for a small price; Erickson's *Map of Point Reyes National Seashore, Tomales Bay and Taylor Parks;* Molenaar's *Point Reyes National Seashore Pictorial Landform Map.*

How to get there

From Inverness drive west on Sir Francis Drake Highway for 2½ miles to Pierce Point Road and go right on it for a mile to the Tomales Bay State Park turnoff (sign) on the right.

Features

This charming park, a sort of enclave within Point Reyes National Seashore, is sometimes a sunny refuge when the rest of the peninsula is fogged in. Its small, sheltered beaches are a pleasant contrast to the windswept ones on the rest of the peninsula, and for swimmers Tomales Bay is milder and warmer than Drakes Bay—let alone the ocean. Children will enjoy the short walks from beach to beach through lush forest, and will see why the Miwok Indians were so fond of this area. Fishing and clamming are popular activities here.

Facilities
Water, restrooms and dressing rooms, picnic tables, grills; about 20 bicycle campsites available on a first-come, first-served basis, except reservable by groups. Hand-carried boats may be put in the water away from the swimming beaches.

Regulations
The usual for state parks.

Description
From the parking lot at Hearts Desire Beach, one trail leads ½ mile northwest over the forested bluff to Indian Beach, and a similar trail leads ½ mile southeast to Pebble Beach. Children may want to explore both of these. The combination of forest, marsh and beach provides a wide variety of plant and animal life within a small area.

From the picnic area, a mile-long trail (an old farm road) leads uphill to the Willis Linn Jepson Memorial Grove of Bishop pines, dedicated to the late University of California botanist who wrote one of the standard manuals on the state's flora. In addition to the sturdy pines, the leisurely ambler will notice wax myrtle, salal, gooseberry, currant, coffeeberry, huckleberry and a variety of ferns.

The Johnstone Trail leads 4½ miles, mostly through oak-madrone forest, above private inholdings and drops down to Shell Beach, which is also part of Tomales Bay State Park. A pleasant loop of about 3 miles can be made by combining the Johnstone and Jepson trails.

Hikes 30–38
Sonoma and Napa counties

Instead of a trip to Europe or Latin America, why not enjoy a cosmopolitan vacation in Sonoma and Napa counties? Blessed by nature with forested hills and fertile valleys, these counties have attracted settlers from many cultures, and each culture has left its distinctive imprint on the land. Paradoxically, the people who lived here longest, the Pomo, Miwok and Wappo Indians, left fewer obvious traces of their presence than many subsequent groups— although the keen-eyed hiker can sometimes spy an arrowhead.

Russians occupied part of the Sonoma coast in 1812. This intriguing episode of California history is discussed in the chapter on Fort Ross. During the 1820s and '30s, the Mexican governors, nervous about Russian intentions, sought to establish settlements north of San Francisco. Among the colonists was a young army officer, Mariano Guadalupe Vallejo. This able and complex man was to become a pivotal figure in California's history, as commanding general of the northern frontier, secularizer of Mission Solano, owner of a vast agricultural empire, delegate to the state constitutional convention and one of the first state senators. In addition to his many other achievements, Vallejo, together with a large number of his relatives, founded most of the towns in Sonoma County and some of the ones in Napa.

Although reminders of Vallejo and the Spanish-American tradition abound in these counties, to the modern visitor perhaps the most immediately noticeable legacy is that from France, Italy and Central Europe, in the form of vineyards stretching up and down the valleys and hillsides, and winery buildings along the highways. Wine production in California dates back to the early mission fathers, but it was not until after the Yankee takeover and the gold rush that the wine boom really got going. Then a few enterprising growers discovered that some of the better European grape varieties would

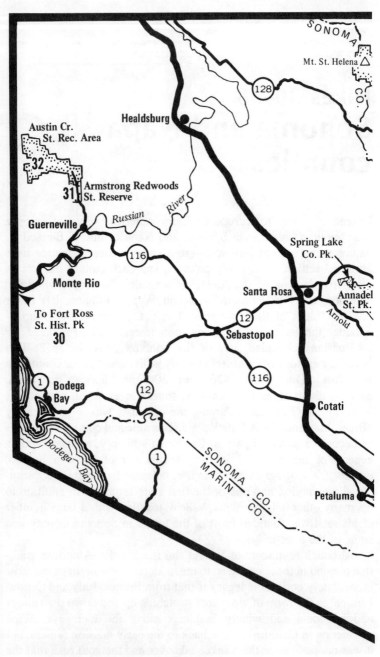

Sonoma and Napa driving map

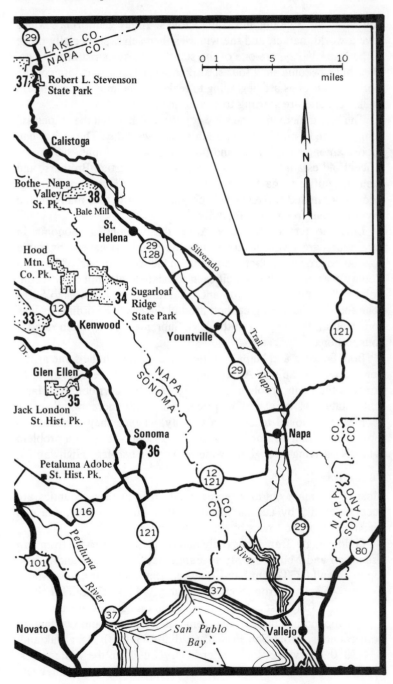

flourish in the Sonoma and Napa valleys. Today California's wines have a world market, and the wineries themselves, especially those in the Napa Valley, are one of the state's biggest tourist attractions. They have become such tourist attractions, in fact, that some of the more popular ones are beginning to feel overwhelmed, especially on weekends, and are starting to charge for tasting.

The best time to visit the wine country is fall, when the grapes are being crushed—and if at all possible, on a weekday. The visitor can choose among small, mom-and-pop jug-type operations, such magnificent old establishments as Beringer and Christian Brothers, and such magnificent new ones as Robert Mondavi and Sterling. Economy-minded travelers will be glad to know that many of the wineries have free picnic facilities.

Like the rest of the Bay Area, these counties—Sonoma in particular—are trying to cope with the problems caused by rapid population growth. In fact, Petaluma, in the southern part of Sonoma County, was one of the first cities in the state to attempt growth control: in 1972 it passed an ordinance that limited new houses to 500 a year and established a greenbelt around the city. The ordinance was contested all the way up to the U.S. Supreme Court, which ruled it constitutional.

Both Sonoma and Napa counties are cursed with the same affliction the rest of the Bay Area complains about: *too much traffic*. In Sonoma the main problem is the Highway 101 corridor. As Marin real estate has escalated in price, more and more middle-class people have moved to Sonoma County, whence they commute to jobs in San Francisco or Marin. In Napa County, the main problem is tourists driving through the wine country on two-lane Highway 29.

Public transit

Most of the main outdoor recreational areas in these counties are accessible only by automobile or charter bus. However, one can reach many of the towns by public transportation:

Golden Gate Transit has daily and frequent bus service from San Francisco and Marin County to Petaluma, Santa Rosa and Sebastopol. To call GGT from San Francisco, dial 332-6600; from Marin County, 453-2100; from Sonoma County, 544-1323. GGT's situation is more fully discussed in the section on Marin transit.

Greyhound has bus service from San Francisco and Oakland to both counties. From San Francisco, dial 433-1500; from Oakland, 834-3070; elsewhere, look under "Greyhound" in the white pages.

Sonoma County Transit has bus service in the Sonoma valley and along the Russian River on weekdays; seasonal weekend service is a possibility; dial 707-527-7665.

As this book goes to press, the Napa Valley Wine Train is seeking permission to run passengers between Napa and St. Helena on 21 miles of old Southern Pacific track. The Napa Valley Vintners and various other civic groups are insisting on an environmental review of the project, fearing that it will bring even more hordes of tourists into the wine country. Indeed, the Wine Train's promoters hope that it will eventually carry 400,000 passengers a year. (To look on the bright side—at least they won't be driving on Highway 29.) As an indication of their serious intentions, the Wine Train's investors have engaged renowned chef Narsai David to plan its dinner menus.

Facilities

Wine Country Inns of Sonoma County, 707-433-4667
Bed and Breakfast Exchange, 707-963-7756

Organization

Napa Valley Natural History Association
3801 St. Helena Highway North, Calistoga 94515

Recommended reading

Edwards, Don, *Making the Most of Sonoma.*

Two famous, prolific, yet very different authors are forever associated with these counties: Robert Louis Stevenson spent his honeymoon on the flank of Mt. St. Helena in 1880; and Jack London moved to a ranch near Glen Ellen in 1905 and lived there until his tragically early death in 1916. Because both these sites are now state parks, it's easy to spend a weekend on a literary pilgrimage to them—and include visits to wineries along the way (Stevenson and London would have approved).

Stevenson, Robert Louis, *The Silverado Squatters.* Many editions.
The author's account of his honeymoon visit to the Calistoga-Mt. St. Helena region in 1880. Don't be deterred by the notion that because this book is a "classic," it must be boring. It's colorful and opinionated (and fairly brief).

Because tourism is important to these counties, they go out of their way to provide visitors with information at low or no cost. Chambers of commerce in the various towns have all sorts of helpful material available. The addresses of the chambers of commerce, as well as a host of other useful data, are in the Redwood Empire Association's Visitor's Guide (see p. 36).

Sonoma County Farm Trails contains a map showing over 150 orchards, nurseries, dairies, craft shops and wineries that welcome visitors. For a copy, write Box 6674, Santa Rosa, 95406. Copies are also available at most chambers of commerce in the county.

Napa County has followed suit with *Napa County Farming Trails,* 4075 Solano Avenue, Napa, 94558.

Information about the wineries is also available from the Wine Institute, 165 Post Street, San Francisco 94108; phone 986-0878.

30   Fort Ross State Historic Park

Address and phone
19005 Coast Highway 1, Jenner 95450; 707-847-3286.

Maps
Topo *Fort Ross.*

How to get there
The park is just off winding Highway 1, 12 miles north of Jenner.

History
I confess I could not help speculating upon the benefit this country [California] would derive from becoming a province of our powerful empire, and how useful it would prove in Russia. An inexhaustible granary for Kamchatka, Okhotsk ... these regions so often afflicted with a scarcity of corn would derive new life from a close connection with California.

—Otto von Kotzebue, Russian explorer, after visiting the north side of San Francisco Bay in 1824.

The Russian occupation of the Sonoma Coast from 1812 to 1841 constitutes one of the most exotic chapters in the adventurous history of 19th century California, and has contributed its share of legends.

The Russian American Company established a settlement in Kodiak in 1783 and, moving eastward, one in Sitka in 1804. From their headquarters here they hunted sea otters and fur seals with total disregard for any notion of maintaining the species.

In 1806 Count Nikolai Rezanov sailed to San Francisco from Sitka with a crew of hungry, scurvy-ridden men to pick up urgently needed food for the Russians' Alaskan base. Rezanov not only charmed the Spanish authorities, he even became engaged to the

Commandante's daughter, Concepcion Arguello. But Rezanov died on his way back to St. Petersburg to seek royal approval for the wedding. Concepcion never married, and died in a nunnery in Benicia in 1857—having become the subject of numerous fanciful poems and stories, which at least one historian has characterized as "romantic drivel." It is nevertheless tempting to speculate on what sort of influence Rezanov would have had on California history had he returned. He was obviously a capable and ambitious man who envisaged establishing a permanent Russian settlement on the coast north of San Francisco.

In 1812 a party of Russians under Ivan A. Kuskov constructed a redwood stockade thirty miles north of Bodega Bay and christened it Ross, from the archaic name for Russia. The Russians called it "Colony Ross," but the Spanish called it a fort—and it was indeed well protected. Technically speaking, it was on Spanish territory; and the Spanish officials did complain about the Russian occupation, but they were virtually powerless to do anything about it.

At this time, we must remember, California was considered the back of beyond, and the European powers were preoccupied with the Napoleonic Wars. In fact, while Kuskov was constructing Fort Ross, Napoleon's army was marching into the heart of Russia.

Fort Ross and environs for a time sustained over three hundred Russians, Aleuts and California Indians. The Russians also established bases at Bodega Bay and on the Farallones. In addition to otter and seal hunting, they applied themselves to agriculture and manufacture. Some of the resulting products were sent back to the Russian outposts in Sitka, and some were traded with the Californios—although Spanish law officially forbade such trade.

In 1821 Czar Alexander I issued a ukase declaring the Pacific Coast north of San Francisco closed to all but Russian ships. This was one of the events that prompted President James Monroe to issue in 1823 his famous Doctrine asserting that European powers must attempt no further colonization of the New World. Nervousness about Russian intentions also encouraged the Spanish to found the two northernmost missions, in San Rafael (1817) and Sonoma (1823).

Once the Russians had exhausted the sea-otter crop, they found their California colony uneconomical to maintain. After trying in vain to make a deal with either the Mexican government or Mariano Vallejo, in 1841 they sold their buildings, livestock and other chattels to John A. Sutter for $32,000 and returned to Russia. Legend has it that Princess Helena Gagarin, the wife of the fort's last commandant, was one of a party that climbed to the summit of Mt. St. Helena shortly before the Russians left California. History and science-fiction buffs who like to imagine alternative pasts and presents can have a field day speculating on what would have happened if the Russians had decided to stay on—or if they had explored farther inland than Mt. St. Helena and discovered the gold of the Mother Lode before the Americans took over California.

The Fort Ross property went through several owners until 1873, when George Call bought it. His family maintained a ranch here for 30 years. Eventually the state acquired the site as a historic monument. The state has rerouted Highway 1—which used to run through the fort—and reconstructed a number of the old Russian buildings.

Facilities
Open daily 10 A.M.–4 P.M. except Thanksgiving, Christmas and New Year's; water, restrooms, picnic tables, telephone; museum, bookstore, gift shop, self-guiding audio tour. All wheelchair-accessible; special parking area for the disabled.

Nearby facilities
The Fort Ross Deli, 1½ miles north, sells picnic supplies. The elegant Timber Cove Inn, which contains a restaurant overlooking the scenic coast, is 3 miles north.

Regulations
Small parking fee per vehicle; small additional fee for each dog; dogs allowed in main parking lot only, on leash.

Description
You will want to begin at the Visitor Center, constructed in 1985 of redwood in a style to match the fort's buildings. The museum here has exhibits illustrating the area's history from the days of the Native Americans to the present. The staff also presents a slide show.

From the Visitor Center, a paved 0.3-mile path (wheelchair-accessible) leads to the fort proper. In the restored Commandant's House you can borrow a wand for the self-guiding audio tour and wander about the fort at your leisure. The State Park System is restoring the buildings as authentically as possible. It does give one a bit of a start to see the double-headed eagle of the Romanovs flying over the northern California coast!

The building that symbolizes Fort Ross to most people—and one of the most photographed structures in California—is the chapel. Although the chapel is the focus of visitors' attention, it may not have played a prominent role in the daily lives of the Russian inhabitants: there is no record that a priest was ever assigned to the colony.

After the Call family bought the property, the chapel served for a time as a haybarn. The 1906 earthquake knocked it down, just a few weeks after it had officially become a state historic site. It was restored in 1916, not entirely authentically, but sufficiently so that San Francisco's Russian Orthodox community could begin to hold occasional services in it. A more correct reconstruction took place in 1955-56, but in 1970 the building was destroyed by fire. The present, or third, reconstruction is based on extensive archeological and historical research and is the most authentic.

Recommended reading

As befits such a colorful chapter of American history, literature about the Russian occupation abounds.

Spencer-Hitchcock, Diane, and William E. Pritchard, "The Chapel at Fort Ross: Its History and Reconstruction." *California History,* Vol. 61, No. 1, Spring 1982, pp. 2–17. This article contains an extensive bibliography. *California History,* the journal of the California Historical Society, can be found in most medium-sized and larger libraries.

The bookstore in the Visitor Center contains other material on the history of the area. An interesting reminiscence is

Carr, Laura Call, *My Life at Fort Ross, 1877–1907.* Jenner: Fort Ross Interpretive Association, 1987.

Nearby attractions

1. Across Highway 1 and about ¼ mile up the Fort Ross Road is the Fort Ross Historic Orchard. Here the Russians planted apple, pear, cherry and other fruit trees. This is a fascinating place to visit during the spring blossom season. For a leaflet about the orchard, inquire at the Visitor Center.

2. The wild and beautiful Sonoma coast has many state and county parks, some with picnic facilities and campgrounds.

31   Armstrong Redwoods State Reserve

Address and phone

17000 Armstrong Woods Road, Guerneville 95446; 707-869-2015;
707-865-2391

Maps

Topos *Cazadero* and *Guerneville;* trail map available from ranger
station for a small price.

How to get there

From Highway 101 in Santa Rosa take Highway 116 northwest
through Sebastopol to Guerneville, or from north of Santa Rosa take
River Road west to Guerneville; from stop sign in Guerneville drive
north 2 miles on Armstrong Woods Road.

Features

The main attraction of this reserve, 2 miles from the Russian River,
is an almost-virgin redwood forest (limited logging took place in the
19th century) with many of the qualities described in the section on
Muir Woods. Armstrong Redwoods may transmit even more of a
sense of awe and otherworldliness than Muir Woods; in fact, a
former park leaflet once noted that "Indians shunned the area,
referring to it as the 'dark hole.' "

A redwood forest is usually a cool place to be on a hot day. The
giant trees on the canyon floor at Armstrong Reserve, some of them
more than 1000 years old, provide deep shade even when the surrounding countryside is sweltering in August heat.

Facilities

At the north end of the park, under redwoods, are 100 picnic sites
with grills; one of the restrooms is wheelchair-accessible. A group
picnic site for 50–150 people can be reserved through the park. If
you should feel like getting married, the park's 1200-seat Forest
Theater is a popular spot for weddings; it's also the setting for plays
and musicals during the summer. A snack bar, trail rides and pack
trips may be available seasonally; phone 707-887-2939 for information.

Regulations

The usual for state parks.

Description

When you pay your entrance fee, pick up a trail map. It shows the major points of interest, such as the Forest Theater and some especially large trees. One of these is a memorial to Colonel James Armstrong, a pioneer landowner and developer in Sonoma County, who saved this redwood grove for posterity just as William Kent subsequently saved Muir Woods.

From the Parson Jones Tree the Pioneer Trail runs north a short mile along small Fife Creek (dry in summer) to the picnic areas. Picnickers can draw straws to see who has to drive all the gear to their destination while the other members of the party take the cool Pioneer Trail under the big trees.

For an easy loop, you can take the Pioneer Trail in one direction and the East Ridge Trail in the other.

Nearby attractions

The town of Guerneville (pronounced in two syllables) is a popular resort area, containing motels, restaurants, grocery stores and so forth.

On River Road 3 miles east of Guerneville is the Korbel Winery (open daily 9 A.M.–5 P.M.; tours 10 A.M.–3 P.M.).

32 Austin Creek State Recreation Area

Address and phone

Same as for Armstrong Redwoods

Maps

Same as for Armstrong Redwoods.

How to get there Follow the directions for Armstrong Redwoods. Bullfrog Pond Camp in Austin Creek State Recreation Area is 3½ miles north of the Armstrong picnic ground by a steep, narrow, twisty road. This is the sort of road on which it is advisable to honk as you approach curves. It cannot accommodate vehicles over 20 feet long or trailers of any size.

Features

Although Austin Creek Recreation Area adjoins Armstrong Redwoods Reserve, its high, sunny, rolling hills present a striking contrast to the shady redwood canyon. Roads and trails restricted to hikers and equestrians lead to the backcountry of the recreation area, a beautiful, isolated region of forests, hills and creeks.

(Note that it can get very hot in summer. Campers should also be aware that the raccoons here are unusually enterprising, and so should lock up their ice chests securely.)

Facilities

Bullfrog Pond Camp has 24 primitive sites available on a first-come, first-served basis. This camp is situated around the small man-made pond of its name. Some of its sites are dispersed under huge madrone trees.

Check with the ranger about carrying in water.

Deep in the recreation area are Tom King, Mannings Flat and Gilliam Creek camps—small, primitive camps for backpackers and equestrians. Horse-trailer parking space is located at the entrance to Armstrong Redwoods. Anglers should check with the ranger at Armstrong about fishing possibilities.

Regulations

The usual for state parks. Campers must register at Armstrong Redwoods. As noted above, vehicles over 20 feet in length cannot negotiate the road to Bullfrog Pond Camp. During periods of fire hazard or extremely bad weather, the rangers may close off part of the area. Dogs are not allowed in the backcountry camps.

Description

Once having negotiated the road to the camp, you may feel inclined to relax with your iced tea or chilled chardonnay while you talk someone else into setting up the tent. Or you might want to walk back to the vista point just south of the campground and gaze upon the vast panorama of hills and forests spread out before you. Or, if you are here in spring, you might want to stroll about looking for blossoms: this is great wildflower country, especially for members of the genera *Brodiaea* and *Calochortus*. Or you may just want to sit at your campsite and meditate; there is something about this place that encourages one to go into a semi-trance—until perhaps startled by a large, voluble raven sweeping down and cawing loudly.

It is apparent that if you take the Austin Creek Trail down to any of the trail camps, you will have to hike back up. The last time I tried this, I soon yearned for a rent-a-horse to appear magically on the trail. Of course, if you've registered with the ranger, you can back-pack into one of the camps.

A pleasant, easy walk from Bullfrog Pond Camp is the first part of the route leading to the East Ridge Trail and ultimately the Armstrong picnic area. Head back on the access road and go left through a gate onto the fire road. Pass another road that veers left and soon you come out on a stunning panorama of the rolling, forested Sonoma hills. A small grove of black oaks provides a pleasant site for resting and admiring the scenery.

If you continue on the fire road, you will find the connection to the East Ridge Trail going off to the right. The hike down to Armstrong via the East Ridge is a good one, offering lots of variety, but it involves a descent of 1000 feet in less than 3 miles . . . and then you have to come back up. At least from Armstrong—unlike the trail camps—you can hope to hitch a ride back to Bullfrog Pond.

33 Annadel State Park

Mailing address and phone
6201 Channel Drive, Santa Rosa 95405; 707-539-3911; 707-938-1519

Maps
Topos *Santa Rosa* and *Kenwood;* trail map available at park office or from nearby vending machine for a small price.

How to get there   Annadel is east of Santa Rosa.

From the West Bay   Drive north to Santa Rosa on Highway 101. Take the Highway 12 (Sonoma-Sebastopol) exit and go east, past the county fairgrounds, following signs for 12, Sonoma and Napa. After 5½ miles on 12, turn right on Los Alamos Road, turn right again on Melita Road and almost immediately bear left on Montgomery Drive. After ½ mile turn left on Channel Drive and follow it 2 miles to its end.

From the East Bay   Drive north on Highway 80, west on Highway 37 and north on Highway 121 and then northeast on Highway 12, past Kenwood and the little retirement community of Oakmont. Turn left on Los Alamos Road and continue as described above.

You will enter the park about a mile after turning onto Channel Drive. The park office (water, maps) is at the entrance; the parking lot is about a mile farther along the road.

Features
Annadel was once part of Rancho Los Guilicos, owned in the 19th century by Scotsman William Hood, for whom a nearby peak and park are named. When the farm land went up for sale, conservationists led by Santa Rosa businessman Henry Trione succeeded in having it preserved as an undeveloped state park.

In addition to meadows and oak-studded hills, Annadel contains a marsh area inhabited by a variety of wildlife, including some feral pigs. In spring, the park glows with colorful wildflowers, especially some from the genera *Brodiaea* and *Calochortus*.

The moderate hike described here offers only an introduction to this park of almost five thousand acres with forty miles of trail. Students of birdlife and native plants will want to return and visit the area around Ledson Marsh—being careful not to irritate the wild pigs.

Facilities

Open from sunrise to sunset. Toilets and a few picnic tables at the parking lot and Lake Ilsanjo, but *no drinking water* anywhere except at the park office. Fishing for black bass and bluegill is permitted at Lake Ilsanjo.

Regulations

No dogs, fires, camping, or motor vehicles.

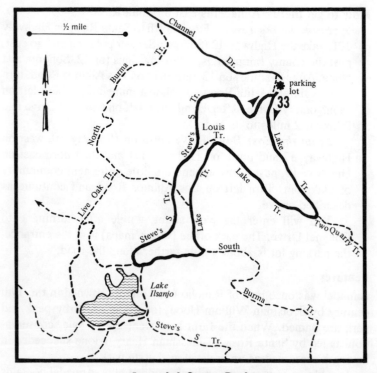

Annadel State Park

To Lake Ilsanjo

Distance 4½ mile loop; another optional 2 miles around the lake.
Grade Moderate.

Features

Hikers along these trails will see evidence that two very different cultures have used this area as a source of minerals: The local Indians found a supply here of obsidian, the shiny black rock that makes good arrowheads. Then, in the late 19th and early 20th centuries, settlers quarried basalt here to use in building and, after 1906, rebuilding San Francisco.

The lake's name is not Spanish, but a composite formed from the names of two former owners of the land, Ilsa and Joe Coney.

Description

From the parking lot (where botanists may note some Oregon ash) take the trail heading south, which soon runs into an old gravel road, the Lake Trail. A sign points the way to Lake Ilsanjo (4.2 km, 2.6 miles). Pass Steve's S Trail going off to the right and then ascend gradually through oaks and Douglas firs, with views of the hills to the north.

In a short half mile, where a road branches left, stay right and immediately turn sharp right on the Lake Trail at its junction with the Two Quarry Trail (sign). You continue ascending gradually, now through forest that includes redwood as well as oak and Douglas fir; underneath are sword fern and wood fern. As the road levels off, on the left are outcroppings of basalt. You can explore the remains of the old quarries.

Now the road turns south, passing the Louis Trail; keep following LAKE TRAIL signs. Soon you come over a rise and see Lake Ilsanjo glistening below on your right. You walk through sun-warmed oak-grassland, joining the Burma Trail for ¼ mile. At a signed junction, where the South Burma Trail branches left to Ledson Marsh, bear right on the Lake Trail and curve down to the peaceful little lake, passing Steve's S Trail. Here you can picnic on the grass under spreading, leafy oaks, perhaps serenaded (as I've been) by a gigantic, or at least a remarkably sonorous, bullfrog. Another possible picnic spot is a gazebo just off the trail at the north end of the lake.

If you like, you can stroll around the lake, checking the fishing action. Otherwise, return to Steve's S Trail, which climbs above the east edge of a meadow. At the top of the hill Steve's S briefly joins the North Burma Trail and together they start downhill. Where the North Burma Trail veers left, Steve's S continues downhill and soon enters the woods. Pass the Louis Trail branching right. Steve's S Trail descends through dense, tall Douglas firs; on the forest floor are many varieties of ferns. Shiny obsidian abounds on the lower part of this trail. After a short mile of downslope, Steve's S Trail meets the Lake Trail; here you turn left to retrace the few steps to the parking lot.

Nearby attraction

Adjoining Annadel on the west is Spring Lake County Park. This attractive park contains a bike trail and facilities for picnicking, camping, swimming and boating. You may be charged moderate fees for parking and using the facilities. Phone: 707-539-8092.

34   Sugarloaf Ridge State Park

Address and phone

2605 Adobe Canyon Road, Kenwood 95452; 707-833-5712; or c/o Sonoma Area of State Park System, 20 East Spain Street, Sonoma 95476; 707-938-1519.

Maps

Topos *Kenwood* and *Rutherford;* trail map available from head-quarters for a small price.

How to get there

The park is about halfway between Santa Rosa and Sonoma.

By way of Santa Rosa   Go north on Highway 101 to Santa Rosa and east on Highway 12 for 11 miles to Adobe Canyon Road; turn left on it and follow it 4 miles to its end.

By way of Sonoma   From the West Bay go north on Highway 101 and east on Highway 37 (Vallejo-Napa exit) to reach Highway 121; from the East Bay go north on Highway 80 and west on 37 to reach 121. Take 121 north for 6 miles, and continue north by one of two routes: Highway 12, which runs through Sonoma, or Arnold Drive, which parallels 12 on the west and runs through Glen Ellen. (You might wish to go one way and return the other.) Continue north on 12 for 3 miles after Arnold rejoins it, to the town of Kenwood. About ½ mile beyond the center of town, just past Kenwood Vineyards Winery, turn right on Adobe Canyon Road and follow it 4 miles to its end.

Narrow Adobe Canyon Road is not suitable for trailers over 22 feet long. (It is not, however, nearly as hairy as the road to Bullfrog Pond Campground in the Austin Creek Recreation Area.)

Features

Sugarloaf Ridge State Park is tucked away in the Mayacamas Mountains, somewhat off the beaten track. Earlier in the century Sonoma State Hospital operated a ranch here, and some of the present park still resembles a ranch. Sugarloaf lacks the spectacular attractions of some other state parks, such as lakes for swimming or thousand-year-old redwoods. However, it's a good place to take it easy, to toss Frisbees on the meadow and to hike around the volcanic hills and the oak woodlands of Sonoma County.

The best times to visit the park are spring and fall. It can get uncomfortably hot and dry in summer, and rainy or even occasionally snowy in winter.

Facilities

Water, toilets; 16 picnic sites with tables and grills; 50 primitive campsites, each with table and fire ring, reservable through Mistix. The sites are under trees surrounding a large, oval meadow; many afford some privacy, especially during the off season. A group camp, with equestrian facilities, is available by reservation through the park. A ¾-mile nature trail is described on the park map.

Nearby facility

The Sonoma Cattle Co. offers guided horseback rides in the park. For more information, write them at Box 877, Glen Ellen 95442, or phone 707-996-8566.

Regulations

Because the fire hazard is so high in summer, smoking is limited to developed areas, and is not permitted on trails; otherwise, the usual for state parks. Quiet hours 10 P.M.–6 A.M..

A Vista Trail Loop

Distance   6-mile loop.
Grade   Moderately strenuous.

Features

Sugarloaf has 25 miles of trails, ranging from the easy, level creekside nature trail to the strenuous ascents of Bald Mtn. and Brushy Peaks. The hike described here gives a good idea of the park's varied terrain. The first mile is a steady climb of 600 feet; after that, most of the route is level or downhill, and much of it is under shade. (Some of it is probably pretty muddy during the wet season.)

There is *no drinking water* along the route.

Description

From the east end of the day-use parking lot a sign indicates the Bald Mtn. and Meadow trails. They switchback up under trees for a few hundred feet and emerge in the meadow, where they fork. Take the Bald Mtn. Trail, which ascends first in the open, then through oak-madrone forest. After about a mile you reach the paved Ridge View Trail. A bench offers the opportunity to catch your breath and admire the view of Mt. Hood. Now turn right on Ridge View to continue uphill for another ¼ mile to the Vista Trail (sign).

The Vista Trail runs generally level, in and out of trees, occasionally crossing seasonal tributaries of Sonoma Creek. When the trail contours along the open hillside, it offers panoramic views over the park and the dramatic volcanic rock formations of Sugarloaf Ridge. After passing the Headwaters Trail, the Vista Trail begins to

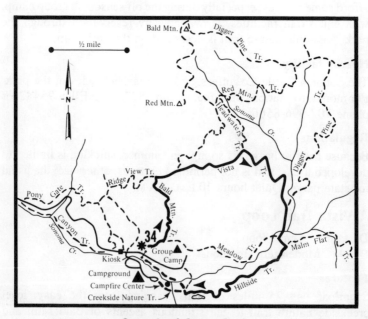

Sugarloaf State Park

descend—at times steeply—toward Sonoma Creek. Along this stretch of trail in spring you may find a virtual garden of golden fairy lanterns (*Calochortus amabilis*).

The trail follows the companionable creek downstream to join the Digger Pine Trail and traverse a meadow. In less than ¼ mile you ford the creek and soon arrive at the Meadow Trail. The trees around this part of the park are magnificent: huge old black oaks, plus bays, maples and alders.

The most direct route back to your starting place is to turn right on the Meadow Trail. However, if you're game to see a bit more of the park, turn left here, and almost immediately thereafter bear right on the Hillside Trail. This trail ascends the hillside above the creek. Just after it starts to descend, a picnic table and a water fountain invite the hiker to rest and enjoy the view over the park. The Hillside Trail concludes at post 14 of the nature trail, and you can follow it in either direction—either across the creek or past the campfire center and through the campground—to get back to the parking lot.

Nearby attractions

In addition to the Kenwood Winery mentioned above, two newer wineries are located near the intersection of Highway 12 and Adobe Canyon Road: St. Francis and Chateau St. Jean (both open daily 10 A.M.–4:30 P.M.).

The Old Bale Grist Mill in Napa Valley

Mallette Dean

35   Jack London State Historic Park

Address and phone

Box 358, Glen Ellen 95442; 707-938-5216.

Maps

Topo *Glen Ellen;* hiking map available at the park for a small price.

How to get there

From the West Bay   Drive north on Highway 101, east on 37, north on 121 and continue north on Arnold Drive to Glen Ellen; the London Ranch Road takes off to the left of the London Lodge.

From the East Bay   Drive north on Highway 80, west on 37 and north on 121; continue as above.

Features

For many years people from all over the world have come on pilgrimages to the ranch of the prodigious writer Jack London. They have visited the museum in "The House of Happy Walls," built by his widow Charmian; they have strolled to his simple grave and the eerie remains of Wolf House, the grand mansion that was gutted by fire—probably arson-caused—just before the Londons were scheduled to move into it.

Now the state has added so much acreage to this park that visitors can easily find enough here to occupy them for the better part of a day. In fact, energetic hikers can climb the wooded 3.3-mile trail to the 2300-foot summit of Mt. Sonoma, which lies just outside the park. Most visitors will want to stroll around London's Beauty Ranch and marvel at yet another facet of this amazing man: his dedication to scientific agriculture. For years he poured his royalties into this farm, and the results are evident in the terraced vineyard hillsides, the stone barns and silos, the "Manure Pit" for recycling fertilizer and the "Pig Palace," a luxurious residence London designed for his porkers. His energy is mind-boggling: in addition to designing and running this model farm, he faithfully produced his thousand words a day, maintained a wide correspondence, traveled frequently, entertained guests constantly . . . and managed to get in quite a bit of drinking. It is hardly surprising that he burned himself out by the age of 40.

Facilities

Water, restrooms, picnic tables; park open 8 A.M.–sunset; museum open 10 A.M.–5 P.M.

Nearby facilities

Adjacent to the upper parking lot is the Sonoma Cattle Co., which conducts guided horseback trail rides and carriage rides through the park (Box 877, Glen Ellen 95442; 707-996-8566).

Regulations

Small parking fee; dogs on leash only, and not allowed on lake and mountain trails.

Description

Once having paid your parking fee, you're free to stay all day and explore the park according to any route you choose. Gung-ho hikers, for example, might want to climb Mt. Sonoma before lunch.

Here's a suggested itinerary for a day in this park: Park in the main lot and spend an hour at the museum in the "House of Happy Walls." Here are memorabilia from the Londons' travels, a restoration of his study, and other fascinating exhibits. While here, pick up the brochure with trail maps (small price).

Next, make the half-mile pilgrimage down past London's grave to Wolf House. (This is a gravelly road; sturdy shoes are recommended. There are occasional water fountains along the route.)

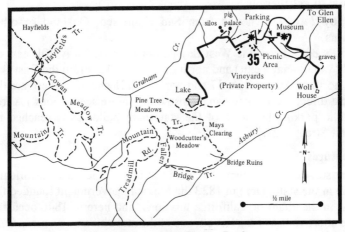

Jack London State Park

Returning to the main parking lot, move the car to the overflow parking lot so you can picnic at the tables on the nearby knoll above the stone farm buildings (water, toilets, grills). (There are a few tables in the main parking lot, but their proximity to the cars does not promote restful picnicking.) After lunch, use the Beauty Ranch trail guide in the brochure to explore the ranch.

Next, find the trail to the lake. This easy ¾-mile trail is definitely worth taking. Constructed by a Youth Conservation Corps, it leads gently up through redwoods, oaks and maples to the 5-acre lake where London had a stone dam built to make a reservoir for irrigating the ranch. The dam is still here, as is the redwood-log bathhouse where the Londons entertained their friends at swimming parties. The lake is too turbid to tempt anyone to swim nowadays. However, when I visited it in spring it was full of bass leaping enthusiastically about. Anglers might check with the rangers in advance about fishing possibilities.

36   Old Sonoma

Maps

Topo *Sonoma;* map of walking tour available for small fee from Sonoma State Historic Park and from Vasquez House, 129 East Spain Street; material also available from Chamber of Commerce, 453 First Street East.

How to get there

By bus   Greyhound from San Francisco, Oakland or other towns.

By car   From the West Bay go north on Highway 101, east on 37 (Vallejo-Napa exit) and north on 121 and 12. From the East Bay go north on 80, west on 37 and north on 121 and 12. (These are the most direct routes; you can choose other, more scenic ones.) A free public parking lot north of the state-park buildings is reached by First Street East.

Features

The sun-drenched town of Sonoma is one of the most historically rich in the state. Here in 1823 the Mexican government founded the last in the chain of California missions, and here in 1846 occurred the abortive Bear Flag Revolt, one of the more bizarre events in California's history, which is commemorated by a monument in the town's plaza. The preeminent historic personage whose spirit pervades Sonoma, however, is General Mariano Guadalupe Vallejo (described briefly on p. 135). He laid out the spacious plaza, and he and his family were responsible for many of the early buildings around it; in his later years he served as mayor.

Fortunately the inhabitants of Sonoma have taken pains to preserve its historic buildings and landmarks, and to make them accessible to visitors—especially pedestrian visitors.

Facilities

Water, restrooms in various of the public buildings and the plaza; picnic area in the plaza and an even more delightful one at the Buena Vista Winery; grocery stores, delis, bars and restaurants in abundance.

The buildings of Sonoma State Historic Park are open from 10 A.M. to 5 P.M. daily except Thanksgiving, Christmas and New Year's. The small fee includes admission on the same day to the adjoining Barracks, the nearby Vallejo Home, the Benicia Capitol and Vallejo's Petaluma Adobe.

Description

Begin at Mission San Francisco Solano, corner of First Street East and Spain Street, now part of the state park. An assortment of historical and touristic literature is available here. The leaflet published by the State Department of Parks and Recreation is well worth its modest price. Architecture and history buffs will want a copy of the Sonoma League for Historic Preservation's walking-tour guide. In the courtyard behind the mission is a garden of native plants, plus water fountain and restrooms. After the Mission, the next logical place to go is the Barracks next door, which houses a historical museum. At your leisure you can continue strolling around the plaza, which offers plenty of opportunities for eating, drinking and shopping as well as historical browsing. You will want to wander *through* the plaza, also, to admire the rose gardens, the Bear Flag monument and the Mission Revival City Hall (1906).

Just north of the state-park buildings and the parking lot is Depot Park. The original Northwestern Pacific Railroad depot burned down in 1976, but a rebuilt replica now houses a small museum (open Wednesday through Sunday 1–4:30 P.M.; small fee; picnic area nearby). Eventually this may be part of a complex of museums featuring transportation; this one, naturally, will emphasize trains. At present it contains historical exhibits and a bookstore.

A bicycle path, which has sprouted a Parcourse, now runs along the old railroad right-of-way. You can walk along it to Lachryma Montis, Vallejo's home, built in 1851–52; or you can drive there by taking Spain Street and Third Street West. Its name, "tear of the mountain," derives from a spring on the property. This Victorian Carpenter's Gothic house contrasts sharply, but not unpleasantly, with the adobe buildings around the plaza. Inside it are many of the Vallejo family's own handsome furnishings. The state also maintains a small museum in a nearby building called the Swiss Chalet.

It seems fitting to end this excursion by visiting a winery that dates back to Vallejo's time. Sonoma has two of these, both state historic landmarks (and both open daily 10 A.M.–5 P.M.). The one within walking distance of the plaza is Sebastiani Vineyards, on East Fourth Street just north of Spain Street. Across from its entrance is a small open-air collection of Indian artifacts.

Two miles northeast, at the end of Old Winery Road, is romantic-looking Buena Vista, which achieved fame in the mid-19th century under the direction of entrepreneur Agoston Haraszthy. Although recent research by wine historian Charles Sullivan indicates that Haraszthy has no real claim to the title "father of the California wine industry," he did develop Buena Vista into a remarkable wine-growing estate and his example did much to raise the standards in the industry. His business affairs at Buena Vista and in the years before were generally marked by confusion: he had come up almost $150,000 short in his gold account during his term as assayer at the San Francisco Mint before coming to Sonoma, though he was never convicted. Whatever financial irregularities he may have been guilty of, however, hardly seem to justify his eventual fate—he was probably eaten by alligators in Nicaragua.

Regardless of Haraszthy's role, the Buena Vista Winery is a delightful place. After visiting its elegant new tasting quarters, you can pick your bottle for a picnic along the creek. (Facilities here include water, restrooms, telephone.)

37   Robert Louis Stevenson State Park and Mt. St. Helena

"Perhaps because of the special immediacy and pungency of his writing about it, one feels more Stevenson in the air at Silverado than anywhere else except in Edinburgh and environs."

> —J. C. Furnas, *Voyage to Wind-*
> *ward: The Life of Robert Louis*
> *Stevenson.*

Maps

Topos *Mt. St. Helena* and *Detert Reservoir.*

How to get there

From the West Bay go north on 101, east on 37 (Vallejo-Napa exit), north on 121, east on 12/121 and northwest on 29 to Calistoga. From the East Bay go north on 80, west on 37 and northwest on 29 to Calistoga. At Calistoga bear right on 29 for 8 miles, and at the summit of the road find the small parking lots for the Robert Louis Stevenson Memorial State Park on either side of the highway.

Features

This hike takes you first to the secluded canyon in which Robert Louis Stevenson honeymooned with his bride, Fanny van de Grift Osbourne, in the spring of 1880, and which he described in *The Silverado Squatters.* You can turn back after the mile-long climb to the Stevensons' haunt, but at least once in your life you may want to hike to the top of Mt. St. Helena. At 4343' it is considerably higher than Tamalpais or Diablo, but not hard to climb by the graded road described here. On a clear winter's day you can see from its summit the white peaks of Shasta and Lassen to the north and the Sierra Nevada to the east, as well as the tall buildings of San Francisco to the south. Bring binoculars and a California road map to identify the various landmarks in the distance. Clear days are often windy, especially at the summit, so a warm jacket and a watch cap are advisable.

How did Mt. St. Helena get its name? Not even Erwin G. Gudde, the great authority on California place names, is certain. As we noted in the chapter on Fort Ross, a party of Russians climbed the mountain in 1841, shortly before leaving their California holdings, and one popular legend has it that the commandant's wife, Princess Helena de Gagarin, was in the party and named it for her patron saint.

Facilities

A few picnic tables near the start; no water or toilets anywhere along the route. If you plan to hike to the top of the mountain, take along twice as much water as you think you will need!

Regulations

No dogs on trail.

To the Silverado Mine . . . and perhaps the summit

Distance   1 mile to the mine; 4½ additional miles to the summit.
Grade   A steady climb all the way; if you go to the top, you will ascend 1300 feet in 5½ miles.

Description

Begin at the parking lot just inside the park. Some of the foundations of the old Toll House are still visible here. As Stevenson described this hotel nearly a century ago, it was a somnolent spot housing a few consumptives, where except for the occasional rattle of dishes and the strokes of croquet mallets "it was sleep and sunshine and dust, and the wind in the pine trees, all day long." This drowsy atmosphere was abruptly shattered whenever the stage arrived, and a great bustle of activity thereupon ensued—especially around the bar.

The trail switchbacks for a mile up the side of the mountain under Douglas fir, oak, bay and occasional nutmeg trees to the Stevensons' honeymoon site, commemorated by a granite marker in the form of a book. Their shelter was a rent-free bunkhouse that had provided living quarters for workers at the recently abandoned Silverado Mine. The remains of this mine, marked by reddish tailings, are to the west of the marker. Stevenson recounts, or possibly concocts, various tales circulating about the mine at the time of his stay, shortly after its closing: that $600,000 was taken out; that $90,000 was taken out but $140,000 put in; and that it was salted with silver transported here secretly in old cigar boxes. The more down-to-earth State Division of Mines in its Bulletin #154 merely says the mine "was first opened in 1872 and produced $93,000 in silver and gold during 1874."

A marker indicates the route to the summit: a scrambly trail that climbs a few hundred feet to reach the fire road. As the road curves around the mountain and occasionally switchbacks, you pass fantastic bubbly rock formations. The Division of Mines Bulletin #190 notes, "Although Mt. St. Helena . . . superficially resembles an

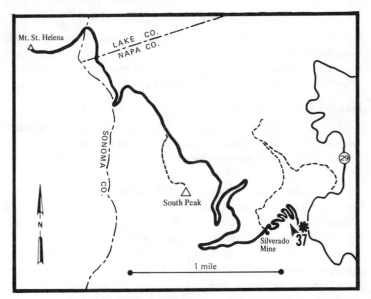

Robert Louis Stevenson State Park

eroded volcano, its internal structures suggest that it probably is not an old vent." It is, rather, built up of a series of folded lava flows. The mountain and the rest of the surrounding Sonoma volcanics date from the Pliocene and overlie older Franciscan rock. Prominent to the southeast are the Palisades.

Except for a few knobcone pines, there is little to obstruct the view, which becomes increasingly panoramic. You can orient yourself by the ocean to the west, Mt. Tamalpais to the south and Mt. Diablo to the southeast. Your musings may be interrupted by the whish of a sailplane from the Calistoga Soaring Center. In spring the roadsides are brightened by blazing star and lots of chaparral pea and bush poppy. After passing the turnoff to South Peak, the road levels off for a while under chinquapin.

When the road begins to ascend along the north shoulder of the mountain you may see Lassen and Shasta. Finally—after passing through a tiny corner of Lake County and entering Sonoma—you reach the summit, which contains a radio-transmitting station and a plaque commemorating the founding of Fort Ross in 1812 and the ascent of the Russian exploring party in 1841. (This plaque is now pretty well obscured by a metal shed.)

After enjoying as much view as weather permits, return to the trailhead the way you came. If you don't choose to sample the attractions along Highway 29, you may wish to drive back on the Silverado Trail, a winding, scenic road that branches east off from 29 about ½ mile north of Calistoga and parallels it as far as Napa.

Nearby attractions

1. Start early and stop at one or more of the many wineries along Highway 29 to taste, tour and pick up a bottle for lunch. Or hike first and then visit the wineries—but remember that many of them close at 4 P.M.

2. The Silverado Museum in St. Helena, 1490 Library Lane at the end of Adams Street east of Highway 29, contains a unique collection of Stevensoniana—books, letters, photographs and other memorabilia—and features changing exhibits. This museum is the priceless contribution of bibliophile Norman H. Strouse to his adopted home, the Napa Valley. (Open noon to 4 P.M. except Mondays and holidays; free.)

3. The town of Calistoga contains restaurants, delicatessens and spas. At 1311 Washington Street is a charming small historical museum, the Sharpsteen Museum and Sam Brannan Cottage. (Open daily noon–4 P.M. October–May, 10 A.M.–4 P.M. May–October, except holidays.)

38   Bothe-Napa Valley State Park

Address and phone
3801 St. Helena Highway North, Calistoga 94515; 707-942-4575

Maps
Topo *Calistoga;* trail map available from headquarters for small price.

How to get there
By bus   Greyhound from San Francisco or the East Bay; ask the driver to let you out at the park, 5 miles north of St. Helena, and ask him where to flag down the return bus.

By car   From the West Bay go north on 101, east on 37 (Vallejo-Napa exit), north on 121, east on 12/121 and northwest on 29 to St. Helena and 5 miles farther to the park. From the East Bay go north on 80, west on 37 and northwest on 29.

Features

For many years the campground in this park was just a stone's throw from Highway 29, and campers were regaled throughout the night by the sounds of trucks. Early in 1982 the State Park Department completely reorganized this park. The picnic area is now where the campground used to be, and a new, attractive and much quieter campground stretches along Ritchie Creek. (The current park map spells it "Ritchey," the USGS "Ritchie"; the pioneer settlers for whom so many of these geological features are named were not always meticulous or consistent in their spellings.)

Facilities

Family picnic ground; group picnic area by reservation; 40 family campsites accommodating tents or RVs (trailers up to 24 feet long, motor homes up to 31 feet), one of them designed for disabled campers; 10 walk-in sites, one for hikers and bicyclists; showers, laundry sinks also available to disabled visitors. An unusual feature for a state park is a swimming pool, which is open daily 10:30 A.M.–7 P.M. from Memorial Day weekend through Labor Day; moderate fees. Nature programs in summer. Small bookstore in Area Headquarters and Visitor Center building.

Regulations

The usual for state parks; no dogs on trails.

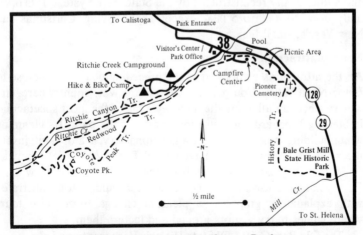

Bothe-Napa Valley State Park

The park's trails

Distance   Ad lib; the park has about 10 miles of trails.
Grade   Ad lib; some are very easy, some are moderately strenuous.

Description

At the Area Headquarters and Visitor Center building you can purchase a leaflet with map which describes the park, its trails and other
nearby places worth visiting. This leaflet is definitely worth its
modest price and will suggest enough activities for a long weekend.

Before this park was reorganized, one of its main attractions was
a nature trail named for "Firebelle Lillie" Hitchcock Coit. Lillie's
parents, Dr. and Mrs. Charles M. Hitchcock, bought a thousand
acres here in 1872 and built a mansion called "Lonely," where
tomboy Lillie spent much of her youth. In adult life Lillie became
San Francisco's most celebrated amateur firefighter. In her will she
left the City the funds to construct Coit Tower.

Although "Lonely" burned down after Reinhold Bothe bought
the property in 1929, some of the ornamental plants introduced by
the Hitchcocks linger on. The delightfully shady Redwood and
Ritchie Canyon trails on either side of the creek follow substantially
the route of the former nature trail.

One of the most intriguing trails in the park is the History Trail.
(Watch out for poison oak along it, however.) This trail runs from the
picnic area through the Pioneer Cemetery, up a ridge forested with
oak and madrone, and down to the Old Bale Grist Mill State Historic
Park. The mill and its 36-foot waterwheel have been painstakingly
and authentically reconstructed by the State Park System. It is open
daily from 10 A.M. to 5 P.M., except Thanksgiving, Christmas and
New Year's; small fee.

Nearby attractions

All the attractions mentioned in the preceding chapter are close to
Bothe-Napa Valley. You're in the heart of the wine country here, and
wineries beckon all along the highway. One of the most spectacular
is Sterling Vineyards, about a mile north of the park. Its gleaming
white building, modeled on an Italian monastery, is atop a hill just to
the right of Highway 29 on Dunaweal Lane. An aerial tramway
(moderate fee) carries visitors from the parking lot to the winery.
Here you can follow at your own pace a self-guiding tour illustrated
with explanatory graphics—a pleasant change from those tours
where guides hurry visitors around and lecture them.

The Old Bale Grist Mill State Historic Park mentioned above can
also be reached by car, and is wheelchair-accessible.

Hikes 39–63
Alameda and Contra Costa counties

All the land on the side of the Bay across from San Francisco was once part of Contra Costa ("opposite coast") County, but in 1853 Alameda County was carved out of it.

History

The East Bay had a sizable Indian population for thousands of years, as evidenced by the hundreds of shell mounds discovered on or near the shore, one of the largest at what is now Emeryville. Most of these mounds, of course, have long since been shoveled or bulldozed into oblivion.

The southern part of the "contra costa" was briefly explored in 1769 by a scouting party under Jose Francisco Ortega, the discoverer of San Francisco Bay. The first major expedition in the East Bay, however, was that in 1772 led by Pedro Fages and documented by Father Juan Crespi. They made observations of the Golden Gate, camped near Strawberry Creek on land now occupied by the University of California campus, and trudged north as far as Carquinez Strait before returning to Monterey. Hikers can still follow a part of Fages' route that traverses what is today East Bay Regional Park land.

From the 1820s on, first the Spanish and then the Mexican government conferred huge land grants on men they considered deserving of such largesse, mainly retired soldiers and civil servants. One of the largest estates was Rancho San Antonio, granted to Luis Maria Peralta in 1820. He and his sons ran thousands of head of cattle over land now occupied by Albany, Berkeley, Emeryville, Oakland, Piedmont, Alameda and part of San Leandro.

As elsewhere in California, the vast ranchos began to break up in the 1840s—subdivided among heirs, sold to Yankee immigrants or

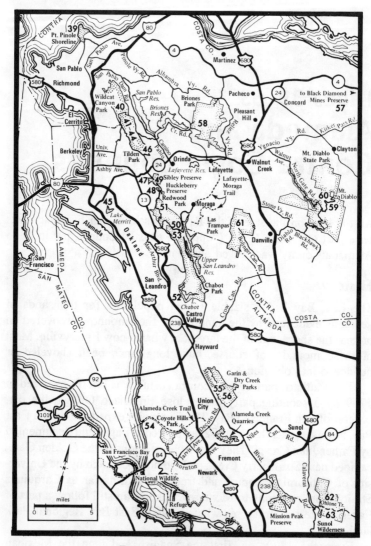

East Bay driving map

taken over by squatters, some of whom involved the original grantees in years of ruinously expensive litigation. The Spanish heritage lingers on, however, in the form of hundreds of place names that commemorate the old ranchos and their owners.

During the century following Yankee conquest, the area on the Bay side of the Berkeley Hills was gradually urbanized and industrialized, while that on the inland side remained primarily a pastoral country of oak-studded hills and a few small towns. World War II abruptly brought thousands of workers from elsewhere in the U.S. to the shipyards of Alameda and Richmond, and immigration continued unabated during the postwar period. Tract housing spread over the inland valleys, and vast, auto-oriented shopping centers surrounded the villages. These developments are still going on, and in fact may have been given new impetus by BART. On the other hand, a determined movement against unrestrained growth has arisen in these counties in recent years, as witnessed by the proliferation of citizens' groups attempting to thwart the addition of new housing tracts in their neighborhoods.

The East Bay Regional Park District (EBRPD)

Much of the hiking area in these two counties lies in the domain of an unusual organization which in 1984 celebrated its 50th anniversary, the East Bay Regional Park District. The idea of parks and "scenic lanes" in the East Bay hills goes back more than a century, to Frederick Law Olmsted, the brilliant landscape architect who had a hand in designing such diverse projects as the Berkeley campus, the Stanford campus and New York's Central Park. But not much came of Olmsted's notion until 1928, when the newly formed East Bay Municipal Utility District took over the East Bay Water Company and with it several thousand acres of surplus, non-watershed land. A citizens' group conceived of using this land for recreational purposes, and hired the landscape architects Olmsted and Olmsted (Frederick L.'s son and stepson) and Ansel Hall of the National Park Service to survey the territory for a possible park. The Olmsteds and Hall concluded that 7000–10,000 acres were suitable for recreational use. Because EBMUD at that time shrank from getting involved in park administration, the citizens' group decided to try to create a special regional park district, and spent several years of dedicated politicking to this end. In 1934 the voters of seven cities in Alameda County overwhelmingly approved the formation of the EBRPD, to be supported by a few cents on the property tax. Contra Costa joined the district in 1964.

Now the EBRPD administers over 60,000 acres of parks, trails, shorelines and preserves, It conducts active nature-study programs in many of the parks. For maps and information, consult East Bay Regional Park District Headquarters, 11500 Skyline Boulevard, Oakland 94619-2443. For general information, call 531-9300 (from central and eastern Contra Costa County, 671-0678; from Washington and Eden Township, 881-8878; from Pleasanton, Livermore and Dublin, 846-1008); for reservations for group picnic areas and youth-group day and overnight camping, 531-9043.

Facilities

The EBRPD early in 1988 announced that it had completed its Whole Park Access study—an inventory of park facilities accessible to people with physical disabilities, and recommendations for improvements to provide greater accessibility. For information, phone 531-9300, extension 278.

From April through September, the Parks Express bus program provides low-cost transportation for organizations serving the East Bay's low-income youth, the elderly and people with disabilities. For information, phone 531-9300, extension 329.

Public transit runs to or near many of the parks; see the section on Transit (pp. 174–175).

Regulations

Many of the popular parks have small parking fees, especially on weekends. Currently these are in the range of $1.50 to $3.00 per vehicle. Some parks charge a small additional fee for each dog.

Under "Regulations" for each park, I mention any that are posted there. From EBRPD headquarters you can get a list of regulations that apply in *all* EBRPD parks. Here are the ones most likely to concern readers of this book:

● Don't disturb or remove plants, animals or geological, archeological or historic objects.

● Dogs and other pets must at all times be under control so as not to interfere with park users, other animals or wildlife. No dogs or other animals are permitted at any swimming pool, bathing beach or nature area. Dogs and other animals must be leashed at parking areas, lawn areas, picnic areas, concession areas, developed areas, and any posted area. Dogs and other animals may be off leash only in open-space areas and undeveloped areas of parklands, and must be under control at all times.

● Motor vehicles and motorcycles are restricted to designated paved roads and parking lots open to public use. Driver and vehicle must be licensed.

● Bicycles may be ridden on designated bicycle trails and fire or service roads, paved or unpaved. Bicycles are not permitted on narrow hiking and equestrian trails, or in other areas so posted.

● On multi-use trails: bicycles yield to hikers and horses; hikers yield to horses; walk to the right, pass on the left.

● Alcoholic beverages are not permitted in swim areas or within 50 feet of paved roads or parking areas. Beer and wine are permitted elsewhere.

● Fires are permitted in barbecue pits or personal appliances at least 30 feet from flammable materials. Dispose of burned fuel in barbecue pits.

● Radios and other sound-creating devices may not be used in a way that disturbs other park users.

● Firearms of any kind are permitted only at designated rifle ranges. Other dangerous weapons such as crossbows, spears and slingshots are not permitted on parklands. Bows and arrows may be used only at designated archery ranges.

● Games and activities likely to endanger property or other park users—e.g., model airplanes, model rockets, fireworks, hang gliding, golf—are not permitted except in designated areas.

● Horses are not permitted in swimming, lawn or nature areas; equestrians should stay on trails.

● Assemblies, performances and similar gatherings require permits from the General Manager's Office.

Maps

The district issues free maps of most of its facilities; these are available at headquarters, at the Environmental Education Center in Tilden Park and at some other of the larger parks.

Olmsted Bros. are issuing *Rambler's Guides to the Trails of the East Bay Hills,* similar to their *Rambler's Guide to Mt. Tamalpais.* So far two have been completed—*Northern Section* and *Central Section*—and more are in the works. In addition to their multicolored, contour-showing maps, these publications contain all sorts of useful information about the parks.

T. O. Erickson has issued a number of maps showing the regional parks.

The East Bay Municipal Utility District (EBMUD)

In 1972 EBMUD began to open some of its watershed lands for recreational use. At present three of the district's five reservoirs are open:

Lafayette Reservoir Recreation Area, off Mt. Diablo Boulevard only a mile from BART and the freeway, has fishing, picnic areas, group picnic areas, bicycling and hiking trails, boat and canoe rentals, and launching for cartop sailboats and canoes; phone 284-9669.

San Pablo Reservoir Recreation Area, off San Pablo Dam Road between Orinda and El Sobrante, has fishing, picnic areas, snack bar, hiking, bicycling and riding trails, boat rentals and a sailboat launching ramp; phone 223-1661.

Lake Chabot is administered by the EBRPD and is described in the chapter on Anthony Chabot Regional Park.

The trails around these three reservoirs are open to the general public. Hikers and equestrians who wish to travel on the 55 miles of trail over the district's beautiful, sometimes rugged, backcountry must obtain a trail permit. These are available at any EBMUD business office and at Lafayette and San Pablo recreation areas for a moderate fee—currently $5 for one year or $10 for three years.

The district has issued an elegant leaflet with map by Malcolm Margolin that contains detailed descriptions of its trails.

For maps, information and trail permits: East Bay Municipal Utility District, Recreational Land Division, 2130 Adeline Street, Oakland 94607; phone 835-3000; mailing address Box 24055, Oakland 94623.

Linear trails

One of the most exciting developments in the East Bay's open-space picture has been the construction of linear trails connecting various of the regional parks with one another, with EBMUD lands, and with local parks and other community facilities. Insofar as possible, these trails are multi-use: they are designed to accommodate walkers, joggers, bicyclists and equestrians (but not motorcycles—one of their great charms is their freedom from internal-combustion engines).

Planning and building such trails can be a real challenge, as permission must be obtained from a host of agencies—regional, county, city and utility-district—as well as private owners. Many householders may initially be apprehensive about having a public trail going past their property, yet once it is built they become enthusiastic users. For example, commuters soon discovered that they could bicycle on the Lafayette-Moraga Trail to the Lafayette BART station more conveniently and agreeably than they could drive. They helped to swell the usage figure on this trail to an amazing 250,000 persons per year. The newer Briones-Mt. Diablo and Contra Costa Canal trails will probably become just as popular, if not more so.

Hiking, and especially bicycling, on these level trails offers a unique and exhilarating experience, as you pass a kaleidoscope of schoolyards, old orchards, horse corrals, fruit and vegetable gardens (some complete with scarecrows), canals, game fields and every kind of backyard ever dreamed of in middle-class California. Students of horticulture will be fascinated by the wide variety of ornamental as well as native plants to be seen along these trails.

The official northeast end of the Lafayette-Moraga Trail is the staging area at Olympic Boulevard and Reliez Station Road, Lafayette. The Lafayette BART station is less than a mile from the trail: from the station walk south to Mt. Diablo Boulevard, east to Moraga Road, south to School Street, and east on it to the trail entrance. The trail runs along the old Sacramento Northern roadbed for much of its route. After 5½ miles it arrives at Moraga Commons. Along the way you can try out two exercise game fields and take a side trip to St. Mary's College campus. The trail continues to the Valle Vista Staging Area on Canyon Road, where it connects with EBMUD trails (permit required—see above).

A good entrance to the Briones-Mt. Diablo and Contra Costa Canal trails is at Heather Farms City Park in Walnut Creek. The Pleasant Hill BART station is just a few blocks north of the trail.

The Alameda Creek Trail is described in Chapter 54. The East Bay Skyline National Recreation Trail and the Ohlone Wilderness Trail are described below.

A bike permit lets cyclists take their bikes on BART during noncommute hours on weekdays and all day on weekends; for information, phone 464-7133.

Maps
The EBRPD has issued free maps of some of the regional trails. The City of Walnut Creek has published a map called *Walnut Creek Trailways* which is available for a small price at City Hall (phone 943-5849) and at Heather Farms Park.

The East Bay Skyline National Recreation Trail

In 1970 the then Secretary of the Interior, Walter J. Hickel, selected the East Bay Skyline Trail as the first nonfederal national recreation trail in the National Trails System. To qualify as a national recreation trail according to the Interior Department's guidelines, a route "must be situated close to an urban or metropolitan area, be in public ownership or control, have scenic value, be wide enough to provide for multi-use such as hiking, horseback riding, nature study and, in some cases, bicycling. No use by motor vehicles is allowed."

The present East Bay Skyline National Recreation Trail consists of 31 miles running from Richmond to Castro Valley through the following EBRPD parks: Wildcat Canyon, Tilden, Sibley, Huckleberry Preserve, Redwood and Chabot. The trail generally follows the crest of the Berkeley-Oakland hills, but it traverses a wide variety of terrain: grassland, brushland, chaparral, oak woodland and redwood forest, all interspersed with areas of introduced plants—notably, eucalyptus. Much of the trail runs along previously existing roads and trails in the EBRPD system, but several miles of it were constructed by volunteers—Scout troops, hiking clubs and so forth.

It is possible to hike the whole 31 miles in one day, and in fact a couple of experienced Sierra Club hike leaders, Don de Fremery and Jerry Borges, have made this an annual outing for a very fit group. They schedule it in May, during daylight-saving time; arrange a car shuttle from Willow Park Golf course to Wildcat Canyon Park; plan to be on the trail from about 7:30 A.M. to 7:30 P.M.; and celebrate with an informal tailgate potluck at the finish. The event is described in the Sierra Club Bay Chapter activities schedule as "a classic 5D hike"—meaning it is over 20 miles long and includes over 3000 feet of total elevation gain. It has attracted as many as 38 participants.

Most of us are not quite up to such a strenuous outing. It will be easier for ordinary hikers and families to cover the whole trail in a long weekend when the Park District establishes more camps along it, as they plan to do. At present there is only one family camp, Chabot in Chabot Park near the southern end. Organizations, however, can reserve group campsites at several places along the trail (phone 531-9043).

Because for the foreseeable future most people will be hiking the Skyline Trail in sections, I have described its sections in the chapters devoted to the six parks it runs through.

Maps

A map of the entire trail is available at EBRPD headquarters and at the Tilden Park Environmental Education Center. The trail is also shown on the Olmsted and Erickson maps. More detailed maps of the individual sections appear on the maps of the six parks through which the trail runs.

The Skyline Trail is marked at junctions by a blue dot on a post and/or a distinctive triangular emblem.

The Ohlone Wilderness Regional Trail

It was the culmination of a long-held EBRPD dream when the Ohlone Wilderness Regional Trail opened in 1986. This trail for hikers, backpackers and equestrians (but not bicyclists) runs for 29 miles from Mission Peak Regional Preserve through San Francisco Water Department lands, Sunol Regional Wilderness and Ohlone Regional Wilderness and ends at Del Valle Regional Park. It contains five wilderness campsites, so that backpackers can plan a three- or four-day outing.

The trail passes through oak woodlands and over high ridges, including Rose Peak, which at 3817 feet is just 32 feet lower than Mt. Diablo. The area is home to an abundance of wildlife—hawks, eagles, deer, bobcats, probably even mountain lions. Spring wildflower displays are unsurpassed anywhere. It seems almost incredible that such a wilderness backpacking experience could be possible so close to the metropolis. You will have to share it, however, with some grazing cattle.

A permit is required for any use of the Ohlone Wilderness Trail. These permits are available for a small fee (currently $1) from the entrance kiosks at Sunol and Del Valle parks and by mail from EBRPD Headquarters at 11500 Skyline Boulevard, Oakland 94619-2443. Reservations must be made in advance from Sunol (862-2244 between 8 A.M. and 4 P.M.) for Sunol and Ohlone Wilderness backpack campsites, and from any Ticketron outlet for Del Valle car-camping sites.

The trail permit contains a detailed map and description of the whole route, plus information about facilities and regulations. Hint:

Beginning backpackers may want to start out on a small scale by
trying the camps in Sunol (Chapter 63). Note also that if you start
from the Mission Peak end, you have a strenuous 8½-mile hike to
the Sunol Valley family camp (4 nonreservable sites) or 12 miles to
the Sunol backpack campsites. However, starting from Del Valle will
require climbing 1500 feet in two miles to Boyd Camp (water supply
0.4 mile below the camp) or continuing to Stewart's Camp with a
total elevation change of approximately 4,600 feet in seven miles.
The best plan is to do the trail in two sections: Mission Peak to Sunol
Valley and Sunol Valley to Del Valle. Car shuttles or pickups will be
required in either case.

Like the Skyline Trail, the Ohlone Trail has its own symbol: a red

Public transit

As noted elsewhere in this book, transportation problems are vexing
the entire Bay Area, including the East Bay. In fact, in recent years
the East Bay transit situation has occasionally verged on melo-
drama or farce. In January 1988 the Alameda County grand jury
called for the resignation of all seven of AC Transit's board of
directors on grounds of their financial mismanagement of the
system, and in March the district attorney charged one of them with
felony misuse of public funds. Meanwhile BART—after 15 years—
is still having trouble with cost overruns, suppliers' missed dead-
lines, malfunctioning equipment and schedule delays.

Both systems will have to face additional long-range problems
that have developed from changing population patterns in the Bay
Area. BART directors have to decide whether to extend service to
San Mateo County or to East Contra Costa County, or whether they
can afford both. And AC Transit is engaged in devising a complex
new route network, for which it invites comments from the public:
AC Transit Planning Department, 1600 Franklin Street, Oakland
94612.

Here is the public-transit situation as this book goes to press: BART runs four rail lines: up the urban corridor from Fremont to Richmond, and from San Francisco/Daly City to Richmond, to Concord and to Fremont; transfers between all lines are possible in Oakland. BART connects with Amtrak and with various bus lines. For information:

from San Francisco/Daly City	788-BART
from Oakland/Berkeley	465-BART
from Hayward/San Leandro	783-BART
from Richmond/El Cerrito	236-BART
from Fremont/Union City	793-BART
from Walnut Creek/Concord	933-BART
from Livermore/Pleasanton	462-BART

AC Transit runs buses daily over much of the East Bay and across the Bay Bridge to San Francisco. For information:

from Oakland/San Francisco	839-2882
from Hayward	582-3035
from Richmond	232-5665
from Fremont/Newark	797-6811
from west Contra Costa County	758-2266
from east Contra Costa County	754-4040

In recent years AC Transit has operated summer bus service to some of the most popular East Bay parks; since this service varies each season, it is best to phone for information. AC Transit has also offered special summer weekday service to nonprofit groups who want to charter a bus to visit one of the regional parks; phone 531-9300, extension 329.

Greyhound runs buses daily to various points in these counties. In San Francisco, phone 433-1500; elsewhere, look in the white pages.

Peerless Stages runs buses daily from San Jose and Santa Cruz to Oakland. In Oakland, phone 444-2900; elsewhere, look in the white pages.

The Commute Store in Berkeley provides information about the routes and schedules of all Bay Area transit systems and sells tickets and passes for them. It also provides bicycle maps and promotes ridesharing. It is located in downtown Berkeley ½ block from the BART station, at 2033 Center Street; open Monday through Friday 8:30 A.M.–5:30 P.M.; phone 644-7665 (644-POOL).

Recommended reading

The EBRPD has put out a useful brochure that contains maps of most of the parks and information about their facilities; it is available from park headquarters and visitor centers for a small donation.

The EBRPD also issues a monthly LOG that contains news of the parks and a calendar of all the activities scheduled in them; copies are usually posted at the entrances to the parks. For subscription information, phone 531-9300 and ask for Public Affairs.

Doss, Margot Patterson, *There, There*. San Rafael: Presidio Press, 1978. (Out of print.)

Margolin, Malcolm, *The East Bay Out: A Personal Guide to the East Bay Regional Parks*. 2nd ed. Berkeley: Heyday Books, 1988.

Newey, Bob, *East Bay Trails: A Guide for Hikers, Runners, Bicyclists and Equestrians*. 4th ed. Hayward: Footloose Press, 1981.

Spangle, Frances, and Jean Rusmore, *South Bay Trails*. Berkeley: Wilderness Press, 1984.

I have omitted from this edition of *Outdoor Guide* the following parks, which have appeared in previous editions but which my colleagues Spangle and Rusmore have described in their book:

> Coyote Hills Regional Park
> Mission Peak Regional Park
> San Francisco Bay National
> Wildlife Refuge

Stein, Mimi, *A Vision Achieved: Fifty Years of East Bay Regional Park District*. Oakland: EBRPD, 1984.

39 Point Pinole Regional Shoreline

Maps

Topos *Richmond* and *Mare Island;* trail map available from EBRPD headquarters.

How to get there

By BART and bus Take BART or AC Transit #68, #69 or #72 to the Richmond BART station; thence take #78 (currently not running on Sundays) to the park entrance.

By car From Highway 80, just north of Richmond, take the Hilltop Drive exit west to San Pablo Avenue, go right (north) to Atlas Road, left (west) to Giant Highway and left (south) for ¼ mile to the park entrance. The change from the new cookie-cutter housing developments near San Pablo and Atlas to the old, meandering, two-lane Giant Road is an abrupt one.

Features

Point Pinole has had an explosive career in more ways than one. Between 1881 and 1960 a series of gunpowder manufacturers occupied the point. Because they had to keep this hazardous site off limits to the public, for fear of explosions, it remained isolated from the industrial urbanism that gradually came to surround it. In fact, except for some moldering bunkers, cracked roads and remnants of railroad tracks, the point was still a remarkably untouched landscape in 1963, when Bethlehem Steel bought it to add to a nearby galvanizing plant.

At this juncture a group of conservationists were themselves galvanized into action. They began a determined campaign to bring Point Pinole into the regional park system. In 1972 the EBRPD purchased the point and began installing recreational facilities. Probably the most popular of these is the concrete fishing pier the Park District constructed in 1977, which stretches almost a quarter mile into San Pablo Bay. This pier, according to the *Bay Guardian,* is "the best place [in the Bay Area] to go deep sea fishing without a boat," as it extends into the migration routes of salmon, striped bass and white sturgeon. So far the record catch has been a 170-pound sturgeon.

Fishing isn't the only popular activity in the park. This square mile located on the Pacific Flyway includes several kinds of habitat: woods, meadow, freshwater marsh, saltwater marsh and beach. It's ideally suited for birding, beachcombing, bicycling or just picnicking.

Facilities

Hours vary seasonally; generally sunup to dusk. Toilets, phone at parking lot; water, restrooms, tables, grills and phone at main picnic area. Shuttle bus (small fee) from parking lot to picnic area and pier every hour on the half hour, weekdays 8:30 A.M.–6 P.M., weekends and holidays 7:30 A.M.–6 P.M. Shuttle bus, picnic area and pier are all accessible by wheelchair.

Regulations

Small parking fee, small additional dog fee. No alcoholic beverages, except beer in picnic area. Dogs must be leashed; *no dogs allowed on shuttle bus or pier.*

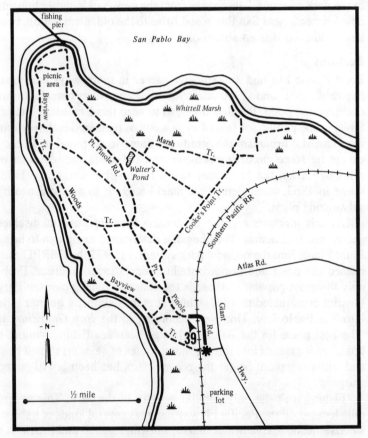

Point Pinole Regional Shoreline

Fishing from the pier is permitted without a license, although a license is required for anyone 16 or over fishing from the shore. The fishing limits for various species are complex; they are posted at the pier, or you can ask the EBRPD about them in advance (531-9300).

Description

Begin at the parking area, which is also the shuttle terminus. If you are toting a lot of fishing gear or picnic supplies, you may want to take the shuttle. Otherwise, head north on a paved road marked by symbols for hikers, bikers and equestrians. On the left is the Southern Pacific track, at the bottom of a canyon.

Soon the J. Paul Badger Bridge (named for a former director of the EBRPD) crosses the railroad track to provide access to the point. Once across it, you can explore the park at your leisure—on road, on trail or cross-country. The main route to the main picnic area, Pinole Point Road, heads northwest. Not far beyond the bridge you come to a small picnic area and a junction with the Bay View Trail. Continuing on the road you'll traverse a meadow and pass groves of eucalyptus planted around the turn of the century. (A flash fire in the summer of 1980 left the eucalypti scarred, but these are tough trees; they will recover.) If the eucalyptus is in bloom, you'll see hundreds of hummingbirds, clustered as thick as bees, feeding from the blossoms. You might see a red-tailed hawk or, with luck, a white-tailed kite.

At the point, a mile from the bridge, you'll find the picnic area, the remains of an old wharf, and the new 1225-foot-long pier. You may want to walk out on it and check the fishing action. On a clear day, the point affords a unique view of San Pablo Bay, from Point San Pablo on the Richmond side across to Point San Pedro on the Marin side, past Hamilton Air Force Base and around to Mare Island and Carquinez Strait.

From the point you can venture into Whittell Marsh, if it isn't too swampy. Or you can proceed south along the shore, either on the beach itself if the tide is low enough or on the Cliff Trail on the bluffs above. The beach here is not particularly attractive, since it is uncomfortably pebbly to walk on and is cluttered with debris from the Bay. It is, however, an excellent spot to watch for birds, since it's situated on the Pacific Flyway just south of the Tubbs Island refuge. Depending on the time of year, you may find grebes, loons, herons, cormorants and a variety of ducks offshore, and avocets, willets, plovers, godwits, curlews, sanderlings, dunlins and other shorebirds on the tidal flats. And, of course, gulls everywhere.

If the beach palls—or the tide comes in—you can repair to the Bay View Trail. Part of it runs along the remains of a narrow-gauge railroad track once used for transporting gunpowder. Other reminders of the explosives-manufacturing period are occasional bunkers and the remnants of concrete foundations. These artifacts provide an intriguing contrast to the present-day quiet of the meadows, salt marshes and tide flats.

You can return to the entrance bridge (the only exit) by any of several trails or roads, or cross-country—perhaps through the eucalyptus trees, which, when viewed from the proper angle, turn out to have been planted in parallel rows. If you're lucky, your walk back will be enlivened by the song of a meadowlark or the sight of a red-shafted flicker.

40   Wildcat Canyon Regional Park

Maps

Topo *Richmond;* trail map available from EBRPD headquarters or from Tilden Park Environmental Education Center; Olmsted Bros.' *Rambler's Guide ... Northern Section;* Erickson's *Recreational Map ... North Section.*

How to get there

By bus   AC Transit #68A runs (except on Sundays and holidays) up McBryde Avenue to the Alvarado Area of the park. AC Transit #69B runs (except on Sundays and holidays) from the Richmond BART station to San Pablo Dam and Clark roads in El Sobrante; 3 blocks south on Clark, just past Hillview School, a trail leads to the park's north entrance and the Clark-Boas Trail.

By car   To reach the Alvarado area from Highway 80 southbound, take McBryde Avenue east to Park Avenue and go 1 block east on Park. From Highway 80 northbound take the Amador/Solano exit, continue 3 blocks on Amador, turn right on McBryde and follow it to Park Avenue. From Berkeley take Arlington Boulevard north to Park Avenue. The original entrance to the park was a mile farther along Wildcat Canyon Parkway, but the storms of 1982 and 1983 caused so many landslides on this road that it had to be closed.

To reach the north entrance, from Highway 80 go east on San Pablo Dam Road to Clark Road (the second past Appian Way), turn right and follow Clark to its end at Hillview School.

Wildcat Canyon Park can also be approached from the south via Tilden Park. You can walk in along Wildcat Creek from the Tilden

Environmental Education Center. Or you can walk or bicycle along Nimitz Way from Inspiration Point.

Features

Wildcat Canyon is one of the least developed of the East Bay regional parks. The property has been a sort of stepchild until very recently. During the 19th century, squatters, speculators and holders of Spanish land grants disputed its ownership. EBMUD eventually acquired it, then sold part of it to Standard Oil for drilling; but the oil supply proved not worth exploiting. In the 1960s and '70s the EBRPD succeeded in acquiring more than 2000 acres here. One argument proponents of making the place a park used against would-be housing developers was the instability of the soil, since the area straddles the Hayward Fault. This instability became dramatically apparent in the winters of 1982 and 1983, as you can see by walking along the remains of the road to the original parking lot.

In 1985 the EBRPD acquired Alvarado Park, which adjoined Wildcat Canyon Park, from the city of Richmond, and is in the process of refurbishing it. The rest of Wildcat Canyon is mostly grassy hillsides punctuated by wooded canyons and occasional landslides. The top of San Pablo Ridge offers great views. By contrast, the riparian forest along Wildcat Creek shelters a cool, green, shady path.

Facilities

In Alvarado Park: Water, toilets, tables, grills, group picnic area.

The East Bay Skyline National Recreation Trail in Wildcat Canyon Park: Belgum Trail, San Pablo Ridge Trail and Nimitz Way

Distance 7½ miles one way to Inspiration Point; various shorter loops possible.

Grade Strenuous.

Features

The Skyline Trail route originally ran along Wildcat Creek and then up the Havey Canyon Trail to meet Nimitz Way. After the storms of 1982 and 1983 washed out Wildcat Canyon Parkway, the first mile of the Skyline Trail was along the cracked paving of that road to the former parking lot. In the Spring of 1988, while this book was on its way to the printer, the EBRPD rerouted the trail so that it goes much

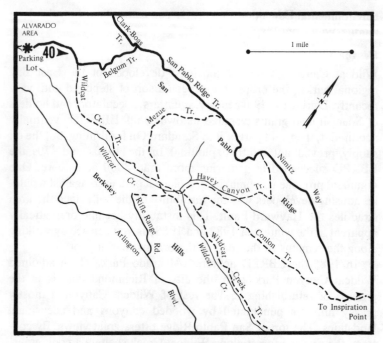

Wildcat Canyon Regional Park

more directly to San Pablo Ridge and the skyline. It is also much more exposed—something to think about on a hot day, as there is no water along the way.

Description

The route begins on the cracked paving of Wildcat Canyon Parkway and after a long half mile ascends the hillside on the Belgum Trail. A resident of the Wildcat Canyon area, Alan La Pointe, has informed me that Dr. Belgum ran a clinic near here in the 1920s. It was a sort of forerunner to the Betty Ford Clinic, specializing in treating addiction to alcohol, opium and other drugs. The clinic buildings burned down during the 1960s.

When you emerge on the open hillside you will note a plenitude of cardoon thistle, a native European plant that has escaped and become an agricultural pest in Solano and Contra Costa counties; it is especially annoying to cattlemen because it displaces the lush grass and rushes that cattle eat but is itself inedible.

The Skyline Trail runs along the top of San Pablo Ridge, offering magnificent views in every direction, for about 1½ miles to meet Nimitz Way, passing the remains of an abandoned Nike base. Paved, nearly level Nimitz Way runs 4½ miles between the old Nike base and Inspiration Point, and is popular year-round with bicyclists and joggers. Fleet Admiral Chester W. Nimitz, for whom this path and a much less attractive freeway were named, was Commander in Chief of the U.S. Pacific Fleet during World War II. After the war he resided in Berkeley; he was a Regent of the University from 1947 to 1955. Reportedly he scattered wildflower seeds as he walked along here.

If you don't want to walk all the way to Inspiration Point, you can make a loop by going downhill on the Havey Canyon Trail, shortly after passing the Nike base. The willow-fringed Havey Canyon Trail formed part of the former route of the Skyline Trail. After a long mile, turn right on Wildcat Creek Trail. It was along this route that Captain Pedro Fages, Father Juan Crespi and a small party of soldiers trudged north in March of 1772, the first white men to explore the east shore of San Francisco Bay. They traded in friendly fashion with the residents of a Native American village along the creek.

Before urbanization in the 20th century, steelhead trout regularly migrated up Wildcat Creek from the Bay. The EBRPD is attempting to restore trout habitat here, aided by grants from various anglers' organizations and from Chevron USA, whose Richmond refinery is at the mouth of the creek. Ideally, the whole creek could be rehabilitated so that the fish could travel all the way from Richmond to Jewel Lake. This task would require a lot of work, especially in the Alvarado Area.

The final mile of the trail is along the cracked paving of the former Wildcat Canyon Parkway past the old parking lot.

Side trip

Alvarado Park—since 1985 officially the Alvarado Area of Wildcat Canyon Regional Park—has an intriguing history. The handsome bridge at the entrance was built in 1936 by the WPA of stone quarried nearby. Native Americans had a permanent settlement for over 4000 years along the creek here, as evidenced by abundant bedrock mortars and shellmounds still existing. In the 1920s and 30s Alvarado was a popular park that contained at various times a dance platform and a roller skating rink, as well as picnic facilities. Just west of the park, perched on top of a rhyolite cliff, is the Boquet House, which for a time was a speakeasy. Now that Alvarado has outlived its sometimes raucous past, the EBRPD is hoping to encourage family recreation here.

Charles Lee Tilden Regional Park

Maps

Topos *Richmond* and *Briones Valley;* trail maps available at the Environmental Education Center, the Botanic Garden, and EBRPD headquarters; Olmsted Bros.' *Rambler's Guide . . . Northern Section;* Erickson's *Recreational Map . . . North Section.*

How to get there

By bus   AC Transit summer service runs directly to the park from the Berkeley BART station. Year-round, AC Transit #7 runs to Grizzly Peak Boulevard and Euclid Avenue, 2 blocks south of the Spruce Gate entrance; and #67 runs to Grizzly Peak Boulevard and Spruce Street, just across from the Spruce Gate.

By car   Tilden Park has several entrances. To find the best route from your starting point, consult a street map of Berkeley or the EBRPD map of the Park.

Features

This park, the granddaddy of the system, is named for the EBRPD's first president. It is by far the most extensively developed of the East Bay regional parks and is extremely popular the year round. Despite the crowds, it's a pleasant place to hike, and its many miles of trails offer a lot of variety in terrain and views.

Tilden Park has one unusual claim to fame: Edwin Meese III, U.S. Attorney General during the Reagan Administration, worked in this park during the summers when he was attending Oakland High School. At the EBRPD's luncheon celebrating its 50th anniversary in 1984, Mr. Meese telephoned congratulations from Washington.

Facilities

Individual picnicking; group picnicking and camping by reservation; archery range, botanic garden, golf course, merry-go-round, miniature railroad, playing fields, pony ride, swimming at Lake Anza, tennis courts. For more information about these facilities phone 531-9300; for group reservations, 531-9043.

At Castle Rock in Santa Cruz County

Richard A. Brown

Madrones on Mt. Tamalpais

Ayala Cove seen from the North Ridge Trail, Angel Island

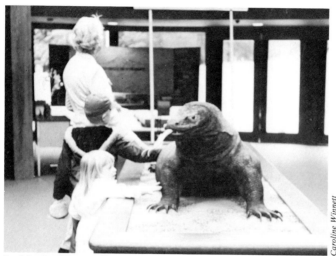

Inside the Nature Center in Tilden Regional Park

Drakes Beach

Dorothy Whitnah

The San Lorenzo River in Henry Cowell State Park

Dorothy Whitnah

Fawn at Big Basin Park

Italianate-Stick houses on Steiner St., facing Alamo Square

San Francisco Visitors Bureau

John L. Strange III

San Francisco from Mt. Tamalpais, with fog

Fort Point

San Francisco Visitors Bureau

In Sunol Regional Wilderness

Dorothy Whitnah

The Vaillancourt Fountain in San Francisco

Trillium in Briones Park, toyon on Mt. Tamalpais

41 The Tilden Park Nature Area

Phone

525-2233

Maps

Topo *Richmond;* trail maps available at Environmental Education Center.

How to get there

    By bus   Take the special summer bus when it is running; or take the #7 or #67 to the Spruce Gate, walk the ¼ mile downhill on Cañon Drive, turn left, and walk ¼ mile to the Center.

    By car   The most direct route is via the Spruce Gate and Cañon Drive.

Features

The Tilden Park Nature Area has long been known by Berkeleyans, especially parents, for its Little Farm and Jewel Lake. Now it's also the site of a handsome free-form cedar building housing the Environmental Education Center. Here are displays on various aspects of the East Bay's natural history, and maps and brochures for Tilden and other regional parks. This is also the headquarters for an active naturalist program.

Facilities

Education Center open 10 A.M.–5 P.M. daily except Monday; wheelchair-accessible. Water and restrooms there and at several picnic sites nearby. Extensive nature programs.

Regulations

No dogs allowed. Bicycles are permitted only on Wildcat Creek Trail and Loop Road (between Central Park Drive and Wildcat Creek Trail). They are not permitted on any other roads or trails in the nature area.

Description

The logical place to begin is at the Education Center. However, young children may insist on going first to the Little Farm near it to greet the animals. The cast of characters in and around the red barn changes from season to season; over the years it has included donkeys, goats, sheep, calves, pigs, rabbits and chickens. Near the barn is a collection of old farm machinery.

    Now proceed to the Education Center, browse through the

displays and pick up trail maps. You will see that a number of short, gentle trails loop around the nature area. Each of them is identified by markers with appropriate symbols, as explained on the free "Hikers' Map of Tilden Nature Study Area." The Jewel Lake Trail, which features an elevated boardwalk above a frog-filled marsh, is a source of endless fascination to young and old.

42   Wildcat Peak and the Rotary Peace Grove

Distance   3 miles round trip; more ad lib.
Grade   Moderate, except that it involves a steady climb of over 700 feet.

Maps

Topo *Richmond;* trail maps available from the Environmental Education Center.
How to get there   See the preceding section.

Features

Wildcat Peak (1250') provides grand views from its summit. Just east of it is a grove of young giant-sequoia trees planted by the Berkeley Rotary Club and the park district to commemorate "great persons who have been honored for their outstanding contributions to world peace." Take this hike if you're curious to find out which great persons have been so honored, or if you just want an exhilarating climb.

Facilities

Water, restrooms, picnic tables and stoves at the trailhead.

Regulations

No dogs allowed.

Description

From the entrance to the nature area take the Wildcat Creek Trail running northwest. As you walk here you're following in the footsteps of Pedro Fages and Juan Crespi, who explored north along Wildcat Creek in 1772. After ½ mile the road reaches the Jewel Lake dam. Turn right here at a marker with the symbols indicating the start of the Sylvan and Peak trails. Go uphill though eucalyptus and then along the side of a canyon, through chaparral. Your view includes PG&E's large power poles. The trail re-enters the eucalyptus forest and levels out; now look for the marker indicating the Peak Trail branching off to the left. Follow it uphill and then along the side of the hill under coast live oaks, and pass under the power lines. (Although they uglify the landscape, power poles do give hikers one benefit: you can often see red-tailed hawks perching atop them, scanning the land for prey.)

The trail now ascends along open, grassy hillside punctuated with coyote brush. Stop now and then to enjoy views of the Berkeley Hills, the Bay, San Francisco and Mt. Tamalpais. When the trail comes to a **T**, go left, uphill, as indicated by the marker with the peak symbol. From here it's a short but stiff climb to the summit.

At the summit is a circular stone construction, the Rotary Peace Monument, where you can rest and enjoy the view—which includes not only the Bay to the west but an abandoned Nike base to the north and Mt. Diablo and Briones and San Pablo reservoirs to the east. When you tire of the view, descend east toward the symmetrically planted Rotary International Peace Grove. You can find the plaques honoring the peacemakers under individual trees at the lower end of the grove. You may disagree with some of the Rotary Club's choices, depending on your politics (John Foster Dulles? Bob Hope? Kurt Waldheim??). Nevertheless, the idea is a worthy one, and the grove a tranquil spot for meditation or lunch or both. It is also encouraging to note that the grove contains enough unallotted trees to last well into the 21st century.

You can return the way you came, or you can make a loop. To do this, leave the Peace Grove at its east corner and bear left on a fire road heading east from the Peace Grove until you hit paved Nimitz Way. Go right on it for ¼ mile and turn right on Laurel Canyon Road, which descends to the trailhead. Or try the Laurel Canyon Trail or the Pine Tree Trail, both of which are marked by the nature area's symbolic posts and shown on its map.

43 The Regional Parks Botanic Garden

Address and phone
Tilden Regional Park, Berkeley 94708; 841-8732

Maps
Available from Visitor Center.

How to get there
By bus AC Transit summer service to the Brazilian Building. (This building—also known as the Brazil Room and the Brazilian

Pavilion—originally housed the government of Brazil's exhibition at
the Treasure Island World's Fair of 1939-40. The stone exterior is by
the WPA.)

By car   The garden is on Wildcat Canyon Road at the foot of
South Park Drive; the parking lot is directly across the road from the
entrance.

Features

This garden is devoted to plants that are native to California—and
since California is a big state with a wide variety of climates and
landscapes, that means lots of different plants! The garden's 9 acres
are divided into 10 sections, each of which represents a distinct
natural area of the state—e.g., Shasta-Cascade, Sierran, Redwood.
In a leisurely stroll through this garden you can see hundreds of
species that you would otherwise have to travel hundreds of miles to
find; furthermore, they're neatly labeled for you.

Facilities

Open daily 10 A.M.–5 P.M. (except New Year's Day, Thanksgiving
and Christmas), summer 10 A.M.–6 P.M. Water, restrooms, phone;
exhibits and small bookstore at Visitor Center, which is accessible
by wheelchair. Free guided tours on summer weekends.

Regulations

No pets, bicycles, balls or Frisbees.

Description

The only entrance is by the Visitor Center, where you can pick up a
map and check out whatever exhibits, tours, slide shows or plant
sales may be scheduled. Then you can wander about at your leisure.
The garden is such a delightful spot that even nonbotanists enjoy
lounging on the sunny Santa Lucia slope or sauntering along the
paths of the Sea Bluff Section above Wildcat Creek. A warm spring
day usually sees a good turnout of young mothers with infants and
Cal students studying for exams, as well as plant-lovers of all ages.

44   The East Bay Skyline National Recreation Trail in Tilden Park: The Sea View Trail

Distance   6 miles round trip.
Grade   Moderate.

Maps

Topo *Briones Valley;* trail map available at the Environmental
Education Center and at the EBRPD Botanic Garden.

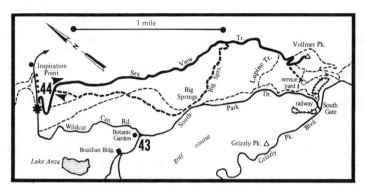

Tilden Park: The Sea View Trail

How to get there

The hike begins at a locked fire gate off Wildcat Canyon Road ¼ mile southwest of Inspiration Point.

From the Spruce, Shasta or Golf Gate, proceed to the Brazilian Building. From here take Wildcat Canyon Road for a mile in the direction of Inspiration Point. There is room for a few cars to park at the fire gate. Please do not block this gate; if necessary, park at Inspiration Point and walk back ¼ mile.

From the South Gate, proceed on South Park Drive to its junction with Wildcat Canyon Road and bear right on the latter.

From the east, proceed to Orinda, go north on Camino Pablo for 2½ miles and west on Wildcat Canyon Road to Inspiration Point and the fire gate beyond.

To arrange a car shuttle for a one-way hike, leave one car at Inspiration Point and one at the parking lot for the steam trains. Because the south end of the route is about 500 feet higher than the north end, you can get more downhill by traveling from south to north.

Features

This section of the Skyline Trail offers magnificent views of the entire Bay Area, and in spring a multicolored display of wildflowers.

Facilities

No water or restrooms along the route.

Description

From the locked fire gate, the trail ascends through eucalyptus and pines to the crest of San Pablo Ridge, passing another fire road that branches off to the right. Now as you walk along the open ridge you overlook the south end of the park and the golf course to your right, and soon San Pablo Reservoir to your left. As you continue to climb gradually along the spine of the ridge you can see the City and both bridges to the west, and Briones Reservoir beyond San Pablo Reservoir. After another bit of climbing, Lake Anza and the Botanic Garden come into view.

Scattered along the trail are stands of pine trees. The many pines in Tilden Park (most of them Monterey, but a few other species here and there) are just as alien to the area as are the multitudes of eucalyptus. Originally these hills were mainly grassland, and the trees in the area consisted primarily of coast live oaks and bays in the canyons and willows along the streams. From time to time purists have proposed returning these hills as closely as possible to their original state. As you walk along the Sea View Trail, try to imagine what Tilden Park would look like without its eucalyptus and Monterey pine trees.

At 1¾ miles pass the Big Springs Trail, which goes downhill on the right. Continue ascending on the Sea View Trail until you reach paving. Make an acute right turn here and curve up to the summit of Vollmer Peak (1905'), the highest point in the park. Like many of the high spots in the Berkeley-Oakland hills, Vollmer Peak sports some unesthetic communication towers. However, if you ignore them you should enjoy the view. Unless the day is very foggy or smoggy indeed, you can see Mt. Diablo to the east, Round Top to the southeast and Mt. Tamalpais to the west. Grizzly Peak (1759'), which is just within the park boundary, is also to the west. Below you is the miniature railroad.

You can return the way you came, or you can make a loop via the Big Springs Trail.

If you're following the Skyline Trail, you'll end up in the park's corporation yard, near the parking area for the trains.

45   The Oakland Museum and Lake Merritt

Address and phone
1000 Oak Street, Oakland 94607; 273-3401; for recorded information, 834-2413

Maps
Topos *Oakland West* and a small part of *Oakland East;* any street map of Oakland.

How to get there

By BART   The museum is a good destination for any one who wants to joy-ride on BART or to introduce out-of-towners to its wonders: the Lake Merritt station is just 1 block west.

By bus   AC Transit A, #14, #15, #18, #38, #40, #43, #82, #83 and the downtown shuttle all run to or very near the museum.

By car   The museum is 4 blocks east of Highway 880 (Nimitz Freeway); southbound, exit on Jackson Street; northbound, exit on Oak Street. Parking garage under the museum can be entered from Oak Street or 12th Street; small fee.

Features
The Oakland Museum, designed by Kevin Roche and opened in 1969, is an architectural triumph that should be a prime attraction for any tourist in northern California. Bay Area residents—especially San Franciscans—should become as familiar with it as they are with such long-established landmarks as Steinhart Aquarium and the Palace of the Legion of Honor.

You can combine a tour of the fascinating museum with a 4-mile walk around Lake Merritt, including a visit to the oldest wildlife refuge in North America.

Facilities
Museum open Wednesday through Saturday 10 A.M.–5 P.M., Sunday noon–7 P.M.; wheelchair-accessible; museum store; docent-led tours; group tours available (phone 273-3514); restaurant open for lunch Wednesday through Friday 11:45 A.M.–1:45 P.M., for brunch Sunday noon–3 P.M. (for reservations, phone 834-2329); snack bar open Wednesday through Friday 10 A.M.–3 P.M., Saturday 10 A.M.–4 P.M., Sunday noon–5 P.M.

Regulations

No dogs or bicycles on the path around the lake.

Description

The main entrance is on 10th Street, at the lowest of the museum's three levels. Here is an information desk where you can pick up a free descriptive leaflet. Level 1 is devoted to natural sciences (including a fascinating transect of eight biotic zones across California), level 2 to California history, and level 3 to California art. The permanent collections alone warrant several visits. The museum also features special exhibits and a wide variety of other attractions, such as lectures and films. If you start suffering from museum feet, you can get a snack or wander out onto the attractively landscaped terraces to rest.

To get to Lake Merritt, walk around the museum to its rear on 12th Street. Walking around it will give you some impression of the massive quality of the poured-concrete structure. After crossing both 12th and Fallon streets, you come to a bust of Lincoln. Head north from it to find stairs leading to an underpass beneath busy Lakeshore Avenue and thence to the path around the lake. The 155-acre lake is named for Dr. Samuel Merritt, an early mayor of Oakland, who in 1869 persuaded the city council to dam a tidal canal here and thereby create this salt lake.

Walking around the lake counterclockwise, you pass a large, modernistic apartment building and next to it what looks like a Greek temple but turns out to be the Fourth Church of Christ, Scientist. At least, you will still pass it as this book goes to press—but maybe it will not be there much longer. In 1984 the Lake Merritt United Methodist Church bought the building with the idea of tearing it down and erecting a modern one in its place. The Oakland Heritage Alliance and other preservationists argued that the church, or at least its facade, should be retained as a piece of historic architecture. The City Council, however, in March 1988 voted to let the Methodists demolish and replace the building.

For the next mile you walk beside busy Lakeshore Avenue, separated from it by a small strip of grass and many varieties of ornamental trees. Along the way you will undoubtedly encounter a host of joggers, photographers, meditators and lovers.

As you round the northeast arm of the lake, near Grand Avenue, you pass under a vine-covered colonnade. Soon the path becomes separated from the traffic by a broad lawn with picnic tables. Lakeside Park here is dominated by two towering apartment buildings: the elegantly ornamented Spanish Baroque Bellevue-Staten apartments, completed in 1929, represent the last flourish of pre-Depression luxury, to which the Park-Bellevue (1967) offers a stark contrast.

As you walk toward the Duck Islands you can hear the quacking and honking of waterfowl. Lake Merritt, a major station on the Pacific Flyway, plays winter host to thousands of migrating birds. In 1870 it was made a wildlife refuge—the first one in North America. Even though most of the birds arrive in fall and winter, you can see (and feed) ducks, geese and swans here the year around. Pelicans and cormorants sometimes show up also, and a small community of shy black-crowned night herons has been in residence.

Near the Duck Islands is the Rotary Natural Science Center, which conducts a year-round science program. It is open from 10 A.M. to 5 P.M. daily, except Monday, when it opens around noon; to find out what's going on, phone 273-3739. Just beyond the Rotary Center are several spots of interest: cages housing birds of prey (hawks, owls, eagles, etc.); a brooder for ducklings, to protect them from gulls and herons; a geodesic-dome aviary; automatic vending machines for duck food; and a snack bar for people food. The birds are fed daily at 3:30 P.M.

When you tear yourself away from the birds to continue walking around the lake, you will soon encounter the Sailboat Clubhouse. Here you can begin a tour of the lake on an excursion boat, or rent your own canoe, rowboat or El Toro. Or you can travel around the lake on the Merritt Queen, a miniature Mississippi-style riverboat. (For hours and prices phone 444-3807.) Across Bellevue Avenue from the Sailboat Clubhouse are the Trial and Show Garden and the Horticultural Center (open daily 10 A.M.–4 P.M., weekends and holidays until 5:30 P.M.).

As you make your way along the northwest arm of the lake you pass the bandstand and Children's Fairyland, a popular amusement park for youngsters (for fees and hours, phone 832-3609). A Toy Train operates nearby, on varying schedules. Near the western corner of the lake you can make a side trip via the pedestrian crossing to the Kaiser Building (open weekdays 8 A.M.–5 P.M.), where some sort of art exhibit is usually taking place. The charming roof garden is also worth a visit. The Kaiser Building was the largest office building west of the Rockies when it was finished in 1960, at a cost of about $45 million. In 1983 ailing Kaiser Aluminum and Chemical Corporation sold the building to a New York real-estate syndicate for $97 million—reportedly the largest real-estate transaction in Oakland up to that time.

Continuing around the lake, you pass the Oakland Office of Parks and Recreation and arrive at a magnificent Italianate mansion, the Camron-Stanford House. It served as the Oakland Public Museum for many years. When the new museum opened, the Camron-Stanford House was slated for destruction. Fortunately, a group of citizens gathered to preserve this sole survivor of the days when fashionable mansions surrounded Lake Merritt. The house has been lovingly restored and now contains several period rooms plus a museum devoted to its history. It is well worth a visit (open Wednesday 11 A.M.–4 P.M., Sunday 1–5 P.M.; phone 836-1976).

As you approach the south end of the lake, the most prominent building in view is the Alameda County Courthouse, a fine example of Middle New Deal. Just across 12th Street from it is your starting point, the museum.

Side trips Downtown Oakland is a paradise for admirers of Art Deco and *Style Moderne*. Within just a few blocks of the 19th Street BART station are such outstanding examples as the Singer Shop (1721 Broadway, 1931); I. Magnin (20th and Broadway, 1931); Breuner's (22nd and Broadway, 1931); and the greatest of them all, the Paramount Theatre (2025 Broadway, 1930). Tours of the Paramount take place on the first and third Saturday of each month; for information, phone 893-2300.

Volunteers for Oakland offer free walking tours of various parts of the city from April through October; for information, phone 273-3234. The Oakland Heritage Alliance offers, for a moderate fee, walking tours on summer weekends through neighborhoods that have retained their original ambience; for information, phone 763-9218.

46 The East Bay Skyline National Recreation Trail between Tilden and Sibley parks

Distance 3 miles one way. Unlike some parts of the Skyline Trail, this one does not provide possibilities for making a loop. However, it is well suited to a car shuttle between Tilden and Sibley (3 miles) or Huckleberry Preserve (another 2–4 miles, depending on your route).

Grade Moderate; no extended difficult ascents or descents, and a total elevation loss of 300 feet from north to south. But boots are advisable, and the trail gets muddy during the wet season.

Maps

Topo *Oakland East;* trail map available from EBRPD headquarters.

How to get there

Drive to the corner of Grizzly Peak Blvd. and Lomas Cantadas, at the south end of Tilden Park, and park in the lot for the little train.

Features

This section of the Skyline Trail was one of the last to be constructed, partly with the help of volunteers. It is, frankly, one of the less attractive sections, since it traverses some rather scruffy vegetation and most of it is within earshot of highways. On the other hand, it offers good views and a unique opportunity to walk over the busy Caldecott Tunnel.

Facilities

Water, toilets, picnic tables at each end; none along the route.

Description

This section of the Skyline Trail begins across Lomas Cantadas from the parking lot for the little train, whose whistle provides on weekends a cheerful accompaniment to the first few minutes of the hike. The trail runs through coyote brush and occasional bay trees, and soon you overlook Siesta Valley to the east. Greenhouses gleam in the sun. At a **Y** in the grove of bay trees, bear right, uphill. (The left fork goes down into the valley.) Mt. Diablo comes into view. At a row of telephone poles the trail turns right, then left to contour along the east slope of the ridge among blackberries and gooseberries. A grove of pine trees is visible in the valley below. Now the trail starts down the west slope of the ridge, overlooking Fish Ranch Road. You can see below you on the road the white pedestrian lane that indicates the Skyline Trail crossing.

The trail switchbacks down and skirts around a barbed-wire fence where Grizzly Peak Blvd. makes a hairpin turn. After traversing a stretch of coyote brush, the trail crosses Fish Ranch Road and runs along the slope above it, within earshot of it. Traffic noise increases as you walk over Caldecott Tunnel. Like several other Bay Area phenomena, this tunnel recently celebrated its 50th birthday: it was opened on December 5, 1937. It was named for the late Thomas E. Caldecott, an Alameda County supervisor and chairman of the special district formed to oversee the tunnel's construction. (An old Sacramento Northern railroad tunnel also runs underneath; the

Lafayette-Moraga Trail now occupies a continuation of its roadbed.)
The view to the east features the old Kaiser quarries on the western
slope of Gudde Ridge, named for the late Erwin G. Gudde, UC
Berkeley professor and authority on California place names. The
quarries are now part of Sibley Park, described in the next chapter.

After a short, steep down and up, the trail goes through a break in
a fence, briefly along an old paved road, and through a gate. Now
begins the most attractive part of this hike, as you ascend along a
little creek, occasionally crossing it. Flowering currant brightens the
scene in the spring. A steady climb past some eucalyptus trees that
still show damage from the 1972 freeze brings you to the Sibley Park
gate and parking lot.

47   Robert Sibley
Volcanic Regional Preserve

Maps
Topo *Oakland East;* trail map available at parking lot (usually) and
from EBRPD headquarters.

How to get there
From the west, cross the Bay Bridge, take Highway 24, and go south
on Highway 13 (Warren Freeway). Make your way to Skyline
Boulevard by one of the roads that go from the freeway to it: Snake,
Shepherd Canyon, Joaquin Miller or Redwood. The Sibley parking
lot is 1½ miles north of the Shepherd Canyon-Skyline junction.

Features
This park used to be named Round Top, for the 1763' hill at its
center. It was renamed to honor one of the founders of the EBRPD.

Round Top is actually the remains of an extinct volcano.
Quarrying over the years by Kaiser Sand & Gravel exposed volcanic vents and other geologic features. The park district acquired
the old quarry and opened up a trail to it.

Facilities
Water, toilet, picnic table at parking lot.

Description
In the parking lot a signboard shows a picture of Round Top in its
volcanic heyday. Boxes contain a map of the park with an excellent
self-guided walking tour written by Stephen Edwards, paleobotanist
and now Director of the Regional Parks Botanic Garden. (Copies
have been available whenever I've visited the park, but to be sure of

getting one you might pick it up at EBRPD headquarters in advance.) Edwards notes, "A great diversity of volcanic phenomena is preserved for study in Sibley, in the form of volcanic dikes, breccias, mudflows, lava flows, solidified cinder piles, and a number of vents." Following his directions along the level quarry road is an easy and pleasant way to learn something of the geologic history of the Bay Area.

The East Bay Skyline National Recreation Trail in Sibley Preserve   See the next chapter, Huckleberry Preserve.

48   Huckleberry Botanic Regional Preserve

Maps

Topo *Oakland East;* trail map available (usually) from box at Sibley parking lot or from EBRPD headquarters; map and brochure for self-guiding nature path available (usually) from box at Huckleberry parking lot.

How to get there

By bus   AC Transit #18 goes to Snake Road and Skyline Boulevard, about ½ mile from the parking lot.

By car   The parking area is a short ½ mile southeast of the entrance to Sibley Park, adjoining 7090 Skyline Boulevard.

Features

This place is a 130-acre preserve of native plant life chock-a-block next to residential Oakland. The Huckleberry Trail was christened in the 1950s by a UC professor of botany, Dr. Herbert L. Mason, who used to bring his students here. He noted,

> A unique feature is the earliness of its flora. About the time when the average citizen becomes sick and tired of winter, spring has already arrived on Huckleberry Trail. . . . It, therefore, affords the citizenry an early relief from the monotony of winter with a trail accessible to all.
>
> —California Native Plant Society
> Newsletter, October 1971.

For a while it was doubtful whether the trail *would* be accessible to all. In 1972 developers bulldozed across it to reach two eastward-facing knolls where they planned to build. Alarmed botanists and conservationists raised a hue and cry, and eventually succeeded in having the fragile preserve and its narrow footpath included in the EBRPD. The two knolls now provide convenient spots for hikers to pause and admire the view of Mt. Diablo from the trail.

Facilities

No water, one toilet; self-guiding nature trail.

Regulations

Curfew 10 P.M.–5 A.M.; no dogs; no horses, no bicycles on Huckleberry Trail.

The Huckleberry Self-Guiding Nature Path

Distance   1.3-mile loop.
Grade   Easy, but some steep spots; boots desirable, especially during the wet season.

Features

The botanical rarities to be found along this trail are perhaps most appreciated in early spring. In fact, the CNPS's traditional February pilgrimage to Huckleberry has in recent years attracted so many enthusiasts that they have had to stagger their starting times and space themselves out along the narrow path in small groups.

In 1982 the park district with the aid of the CNPS constructed a self-guiding nature path connecting the original Huckleberry Trail with the Skyline Trail, and Bert Johnson wrote an interpretive brochure to accompany it.

Description

Look for the brochure describing the nature path in a box by the signboard—or come prepared, having obtained a copy ahead of time from EBRPD headquarters. The trail starts out in a not-too-attractive patch of blackberries, coyote brush and poison hemlock. After a short distance, at a post with the Huckleberry emblem, the nature path diverges from the original trail and then switchbacks down the side of a forested canyon to meet the Skyline Trail switch-backing up from Sibley Preserve. Both trails run together for about a half mile past ferns and bay trees, with occasional vistas out over the Contra Costa hills. Posts with the Skyline and Huckleberry emblems indicate where the two trails separate. The Huckleberry Self-Guiding Nature Path climbs steeply uphill for a short distance, then curves around to finish its loop. (The original Huckleberry Trail continues roughly parallel to the Skyline Trail and joins it just before reaching Pinehurst Road.)

The return part of the Huckleberry Path loop is a bit higher and drier than the first section and features some of the chaparral plants that make this area so exciting to botanists: chinquapin, silktassel, three kinds of manzanita, and the exceedingly rare western leather-wood.

It appears that the huckleberry may be crowding out some of the other plants in the preserve, such as the endangered manzanita *Arctostaphylos pallida*. This situation presents botanists and park staff with a dilemma: should they let nature take its course and the fittest survive, or should they cut back the huckleberry?

49   The East Bay Skyline National Recreation Trail in Sibley and Huckleberry preserves

Distance   3½ miles.
Grade   Moderate.

Features

It might seem paradoxical that the Skyline Trail goes through the *lower* part of Huckleberry Preserve. The explanation is simply that the Skyline Trail is intended for equestrians as well as pedestrians, and the Huckleberry Path on the upper part of the hillside is too narrow, and its botany too fragile, to accommodate horses.

Description

From the Sibley parking lot the Skyline Trail runs parallel to the road to Round Top, just to the road's left, then crosses it and switchbacks down through coyote brush. Just after fording San Leandro Creek the trail switchbacks up from a gate. Soon the Skyline Trail meets the Huckleberry Self-Guiding Nature Path and then runs along it as described above. When the nature path diverges uphill to the right, the Skyline Trail continues ascending gradually to the junction of Skyline Boulevard and Pinehurst Road. The trail crosses Pinehurst and in a short half mile arrives at the East Ridge Trail of Redwood Park. Turn right on it and pass a large landslide to reach the Skyline Gate and the continuation of the Skyline Trail.

Redwood Regional Park

Maps

Topo *Oakland East;* trail map available at Redwood Gate or from
EBRPD headquarters; Olmsted Bros.' *Rambler's Guide . . . Central
Section.*

How to get there

By bus   AC Transit #15A runs daily and one route of #18 runs
weekdays to points on Skyline Boulevard near various park
entrances (check AC Transit schedules).

By car   Redwood, like Tilden, has several gates. The most
frequently used is the Redwood Gate, near ranger headquarters. To
reach it from Highway 580 southbound, exit on 35th Avenue and go
east; 35th becomes Redwood Road. Cross Skyline Boulevard and
continue on Redwood for 2 miles to the park entrance on the left.
From Highway 13 southbound: Take Redwood Road east, cross
Skyline and continue for 2 miles. From Highway 580 northbound:
Get on Highway 13 (Warren Freeway) going north, immediately exit
on Carson Street, turn right on Redwood Road, cross Skyline and
continue for 2 miles.

The main north entrance is the Skyline Gate, which is reached as
follows: From Highway 13 southbound: Exit east on Moraga Avenue
and go southeast on it ¾ mile. Turn left on Snake Road and in a block
(2 blocks on the right side) continue on Shepherd Canyon Road,
which soon becomes Park Boulevard and winds up to Skyline
Boulevard. Turn right on Skyline and in ¼ mile arrive at the Skyline
Gate. From Highway 13 northbound: Exit east on Park Boulevard,
immediately go northwest on Mountain Boulevard for 2 blocks to
Snake Road, turn right and proceed as above. A longer but more
scenic route from either direction on Highway 13 is to exit east on
Joaquin Miller Road, take it to Skyline Boulevard, turn left on
Skyline and go 3 miles to the gate.

Features

This has always been one of the most beautiful of the East Bay
parks, and a complete refurbishing in 1982 made it even more
idyllic. Redwood Park is also one of the best places in the Bay Area
to enjoy fall color, as the old orchard trees and the native maple and
hazel turn bright gold against the dark green of the oaks and
redwoods.

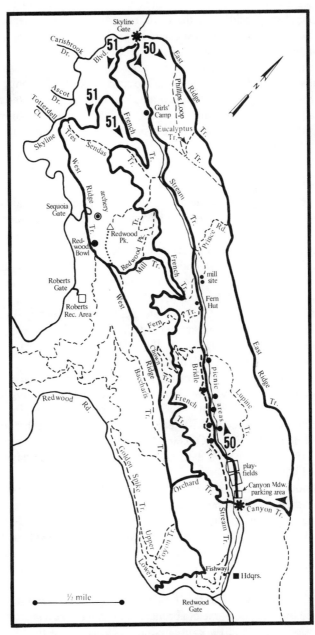

Redwood Regional Park

Redwood Park has a unique distinction: a state historic plaque near Redwood Gate commemorates the discovery by Dr. G. W. Gibbons, first president of the California Academy of Sciences, of rainbow trout as a separate species. Near the plaque is a Denil fishway, a ramp constructed in 1983 to aid the trout in their journey from Upper San Leandro Reservoir up Redwood Creek to their spawning grounds. This fishway enables the trout to bypass a masonry dam that was blocking their path upstream. You may be able to see them in early spring. (No fishing is permitted anywhere in Redwood Creek; if the sight of these trout arouses your piscatorial instincts, try Lake Chabot or Lake Anza.)

History

Redwood Park is one of the very few places described in this book that are much less developed and have fewer inhabitants now than in the 19th century. (Black Diamond Mines Preserve is another.) The carefree picnickers and Frisbee-tossers who frolic along Redwood Creek today might be astounded to learn of the area's lurid past.

The original virgin redwoods here may have constituted the most magnificent forest on the continent. Two of these trees were so tall that sailors entering the Golden Gate used them to steer by. In May 1988 a state historic marker was dedicated to these trees; it is located near the parking lot in Roberts Recreation Area, which forms a sort of enclave within Redwood Park.

The gold rush and the resulting building boom caused a huge demand for lumber, and soon there were 10 sawmills operating in the East Bay's redwood forest. The loggers were a hard-drinking, violent crew who lynched horse-thieves and on one occasion threatened to burn down the city of Oakland because they suspected a pound keeper of conniving with cattle thieves (pounds in those days also handled cattle.)

Although the lumbermen were cutting down the virgin forest as fast as they could, some elements of the original wilderness yet remained. Hungry grizzly bears prowled the logging camps by night, occasionally killing cattle or hogs. Mountain lions awakened the men with their howling. And California condors flew overhead—as many as fifty at a time, or more than now exist in the entire world. The loggers shot them—one reason this bird is near extinction.

Within two decades the forest was cut down, and farmers replaced the loggers. Some old orchard trees remain as a legacy from this period. Redwood Park, created in 1939, is one of the oldest in the EBRPD system. By now the second-growth redwood trees are over a century old and have formed a respectable forest—not as grand as the original one, but still a wonderful place to find cool tranquility not far from the metropolis.

Recommended reading

Monteagle, F. J., *A Yankee Trader in the California Redwoods.* Oakland, EBRPD.

Facilities

Open 8 A.M.–10 P.M. summer, 8 A.M.–6 P.M. winter; picnicking; group picnicking and youth-group camping (for reservations phone 531-9043); archery range; children's playground; Canyon Meadow picnic area accessible by wheelchair.

Roberts Recreation Area contains a swimming pool (small fee), playing fields, and lots of facilities for picnickers; for reservations for groups of 50 or more, phone 531-9043.

Regulations

Small parking fee and dog fee at both Redwood and Roberts; no fishing; bicycles permitted on the East Ridge, West Ridge and Canyon trails and on the Stream Trail as far as Trail's End picnic area; otherwise the usual for East Bay regional parks.

50 The Stream and East Ridge Trails

Distance   Ad lib; 6½-mile or shorter loops possible.
Grade   Easy along the Stream Trail; fairly strenuous for the long loop.

Features

The broad, level Stream Trail running along Redwood Creek offers a fine introduction to this beautiful park. The towering redwoods provide cool shelter for summer picnickers. Ambitious hikers can combine a trip through the redwood canyon with a climb to the East Ridge.

Facilities

Water, toilets, picnic tables and grills scattered along the first mile of the Stream Trail.

Description

You can pick up a trail map from the entrance kiosk or from the signboard near the Canyon Meadow picnic area. The Stream Trail leads through the old orchard past the play fields. A redwood grove and some of the recreational facilities have been donated to the park by the Telephone Pioneers of America, a service organization of both active and retired telephone-company employees. As you enter the redwood forest you may be tantalized by the aroma of barbecue from the picnic spots along the way. The trail leads past some stone huts built by the WPA in the 1930s and now used for youth-group camping. Here the busy sawmills operated in the 1850s.

You can ascend to the East Ridge by the Prince Road (formerly the Mill Trail), or on the Eucalyptus Trail farther along; or you can continue on the Stream Trail. After it leaves the redwoods, the ambience changes abruptly. You wander along the stream past willows and eucalyptus. Across a stone bridge, the Girls' Camp, situated in a willow-fringed meadow, contains water, tables, and restrooms for both sexes. The northernmost half mile of the Stream Trail leads steadily uphill on a broad fire road, to arrive at the Skyline Gate.

From the Skyline Gate, the East Ridge Trail starts at the north end of the parking lot. This trail (actually a dirt road) begins in a forest of Monterey pine and eucalyptus. As it runs along the spine of the ridge, the trees give way to coyote brush. To the south you can look across the Redwood Creek canyon to the densely forested West Ridge; to the north are Moraga and other suburban communities of Contra Costa County and that perennially commanding landmark, Mt. Diablo. When you come to the Canyon Trail (a signed road), turn right on it and descend to the Canyon Meadow parking area.

51   The East Bay Skyline National Recreation Trail in Redwood Park: The West Ridge and French trails

Distance   4½ or 5½ miles one way; all sorts of loops possible.
Grade   Moderate to strenuous, depending on route.

Features

The Skyline Trail has two alternate routes through Redwood Park. A study of the map will reveal that it is possible to combine both routes in a long loop; or to make various shorter loops between them; or to combine either of them with the Stream or East Ridge trail.

Facilities

Water, restrooms, tables, grills at the Redwood Bowl.

Description

The Skyline Trail starts as the West Ridge Trail from the south side of the Skyline Gate. It contours above the steep canyon, offering a view of the eucalyptus forest below that is still recovering from the freeze of 1972–73. In ½ mile the French Trail branches off to the left, and the two Skyline Trail routes diverge:

1. The West Ridge Trail continues to contour along near the top of the steep canyon. Because it is so level and so scenic, it's a great favorite with joggers. A half mile after the French Trail branches off, you come to the Tres Sendas (formerly Tres Cendes) Trail. Although this is now not officially a part of the Skyline Trail, it offers a direct route down to the French Trail, which is. It's also one of the most picturesque trails in this picturesque park, as it follows and occasionally fords a tributary of Redwood Creek down the redwood slope past several small waterfalls.

If you continue on the West Ridge Trail, you will pass the archery range, where you can pause to watch the bowmen—some of them with equipment so sophisticated that Robin Hood and his Merry Men wouldn't recognize it. Next the trail, briefly fenced in, passes the Redwood Bowl, a good picnic spot—popular for weddings, too. Soon a trail on the left leads to densely forested Redwood Peak (1619′), a short optional side trip. The West Ridge Trail comes out into the open and continues along the chaparral-covered ridge, with views of much of the park on both sides, Mt. Diablo to the east, the hills of Chabot Park to the south, and the houses of Skyline Boulevard and beyond them the Bay to the west. The Baccharis Trail running parallel to the West Ridge offers an alternate route high above Redwood Canyon. It is named for one of the more prominent plants along it—coyote brush, or *Baccharis pilularis consanguinea*.

When you come to the Orchard Trail on your left, you can descend on it to the alternate route, the French Trail. To follow the Skyline Trail to the south end of Redwood Park, remain on the West Ridge Trail, passing the Toyon Trail on the right. Beyond this junction the West Ridge Trail descends steeply for ¼ mile. Jog right at a sign with the Skyline Trail emblem and soon reach the Golden Spike Trail. Bear right on Golden Spike, which soon divides into Upper and Lower. The Skyline Trail route switchbacks down the Lower Golden Spike Trail to cross Redwood Road and then, at an emblem, begins the last few hundred yards to the Macdonald Gate of Chabot Park.

2. The French Trail meanders along the redwood-forested slope above the canyon, up and down and in and out of ravines. Unlike the

broad West Ridge Trail, much of the narrow French Trail is single-
file only. The sheltering redwoods and the soft duff underfoot make
this a quiet, cool path to hike on. (Note that where the French Trail
meets the Chown Trail, the French briefly jogs left before continuing southeast.)

The two Skyline Trail routes reunite at the Orchard Trail.
Although this trail has been considerably eroded by storms, it is still
passable—but watch out for the poison oak.

Side trip

If you didn't see the Denil fishway (described above under
Features) on the way in, you might want to examine it on the way
out.

Anthony Chabot Regional Park

Maps

Topos *Oakland East, Las Trampas Ridge* and *Hayward;* trail maps
available from EBRPD headquarters and from Lake Chabot marina;
Olmsted Bros.' *Rambler's Guide ... Central Section;* Erickson's
Recreational Map ... South West Section.

How to get there

By car   Chabot Park has a number of entrances, most of them
off of either Redwood Road or Skyline Blvd. They are apparent on
the park map and on highway maps of southern Alameda County.

Features

Anthony Chabot was a French Canadian 49er who subsequently
became the owner of Oakland's water system.

> Lake Chabot's profound calm gives almost no hint of its grotesque
> beginnings. The lake was built in 1874 by Anthony Chabot, a
> hydraulic engineer fresh from the gold country. His method of con-
> struction was revolutionary. He first aimed gigantic water hoses at
> nearby hills and washed thousands of tons of earth into San Leandro
> Creek. Then he imported herds of wild mustangs to gallop back and
> forth over the loose earth to compact it into a dam.
>
> —Malcolm Margolin, *The East*
> *Bay Out.*

Chabot was one of the area's principal early philanthropists, and
therefore it is not surprising that a lake, a road, a city park and an
observatory bear his name—as well as this regional park, one of the
largest in the system (almost 5000 acres).

Facilities

Anthony Chabot family campground: 73 campsites—some walk-in, some for trailers and RVs, some for cars—reservable through Ticketron from April 1 through September 30, first-come, first-served from October 1 through March 31; self-guiding nature trail. Six youth-group camps by reservation (531-9043). Equestrian Center, with horses for rent (569-4428); marksmanship range (569-0213; Willow Park public golf course (537-4733, 537-2521). For Lake Chabot facilities, see below.

Regulations

For family campground: moderate fees, varying with the season; stay limit 14 days per 30-day period, 30 days per year maximum; auto entrance via Marciel Gate closed at 10 P.M. Otherwise, the usual for the EBRPD.

52 Lake Chabot and environs

Phone

881-1833

Maps

Available at the marina.

How to get there

From Highway 580 go east on Estudillo Avenue, which soon runs into Lake Chabot Road; or go northeast on Fairmont Drive. The entrance to the parking lot is just east of the junction of Lake Chabot Road and Fairmont Drive.

Features

The lake constructed by the bizarre method described above remained closed to the public for 90 years, while the fish in it multiplied and grew fat. In 1966 the EBRPD, having leased the lake from EBMUD for recreational purposes, opened it to eager anglers, and it has been one of the most popular fishing spots in the East Bay ever since. As the list of Facilities suggests, however, there are plenty of things to do here besides fish.

Facilities

Water, restrooms, tables, grills and phone at picnic area near marina, accessible by wheelchair. Snack bar at marina providing breakfast- and lunch-type food, as well as tackle and bait. Canoes, rowboats, pedal boats and electric-powered boats for rent; excursion boat around the lake seasonally on weekends and holidays (small fee); charter tours by reservation. Paved bike path.

Regulations

Small parking fee. *No swimming* (the lake is an emergency water supply); no private boats.

California fishing license and EBRPD fishing permit required for everyone age 16 and over; these are available at the marina, as is the list of limits.

Description

Nearly everyone begins at the marina. Here you can pick up a cup of coffee, maps and fishing advice; or rent a canoe, or embark on a cruise of the 315-acre lake. The excursion boat, when it is running, makes regular stops at four points along the shore, so you can debark and fish or picnic for a while, then take a later cruise back. Campers at Chabot family campground can hike down to the lake and pick up the boat at a dock for a ride to the marina.

Hikers can take the East Shore Trail around Honker Bay and up to the campground. Bicyclists can follow the level, paved West Shore or East Shore Trail for two miles in either direction from the marina. The shady West Shore Trail leads across the dam to San Leandro's Chabot city park.

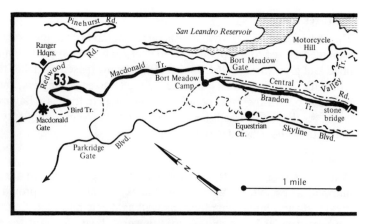

Anthony Chabot

53   The East Bay Skyline National Recreation Trail in Chabot Park: The Macdonald and Brandon trails

Distance   10 miles one way.
Grade   Strenuous.

Maps

A box at the Macdonald trailhead usually contains maps; or you can pick one up at EBRPD headquarters.

How to get there

This trip begins at the Macdonald Gate, which is on Redwood Road 1½ miles east of Skyline Boulevard. The easiest way to do the route as a day hike is to arrange a car shuttle, leaving one car at the Willow Park Golf Course, which is reached by taking Highway 580 to Castro Valley and going north on Redwood Road.

Features

In the first edition of this book I remarked that this section of the Skyline Trail made me long for a horse. After hiking these 10 miles again, I'll go so far as to say that—while the northernmost third of the route is pleasant, and the southernmost third delightful—the

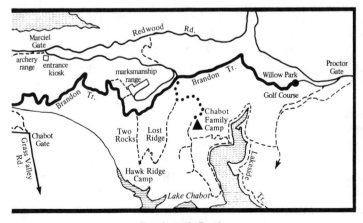

Regional Park

middle stretch is really a bore. The trail ascends and descends, ascends and descends, through a eucalyptus forest, and after a couple of miles of this the ordinary hiker begins to feel that when he's seen one eucalyptus he's seen them all. Furthermore, the din of rifle fire from the nearby range soon becomes nervewracking. With so many attractive places to hike in the East Bay, the main reason for spending any time on this stretch of trail would seem to be curiosity or a determination to cover the whole Skyline Trail. Next time I'll rent a horse from the Equestrian Center (14600 Skyline Blvd., 569-4428)!

Facilities

Open 8 A.M.–dusk. This hike has several long stretches without water, so you should start with a full canteen. Chabot family campground, described above, is situated near the south end of the trail; you can backpack into it (moderate fees).

Regulations

Dogs allowed "on leash and under control."

Description

Begin at the Macdonald Gate parking lot (toilet, no water). Soon the Bird Trail provides a pleasant, leafy detour—but watch out for poison oak at head level. It rejoins the Macdonald Trail, which switchbacks north to overlook Redwood Road; the angular building on the ridge to the west, whose sheets of glass catch the sun's reflections, is the Skyline Community Church. The trail switchbacks again, passing an unmapped, unsigned road on the left. A number of unsigned roads, trails and firebreaks branch off from the Skyline Trail in this park, but you can follow the main route if you watch for the blue dots and the triangular emblems.

The Macdonald Trail runs southeast along the ridge above Grass Valley, which gave this park its original name. Across the valley are the houses of Skyline Boulevard; in 1¼ mile from your start, a fire road leads to them and the Parkridge Gate. As you continue along the ridge, the park's former motorcycle hill becomes visible and, when the wind is in the right direction, the rifle range becomes audible. For many years motorcyclists ran freely (and roughshod) over that hill just on the other side of Redwood Road. Eventually it became so badly eroded that the EBRPD had to call a halt to motorcycling on it, especially as the runoff was beginning to carry silt into EBMUD's reservoirs. Early in 1986 the park district began reseeding and rehabilitating the hill.

After descending a knoll which offers a view over Upper San Leandro Reservoir, look for an unsigned but well-trodden path on your right and descend on it to the eucalypti of Joseph P. Bort Meadow Overnight Group Camp. This was formerly known as Big Trees Camp but has been renamed for a long-time Alameda County supervisor. This is one of the better lunch spots along the route (water, restrooms, tables). If the camp is occupied by a large group, however, you may want to continue on the Macdonald Trail and descend on the road from Bort Meadow Gate, formerly San Leandro Gate.

By whatever route, you arrive in the valley and continue southeast on the Brandon Trail, which runs along the west bank of a creek, passing the trail to the Equestrian Center, and in 1½ miles crosses a stone bridge.

You have already entered the eucalyptus forest which dominates this part of the park and which provoked my dyspeptic remarks under *Features*. The trail meanders along, up and down, in and out of gullies. As you approach the marksmanship range, which is uphill to the left, you can hear the target-shooters. This range has a certain macabre historical significance: it was where the original members of the Symbionese Liberation Army practiced regularly before going underground. (For the very young, and those of short memory, the SLA was the underground terrorist organiztion that kidnapped Patty Hearst in 1974.)

After you go through a fire gate you come to a **T**, from which the left arm goes to the rifle range and the Brandon Trail goes right. Almost immediately you come to a fork; bear left here to stay on the Brandon Trail. You will soon pass the Logger's Loop, the Mirador Trail and an unsigned trail that branches right at a log.

Eventually you come out into open country and arrive at the paved road that leads to the campground. If you plan to spend the night there, you will turn right on it, and then left where it forks soon after, to proceed to the campground. Otherwise, cross the road and pick up the Brandon Trail continuing southeast and offering fine views of the campground and the whole South Bay. The trail levels off for a short stretch before dropping down to the invitingly green golf course. You can finish the hike with a swim, a cup of hot coffee, a beer or whatever the weather and your temperament suggest.

54   The Alameda Creek Regional Trail

Distance   12 miles of bicycling/hiking trail from the Bay to Niles.
The EBRPD map points out that the round trip plus the additional 3.5-mile loop trip in Coyote Hills Park qualifies as
marathon distance. Those who are not in training for a marathon
can turn back when they get tired, or can arrange a car shuttle.
Quarter-mile markers along the trail show how far you've
traveled.

Grade   All level; mostly graveled surface.

Maps

Topos *Newark* and *Niles;* trail maps available from EBRPD headquarters and Coyote Hills Regional Park headquarters.

How to get there

By BART   From the Union City BART station go ¾ mile south
on Decoto Road. BART advises bicyclists, however, to start from
the Fremont station and go south on Mowry Avenue to Paseo Padre
Parkway, then east on it: "The trail approach from the Fremont station is longer but safer than from the Union City station. Paseo
Padre Parkway has a smooth, wide shoulder; Decoto Road's
shoulder is bumpy, and traffic is busy across the bridge." For
information about bikes on BART, phone 464-7133.

By car   The west end begins at Coyote Hills Park: From
Highway 880 (Nimitz Freeway) take the Jarvis Avenue exit, go west
a mile to Newark Boulevard, north on Newark a mile to Patterson
Ranch Road and west on it to its end. From the Dumbarton Bridge
(Highway 84) go east on Jarvis to Newark Boulevard and continue
as above.

The east end begins in the Niles District of Fremont: From
Highway 880 take the Alvarado-Niles Road east, turn left on Niles
Canyon Road (Highway 84), cross Mission Boulevard and park near
Old Canyon Road.

To arrange a car shuttle, study the EBRPD map of the trail and
leave a car at one of the parking areas.

Features

In Europe and the eastern United States, historic canals that were
once the main routes of transportation now afford miles of level
towpath for hikers along their banks. In 1973 the Bay Area acquired
its own canal with, so to speak, Instant Towpath. When the Army
Corps of Engineers constructed the Alameda Creek Flood Control

Channel, they included a level trail on each side—one on the north levee for equestrians and hikers and one on the south levee for bicyclists and hikers. At this point, the trails are hardly as scenic as their counterparts in the east, but the Engineers tried: they planted thousands of young trees along the banks—some native (e.g., black oak), some not (e.g., various locusts, acacias and eucalypti). In a few more decades perhaps the foliage will be abundant enough to reduce the raw effect of the riprap on the channel's sides.

The channel passes through a highly variegated and changing landscape that includes marshland, agriculture, industry and suburbia. Eventually the trail may go all the way to Sunol Regional Park.

After tramping 9 miles along the trail soon after it opened, I pronounced it "a hiking experience that is highly unusual but not universally appealing." It's a good bike trip, however, especially if you combine it with the scenic Bay View Trail in Coyote Hills Park and/or the levees leading to the San Francisco Bay National Wildlife Refuge. Even a bicyclist, however, would probably prefer not to take this trail on a hot, smoggy day, or attempt the stretch from Coyote Hills to the Bay on a windy afternoon.

Facilities

Trail open dawn to dusk. Water, restrooms and picnic tables at each end; toilet about halfway along.

Regulations

No guns, no alcoholic beverages, *no motor vehicles*. Small parking fee at Coyote Hills Regional Park.

Description

If you begin at Coyote Hills you can pick up a map of the trail at headquarters. Bicyclists can get on the channel trail by way of the Bay View Trail, hikers by the Bay View or one of the nature trails.

Shortly after you leave the park, you pass under Newark Boulevard—the first of several roads and railroad tracks that cross the channel above the trail. Finding yourself underneath one as a huge truck or a train goes rumbling overhead is one of the experiences that make biking or hiking on this trail unique. For the next few miles the trail passes truck gardens, mobile homes and tract houses. The large, reddish-tan building visible against the hills to the east is the Masonic Home.

At Beard Road (toilets) the trail curves to head southeast toward Mission Peak (2517′) in the distance. It goes under Decoto Road near the 5-mile marker. Soon the housing subdivisions begin to give way to industry: quarries and gravel pits, and concrete and gypsum plants. Large white letters on a hill to the east proclaim the community of Niles. As you approach the BART trestle, a train may go hissing past.

At present the Alameda Creek Trail ends near the junction of Mission Boulevard and Niles Canyon Road. Here a small Fremont city park, with picnic facilities, commemorates one of Jose de Jesus Vallejo's flour mills. Don Jose, an elder brother of the general, was granted Rancho Arroyo de la Alameda in 1842. He had two flour mills built here in the 1850s, and the town of Niles (originally called Vallejo Mills but subsequently named for state supreme court judge Addison C. Niles) grew up around them.

Side trips

1. Niles was one of five small towns that banded together in 1956 to form the city of Fremont, which soon became one of the fastest-growing cities in the state: by 1987 it had a population of 160,000, second in the East Bay only to Oakland. Meanwhile the Niles District has emphasized its greatest claim to fame—its brief heyday as a movie-making center. "Bronco Billy" Anderson moved the Essanay Company here in 1910 and used Niles Canyon as the setting for westerns. The most famous movie made here was Charlie Chaplin's *The Tramp*. In 1916 the studio decamped to the sunnier clime of Hollywood.

Niles has changed surprisingly little in the 70 years since its movie-making days. As one wanders around, the word that comes irresistibly to mind is "funky." Antique-collectors will find plenty of places to shop.

2. On the north side of the Alameda Creek Trail in the Niles District is the Alameda Creek Quarries Regional Recreation Area, now under the jurisdiction of the EBRPD, which may eventually organize it for water-oriented activities. Meanwhile the place is a sort of fascinating jungle punctuated by water-filled old gravel pits. The underlying Hayward Fault has contributed to the unsettled nature of the landscape, and previous owners have left behind a wild variety of plants. While the EBRPD figures out what to do with the area, visitors can launch remote-controlled model boats in Kaiser Pond A and can fish in the larger Shinn Pond (state and EBRPD regulations apply; *no swimming*).

To reach the quarries: from Niles Boulevard go south 2 blocks on H Street to Niles Community Park, which has a parking lot adjoining the Recreation Area.

Garin and Dry Creek/Pioneer regional parks

Address

1320 Garin Avenue, Hayward 94544

Maps

Topos *Hayward, Newark* and a bit of *Niles;* trail map available at headquarters; Erickson's *Recreational Map . . . South West Section.*

How to get there

By BART and/or bus: Take BART or AC Transit #82 to the South Hayward BART station and from there take AC Transit #21 to Mission Boulevard and Garin Avenue; from here it's a mile of uphill hike to the park.

By car: From the north take Highway 580 to the Highway 238 exit. Highway 238 becomes Mission Boulevard; from Mission turn left on Garin Avenue and follow it a mile to the park entrance. The signal preceding Garin when driving from the north is at Industrial Parkway. If northbound on Highway 238, the signal preceding Garin is at Arrowhead.

Features

These two adjacent parks are among the most recent additions to the EBRPD. They preserve a couple of thousand acres of open space, former ranch land, in the midst of the rapidly developing residential and industrial South Bay.

Dry Creek/Pioneer Park was a gift to the district by the three Meyers sisters, granddaughters of pioneers who settled the property in 1884. The Dry Creek Ranch was traditionally the site of merrymaking by the inhabitants of Washington Township on May Day and Independence Day. Although the ranch has become a public park, the festive atmosphere still prevails. During a visit a few days after the Fourth of July, my notes record: "On the extensive greensward people are playing softball, volleyball, croquet and horseshoes, and tossing footballs and Frisbees. In the picnic area they are barbecueing, cuddling, and practicing the guitar; and at Jordan Pond they are fishing."

In 1984 Garin opened its visitor center in a barn just across the creek from the main parking lot. Exhibits here feature the history of ranching in the Hayward area. Scattered around the barn and the parking lots is some rusty antique farm machinery.

Although both the hikes described here are fairly long, a glance at the trail map will reveal that shorter loops are possible—for example, by combining the High Ridge and Dry Creek trails.

Facilities

Open 8 A.M.–dusk; water, restrooms, wheelchair-accessible; many picnic tables and grills, some wheelchair-accessible; group picnicking by reservation at least 14 days in advance (531-9043); group camping by reservation.

Visitor center open 10 A.M.–4:30 P.M. on weekends, wheelchair-accessible; nature programs coordinated by Coyote Hills Regional Park (795-9385).

Fishing pier on Jordan Pond, wheelchair-accessible, constructed by EBRPD crews with financial contributions from three Hayward area Lions clubs.

Regulations

Small parking fee; small additional dog fee; state fishing license required; otherwise, the usual for the EBRPD.

55 Around Garin Peak

Distance   3½-mile loop; more or less if desired.
Grade   Moderate, but don't try it on a hot day.

Features

Garin Peak (948') and nearby Vista Peak (934') offer a panoramic view of the two parks and the whole South Bay.

Description

You can pick up a map at headquarters that shows the trails in both parks. From the parking lot head north (sign HIGH RIDGE TR.) along the west side of Dry Creek, which in late summer is not quite dry here but is covered with green algae. (On the *east* side of Dry Creek to the north of the main picnic area are some reservable group picnic areas under giant sycamores.) The first ¼ mile is on a paved road. After passing through a cattle gate you arrive at a sign for the High Ridge Trail. Before venturing on it you may want to continue north a few hundred feet to the Newt Pond. This area is fed by springs year-round, so that even in summer the road has muddy spots. California newts breed in the pond during the rainy season.

Returning to the High Ridge Trail, you ascend steadily over open grassland to a junction with the Vista Peak Loop. Continuing on High Ridge, still ascending gradually, you pass a few willow trees where the Garin family's home once stood before it was destroyed by fire many years ago.

At the next trail junction you can turn right and go straight to the top. (If you want a longer hike with more diverse vegetation, you can continue a short distance to the Maple Canyon Trail and head down it to shady Zeile Creek.) On a clear day the 360-degree view from the peaks includes the Coyote Hills, the San Francisco Bay National Wildlife Refuge and the Leslie Salt ponds to the southwest, San Francisco to the west, California State University at Hayward to the northwest, Walpert Ridge to the east and Dry Creek Park and beyond it Mission Peak to the south. In a sense, the view may also be considered to encompass the past, present and future: the former ranch land of the park is in sharp contrast to the urban/industrial sprawl below and the new housing project creeping across the hills to the north.

From the peaks the Vista Peak Loop descends briefly and turns left. After passing the Zeile Creek Trail, the Vista Peak Loop ascends briefly past an unsigned trail, then descends along an oaky canyon and curves around above the Newt Pond to its junction with the High Ridge Trail.

56   The High Ridge Loop and Gossip Rock

Distance   6-mile loop.
Grade   Fairly strenuous; a steady climb of 1000' for the first 2 miles.

Features

The contrast between past and future mentioned in the preceding hike description is even more apparent on this route: you traverse old ranch land to an Indian acorn-grinding stone but also overlook the modern industrial South Bay.

Description

After picking up a trail map at headquarters, head east past the barn/visitor center and go through a cattle gate. The High Ridge Loop Trail ascends steadily, crossing the Chabot Fault as it nears the crest of the ridge. The Chabot Fault is an offshoot of the Hayward

Fault, which runs only about a mile from here and has caused major quakes within the past century. The instability of the land in this fault zone makes it desirable to keep the steeper slopes as open space rather than building on them.

The Old Ranch Trail branches off to the right, offering the possibility of cutting 3 miles off the hike. The High Ridge Loop Trail continues southeast along the crest. After passing a little spring the trail curves right and soon arrives at the side trail (sign) leading to Gossip Rock. In this jumble of sandstone under bay trees the mortars are still visible where the original inhabitants ground their acorns; presumably they chatted as they worked.

Back on the main trail, you descend between two forested swales while enjoying the view over Union City and the Alameda Creek Channel to the Coyote Hills and the San Francisco Bay National Wildlife Refuge. Turn right at a barbed-wire fence and descend through tall stands of poison oak, which give way to bay and oak trees. After passing a pond you walk along a pleasant stream under sycamores and soon reach a gravelled road. The High Ridge Loop Trail turns right here to run along this road briefly, then continues through a green gate on your right. After crossing Dry Creek on a bridge, you arrive at the junction of the High Ridge Loop and Old Ranch trails.

It is possible to return via the High Ridge Loop Trail, but for a nice change of scenery, at least in summer, try the Old Ranch Trail leading to the Dry Creek Trail. (It may get muddy during the rainy season.) The bucolic Old Ranch Trail runs along Dry Creek, crossing it on bridges from time to time, to reach a corral and an old farmhouse, now a park residence. Just a few hundred feet beyond the corral, look for the sign indicating the Dry Creek Trail descending on the left. This attractive, shady trail runs for a half mile along the creek, sometimes above it and sometimes crossing it, and emerges at the south end of Jordan Pond. During hot weather, park visitors might want just to saunter along under the oaks and sycamores of the Dry Creek Trail and forget about the more ambitious hilly loops!

57   Black Diamond Mines Regional Preserve

Address and phone
Route 1, Box 1402, Antioch 94509; 757-2620

Maps
Topos *Antioch South* and *Clayton;* trail maps available at entrance; Erickson's *Mt. Diablo State Park, Black Diamond Mines . . . and Other Recreational Lands.*

How to get there
Drive north on Highway 24/I-680, east on Highway 4 to Antioch, and south on Somersville Road to its end.

Features
Black Diamond Mines Preserve is one of the few places described in this book that were much more bustling and well populated a century ago than they are now. Like Redwood Regional Park in Oakland, it isn't simply *un*developed—it's *dis*developed. In some ways, Black Diamond is even more poignant than Redwood: in Oakland, the rowdy lumbermen came, cut down the trees, raised hell for a few years, and moved on; but in North Contra Costa County, coal miners' families made their homes in the communities of Nortonville, Somersville and Stewartville, and children were born and grew up—and many died—here. The towns that once contained several hundred people have now vanished so completely that it is almost impossible to visualize them as one hikes the windy hills. One reason these communities did not simply molder away into ghost towns, as elsewhere in the West, is that when the coal boom ended many of the residents dismantled their homes and moved them elsewhere. The park office is currently located in a house that was moved here from Stewartville. A few other houses representative of this region during the mining period are being moved here. Although simple-appearing today, they are probably fancier than most of the miners' actual houses—these at least have foundations.

History
Although James Cruikshank and Francis Somers discovered the Black Diamond vein in 1859, it was the better-capitalized Noah Norton who took over the mine and built roads to carry the coal to wharves on the San Joaquin River, whence it traveled up to Stockton and Sacramento and down to San Francisco. During the next two

decades miners and their families poured in and constructed houses, churches, schools, bars and lodges in half a dozen settlements. During the boom period three railroads carried the coal from the mines to the river landings. The coal was never of very high quality, however, and when better, cheaper coal from the Pacific Northwest came on the market the Mt. Diablo mines had to close down.

Another flurry of mining began in 1922, this time for silica sands, used in glass making. This activity ceased in 1949 and again the land lay deserted. The park district began buying acreage here in 1973. The mines on private land remained as an "attractive nuisance" to overly adventurous youths, even though the owners fenced off the property and attempted to seal the shafts. One of the EBRPD's first tasks was to locate all of the old mine openings and seal them off thoroughly. This job was complicated by the fact that most of the coal companies' records had been sent to San Francisco after the mines had closed, and had been destroyed in the 1906 earthquake and fire. Teams of park-district men, aided by a specially trained dog, had to search the ground painstakingly looking for openings.

Facilities

Open daily 8 A.M. to dusk. Water, toilets, picnic tables near parking lot; this is the only potable water in the park, so a canteen is desirable when hiking. Parking is free, except for Black Diamond Days, when there is a small fee. Black Diamond Days take place during the last full weekend in April and feature the music, dancing and food of the various ethnic groups that once peopled the mining towns.

Tours of the underground mining museum take place every Saturday and Sunday *by reservation only* (phone 757-2620 on weekdays); small fee. These tours are so popular, especially in spring and fall, that reservations must be made two or three weeks in advance. On weekdays the park conducts tours for school and other groups.

Park naturalists also offer a variety of walks and tours that explore other features of the region's natural and human history; for schedules, consult the East Bay LOG or phone 757-2620.

Regulations

No children under age 7 permitted underground; otherwise, the usual for the EBRPD.

Description

Most first-time visitors to the preserve want to take the mine tour. Parts of the Hazel-Atlas sand mine have been reconstructed as authentically as possible to give the appearance the mine and its equipment had in about 1945, a few years before it closed for good. The park staff lends visitors hard hats and flashlights for the tour, which involves walking ⅓ mile through tunnels. You might want to take a sweater, because no matter how hot it may be outside, in the naturally air-conditioned mine the temperature remains about 55 degrees. The park staff hopes eventually to add a reconstructed coal mine to the underground museum.

There are plenty of things to see in Black Diamond Preserve besides the mine, as you will find out if you take a guided tour or set out (with a map) on your own on some of its 30+ miles of trails. The preserve brochure notes that this is the northernmost location of Coulter pine, black sage, desert olive and dudleya. The preserve also issues a list of the more than 100 species of birds that have been seen within it, including the golden eagle.

Perhaps the most fascinating place in the park—one you may want to visit on your own if your guided tour doesn't lead you there—is Rose Hill Cemetery. This is an easy walk ½ mile uphill, curving west on the old road between Somersville and Nortonville. Along the way you will note that although the structures the miners built have disappeared, the trees they planted are still here: ailanthus, almond, locust, and the dark Italian cypress marking the cemetery.

Many of the miners were from Wales, as was Noah Norton himself, and some of the tombstone inscriptions are in Welsh. Although the graveyard has been vandalized, enough tombstones still remain to bear mute and touching witness to a way of life and death only a century past, yet so different from ours that we can scarcely imagine it. The modern visitor is especially struck by the *youth* of so many of the people buried here: children carried off by epidemics of diphtheria, typhoid and scarlet fever, boys and young men killed in mine accidents, young women dead in childbirth—all lie at peace now under the windswept grass.

58   Briones Regional Park

Phone

229-3020

Maps

Topo *Briones Valley;* trail map available at Bear Creek and Alhambra Creek Valley staging areas; Olmsted Bros.' *Rambler's Guide . . . Northern Section;* Erickson's *Tilden and Briones.*

How to get there

The Bear Creek Staging Area (main entrance): From Highway 24 take the Orinda exit. Go northwest on Camino Pablo (San Pablo Dam Road) 2½ miles, turn right on Bear Creek Road and follow it 5 miles to the park entrance on the right.

The Lafayette Ridge Staging Area: From Highway 24 take the Pleasant Hill exit and find the staging area just north of Acalanes High School. This is the trailhead for the 11½-mile Briones-Mt. Diablo Trail. Farther north on Reliez Valley Road at Gloria Terrace is another trailhead for Briones.

The Alhambra Creek Valley Staging Area: From Highway 24 take the Pleasant Hill exit, bear left on Reliez Valley Road, drive north on it for about 5 miles, turn left on Brookwood Road and follow it to the parking lot.

The Briones Road Staging Area: Continue west on Reliez Valley Road for about ½ mile and just past its junction with Alhambra Valley Road look for the Briones Road on the left. It climbs 1½ narrow, winding miles to a small parking lot.

Features

Briones contains more than 5000 acres, much of it open, rolling hills. It probably looks substantially as it did when the original grantee, Felipe Briones, ranched here more than a century ago.

This is one of the regional parks where you may encounter cattle. They are not here just to provide bucolic local color: they keep the grass cropped, so that it is less of a fire hazard, and their owners pay the park district a moderate grazing fee. When hiking here, please close cattle gates where signs so request.

The newts of Briones have become its most famous animals. Every year thousands of these creatures migrate from their winter hiding places to their ancestral breeding ponds. As they cross roads enroute, they are liable to get run over. One winter an intersection near Briones Park became the site of the world's first and only *Newt crossing* road signs. As one might have predicted, these items were promptly stolen.

Facilities

Open 8 A.M.–10 P.M.; winter hours 8 A.M.–6 P.M.

At the Bear Creek Staging Area: Water, toilets, tables, grills; two youth-group camps available by reservation (531-9043); children's playground; archery range.

At the Alhambra Creek Valley Staging Area: Water, toilets (wheelchair-accessible), tables, grills; the picnic area is in an old walnut orchard.

Regulations

Dogs must be on leash; no alcoholic beverages, except wine and beer in picnic areas; small parking fee, small additional dog fee.

A Briones Peak loop

Distance 8-mile loop; less if desired.
Grade Moderately strenuous.

Features

This route offers a good survey of the park's main features and a chance to enjoy the views from its high spots.

Description

From the west parking lot, ¼ mile inside the park entrance, head north on the graveled Abrigo Valley Trail that skirts the picnic ground. It passes through a cattle gate and runs along the steep bank of Cascade Creek, under spreading bay trees, live oaks and valley oaks. Gradually the road leaves the creek to ascend gently over cattle-grazing land. After a mile you go through another cattle gate and soon cross a creek. Just off the trail to the right is the Maud Whalen group camp (water, restrooms). Continue north through a valley with rolling hills on each side—on the left wooded, on the right open and grassy. At a fork, ¼ mile past the camp, bear right and cross another creek whose course is marked by willows, elder-berries, bays and live oaks. Not far beyond the crossing are a large flagpole and the Wee-Ta-Chi group camp (water, restrooms).

Now the trail runs along the north bank of the creek. Soon you hear a waterfall, and peering down through the maples and bays you can see it.

The trail twists away from the creek and curves up the hillside. As you ascend, Mt. Tamalpais comes in view to the west. Go through yet another gate and turn right on the Briones Crest Trail. As you continue to climb, you will see the Benicia Bridge, the "mothball fleet," Suisun Bay, and on the near shore a multitude of oil refineries. On a clear day you can see the Sutter Buttes.

After bearing south around Mott Peak you pass between the Sindicich lagoons (breeding place of the famed newts); a peaceful,

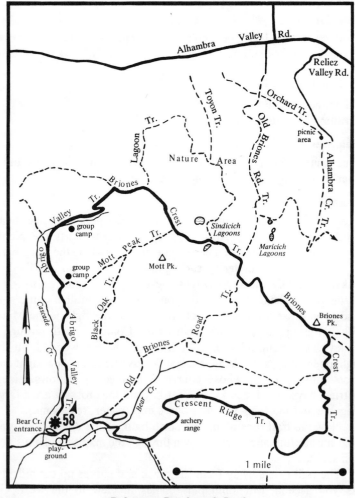

Briones Regional Park

bucolic scene with Mt. Diablo dominating the background. In 1985 the Golden Gate Audubon Society erected a fence around the larger lagoon "to prevent cattle from trampling the shoreline vegetation. This will allow aquatic plants to be re-established, enhancing the habitat for waterbirds, small mammals and the famous Briones newts."

Walk east along a draw and in ¼ mile from the lagoon, at a junction, bear right and in 100 yards arrive at a fork. Now if you want to cut the hike short, you can take the Old Briones Road, which leads directly down to Bear Creek Valley and a level walk along the creek back to the parking lot. Otherwise, continue on the Briones Crest Trail and enjoy a view of the Maricich Lagoons, or what's left of them: over the years they seem to have been getting smaller, and indeed they have altogether disappeared in the Olmsted map. After ½ mile, mostly ascent, you can see Briones Peak (1483', the highest point in the park) a short distance to the left. You can take a side trip up the peak to enjoy the view of Mt. Diablo.

For the next mile, the road meanders along the park boundary, with quite a bit of up and down. Occasional oak trees provide shade, and in spring bush lupine provides color. Along the way you pass another shortcut back to Bear Creek Valley. A few yards farther on, you go through another gate and past a PG&E marker; bear right here. The road runs along the crest of the ridge, passing occasional orange-and-white PG&E markers. At a locked fire gate, go through the hiker's stile on the right. The trail runs along the west side of a fence, then turns right over the open hill. Soon you get a glimpse of Briones Reservoir. The trail runs along the crest of Crescent Ridge, where views of pleasant green valleys alternate on right and left.

When you get a clear view of the parking lot a mile or so ahead, the trail curves southeast and descends rather abruptly, through giant thistles. At the bottom of the descent, just across a creek, is the archery range. Turn right here and walk west along the gravel road, past the road coming in from Homestead Valley and over a stile. Now the road jogs a bit and soon arrives at the barrier just ¼ mile from the parking lot.

Mt. Diablo State Park

Mailing address and phone
Box 250, Diablo 94528; 837-2525

Maps
Topos *Diablo* and *Clayton;* trail map available at headquarters and
ranger stations for a small price; Erickson's *Mt. Diablo State Park,
Black Diamond Mines . . . and Other Recreational Lands.* The Mt.
Diablo Interpretive Association issues an excellent map that
includes description of 12 hikes, from easy to strenuous, in various
of the mountain's life zones. It is available for a small price from
park headquarters, the ranger stations, or the above address.

How to get there
Via the South Gate   From Highway 680 take the Danville-
Diablo Road exit and go east on Diablo Road, following signs to the
park. After 3 miles on Diablo Road go north on Mt. Diablo Scenic
Boulevard, which becomes South Gate Road and twists up 3½ miles
to the South Checking Station and another 3 miles to the junction
with North Gate Road.

Via the North Gate   Proceed toward Walnut Creek via
Highway 24 or 680, continue north on the combined highways and
exit on Ygnacio Valley Road. After 1½ miles bear right on Walnut
Avenue, which in a mile runs into North Gate Road. Follow this road
windingly up the mountain 7 miles to the North Checking Station
and the junction with South Gate Road.

From park headquarters—at the junction of North Gate and
South Gate roads—to the summit is 4½ miles by road.

It is also possible to hike up the flanks of the mountain from trailheads below, as the MDIA map reveals. The Mitchell Canyon trailhead, a favorite in spring, is reached by taking Ygnacio Valley Road
east to Clayton Road, bearing right on Clayton Road for a mile,
turning right on Mitchell Canyon Road, and following it to its end.
There is a small parking fee at the Mitchell Canyon staging area,
water and a toilet.

Features
Although Mt. Diablo is only 3849 feet high, the view from its
summit encompasses more of the earth's surface than that from any
other peak in North America. The mountain has a fascinating
geology and paleontology, and an unusual flora (to which an entire
book has been devoted).

With all these things going for it, why isn't Mt. Diablo as thronged with hikers every weekend as Mt. Tamalpais? Two possible reasons come to mind: First, Mt. Diablo is bare enough, and far enough inland, to get uncomfortably hot in summer. Second, it lacks the public transportation that has long been established on Mt. Tamalpais; the state park on Diablo is, as Margot Patterson Doss has noted, "discouragingly dedicated to the automobile."

Nevertheless, the hiker who is willing to leave the road and the popular picnic sites can enjoy an unusual, even a breathtaking, experience here. Perhaps the MDIA map and trail guide mentioned above will encourage more people to explore this fascinating mountain, including the delightful riparian areas on the lower slopes which form such a fertile habitat for birds and wildflowers.

Geology

Much of the Diablo area was generally under sea roughly 50 million years ago, when the sea retreated and a tropical swampland prevailed, perhaps for millions of years. As time progressed, the climate changed to semitropical, and the plant and animal species likewise changed. By several million years ago, the Mt. Diablo area was definitely above sea level, though not by much. Then, roughly two million years ago, the mountain began to grow. Layers of sedimentary rocks were slowly bulged upward as a mass of Franciscan rock, roughly 100–150 million years old, was being thrust upward through them. This mass ultimately broke through the sedimentary rocks, perhaps by one million years ago. As the Franciscan rock mass continued to rise (and along with it, the mountain), adjacent sedimentary rock strata were steepened even more.

In some places it even turned them over, so that the older ones are now above the younger. Consequently Mt. Diablo today constitutes a fascinating puzzle for geologists and paleontologists. If you approach the mountain from the south, you will pass the Devils Slide just before reaching the South Checking Station. Here you can see layers of Miocene sandstone that have obviously been tilted upward.

About a mile beyond the South Checking Station is Rock City, a place to delight picnickers, photographers and children: even the nongeologist will be fascinated by the bizarre formations that wind has created of sandstone here.

Climate

Mount Diablo is far enough inland to experience greater extremes of temperature than the region west of the Berkeley Hills. In summer, highs in the 90s are not uncommon. This heat, combined with the aridity of the upper slopes, deters hikers. However, it might appeal to San Franciscans who wish to escape their fog-ridden City for an overnight camping trip.

Conversely, the summit receives some snow almost every winter. Most years, in fact, Mt. Diablo is the most accessible place for Bay Areans to frolic in snow.

History

A number of accounts of how the mountain acquired its name exist. The most popular is the one that Mariano G. Vallejo presented to the state legislature in 1850: He reported that in 1806 a military expedition from San Francisco's Presidio was engaged in battle with Indians at the foot of the mountain, when suddenly "an unknown personage, decorated with the most extraordinary plumage," appeared on the scene. The Spanish soldiers took this personage (who, if the story is true, may have been an Indian medicine man) for the Devil, and promptly retreated. This was one of the few triumphs the California Indians enjoyed over the white man. It was short-lived, however, since troops under Gabriel Moraga subdued the tribe later in the year.

The mountain was a landmark for Spanish explorers and Yankee pioneers. In 1851 Leander Ransom established its summit as the base point for land surveys in much of California and what is now Nevada. During the late 19th century, mining took place on its flanks for quicksilver and, less successfully, for copper and silver. In 1874 two toll roads were opened to the summit, and a hotel was built near it, which burned down in the '90s.

In 1931 the state acquired the upper part of the mountain for its park system. In recent years the state park's acreage has increased to about 15,000, partly because of the efforts of Save Mt. Diablo, Inc., a nonprofit organization of conservation-minded citizens. However, some of the rolling grassland on the mountain's lower slopes has already become the site of expensive houses, and more may yet.

In 1979, after years of negotiation, the state acquired rough and rugged North Peak, which had long been privately held. Over its years in private ownership, North Peak had accumulated a number of transmitting towers, and these remain after the state takeover. In fact, in 1982 a Concord-based religious TV broadcasting station succeeded in getting permission from the Contra Costa County Board of Supervisors to erect a new 136-foot antenna on the North Peak. Save Mt. Diablo, the Sierra Club and other concerned groups are trying to prevent such garish intrusions on what could be an island of wilderness in the suburban East Bay.

Another controversy has concerned cattle grazing on the mountain's parklands. The California Division of Parks and Recreation has held several hearings on this subject, many of them marked by fierce debate. The state claims that the cattle are destroying the native vegetation; the ranchers claim that the cattle are eating grasses that would otherwise become a fire hazard. This controversy may not be resolved in the near future.

Facilities

Open daily 8 A.M.–sunset. Many family picnic sites; 2 group picnic areas, which should be reserved in advance through park headquarters; 60 family campsites, which may be reserved from October 1 through May 31 at Mistix (1-800-444-7275); from June 1 through September 30 available on a first-come, first-served basis except when park is closed because of fire hazard; 4 group campsites; 2 horse-group campgrounds, which should be reserved through park headquarters; snack bar at summit on weekends.

Regulations

Both gates closed at sunset. *No alcohol,* not even beer or wine. No skateboarding. Fires allowed only in the park's barbecues or portable campstoves—not in portable barbecues or hibachis. *During times of extreme fire hazard, the park may close.* Otherwise, the usual for state parks, including no dogs on trails.

Organizations

Save Mt. Diablo
Box 25, Concord 94522
This tax-deductible citizens' group was formed to promote preservation of the Mt. Diablo open space and to raise funds for additional land acquisition to expand the state park. In cooperation with the MDIA it conducts numerous walks, camping trips and other family-oriented nature activities in spring.

Sierra Club: Mt. Diablo Regional Group
Box 4457, Walnut Creek 94596
This active group conducts a year-round program of outings, lectures and other events in the Mt. Diablo area and elsewhere in the East Bay.

Recommended reading

Bowerman, Mary L., *The Flowering Plants and Ferns of Mount Diablo, California.* Berkeley: Gillick Press, 1944. Out of print, but available in libraries; the definitive word on the mountain's flora.

Hummert, Betty, *Visitor's Guide to the Geology of Mt. Diablo.*
Available at the ranger stations for a small price; contains
bibliography.

59   The Fire Interpretive Trail

Distance   A short mile.
Grade   Easy: first 1000 feet paved for wheelchair access.

Map

Descriptive leaflet with map available free from ranger stations.

How to get there

The trail starts about ¼ mile below the summit, just northeast of the
lower summit parking lot.

Features

This trail was constructed in 1982, much of it by the California
Conservation Corps, to demonstrate the ecological aftereffects of a
fire that had raged over 6000 acres of the mountain five years earlier. The trail was dedicated to Mary Leolin Bowerman, author of the
definitive study of the mountain's flora. On a clear day this easy,
level route around the summit offers a 360-degree exposure of the
superb views that make Mt. Diablo unique in the Bay Area. When
this trail gets better known, it may become as popular a tourist
attraction as the summit trail on Mt. Tamalpais.

Facilities

Water, restrooms at lower summit parking lot; picnic table at trailhead; disabled parking just across road from trailhead; snack bar at
summit open on weekends.

Description

The first, paved section of the trail leads through scrub oak and bay
trees to a redwood deck constructed trestle-style around a huge
boulder—an inspired alternative to the more common trail-building
procedure of simply blasting away the rock. This is Ransom Point,
named for Leander Ransom, the surveyor who in 1851 established
the base and meridian lines through Mt. Diablo which are still in use.
As you rest on the redwood benches here, you can look out over the
view to the north—which, if you came on the right day, might include
Lassen Peak and possibly even Mt. Shasta.

Nearer at hand, you can study the effects of the 1977 fire that
inspired the construction of this trail. The fire was started by

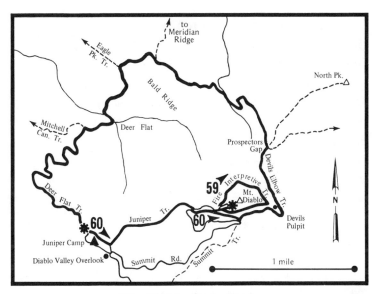

Mt. Diablo State Park

lightning, as similar fires were over the thousands of years before man ever lived near Mt. Diablo. And the vegetation has always grown back, just as it is doing now. Some species of chaparral regenerate rapidly after a fire—e.g., chamise and toyon.

As you continue walking around the summit, you may be able to see the confluence of the Sacramento and San Joaquin rivers. On a truly clear day you can also see the snowy peaks of the Sierra glistening one hundred and fifty miles to the east across the Central Valley, and—most thrilling of all—Half Dome in Yosemite, instantly recognizable through binoculars.

The trail passes the Devils Pulpit and continues along the south side of the mountain to end at the disabled parking lot. You may want to finish with a walk to the summit tower, which was built by the Civilian Conservation Corps in 1941. It is made of Miocene sandstone from the quarry just south of the South Gate, and when you look closely you'll see that it's full of fossils.

60   Around the mountain

Distance   7-mile loop.
Grade   Strenuous.

How to get there

From the junction of North Gate and South Gate roads (see p. 226) proceed 2½ miles up Summit Road to Juniper Camp.

Features

This rather arduous circuit of Mt. Diablo, called "The Grand Loop" on the MDIA map, will reveal aspects of the mountain that the tourists who flock to the summit in their cars never experience. It will also provide a more detailed study of how the north side of the mountain has regenerated from the fire of 1977. Furthermore, if you take the hike in spring you will have the bonus of a host of wildflowers. Shrubby yellow aster is common on the north side, and you can also expect to see wallflowers, various brodiaeas, clarkias, Mariposa lilies, and many others.

A few caveats: Don't try this one on a very hot day; start early; carry plenty of water.

Facilities

Water, restrooms, picnic tables and stoves at Juniper Camp; water and restrooms at summit.

Description

Begin at Juniper Camp, which contains giant canyon live oaks as well as junipers. The trail to the summit begins at the Laurel Nook group picnic area. It climbs through chaparral, jogs to cross Summit Road and arrives at the lower summit parking lot. If you're here on a weekend, you may want to make a side trip to the snack bar. Otherwise, find the trail heading east from the south side of the parking lot down to the acute switchback on Summit Road. The trail to North Peak heads east from here and leads over stark, rocky terrain punctuated by occasional juniper trees. It offers spectacular views over the hills and valleys to the south and east. Above are rugged, craggy formations of reddish-brown Franciscan rock, the most prominent one being the Devils Pulpit. It's easy to understand why the early explorers perceived a malevolent quality in this rough, wild landscape. However, if you sit quietly for a few minutes, a frisky ground squirrel may pop up to provide a nondiabolic counterpoint to the scenery.

Less than ½ mile from Summit Road the trail bends north, and you can look across a saddle to the North Peak (3557'). Fire damage may still be visible down the canyon. The trail generally descends, through scrub and live oaks, poison oak and an occasional bay tree. The last few hundred feet are a rather steep scramble down to a stand of Digger pines and blue oaks at the saddle, Prospectors Gap. This is an excellent spot to relax and enjoy the view across the broad San Joaquin Valley and, if you've come on the right day, all the way to the Sierra. You can take a ¾-mile side trip up the rugged road to North Peak.

From Prospectors Gap a fire road descends rather steeply down the exposed north side of the mountain. Stump-sprouting shrubs have obviously survived the fire—e.g., toyon, yerba santa, poison oak (of course!) and wild grape, which provides a riot of color in fall. At Big Spring a creek under towering oak trees provides a welcome, shady rest spot.

The trail now contours along the north slope, overlooking Clayton. The Meridian Ridge Fire Road—which gets its name, of course, from the nearby Mt. Diablo meridian—branches off to the right. After passing the trail to Eagle Peak you arrive at Deer Flat, another good rest spot, studded with blue oak and bay trees and watered by a creek in spring. Continuing on the trail, you soon pass the Mitchell Canyon Trail going down to the right and you can decide whether you'd like to hike up it from below some time.

The trail now switchbacks steadily up, offering good views of Eagle Peak and whatever the atmospheric conditions permit you to see in the distance—such as Mt. St. Helena. The western hop tree, a somewhat uncommon shrub, grows along the trail here. Rounding a shoulder, you see Juniper Camp a short mile ahead.

61　Las Trampas Regional Wilderness

Maps

Topo *Las Trampas Ridge;* trail map available from box in sign near entrance or from EBRPD headquarters; Olmsted Bros.' *Rambler's Guide . . . Central Section.*

How to get there

Take Highway 24 toward Walnut Creek, go south on 680 to just beyond Danville, turn right on Crow Canyon Road for 1½ miles, then right again on Bolinger Canyon Road and follow it 4½ miles to its end. Or take Highway 580 toward Tracy to Crow Canyon Road, drive northeast on it for 7 miles and turn left on Bolinger Canyon Road.

Access by foot or horse only is also possible on the Del Amigo Trail at the west end of Starview Drive, Danville; there is *no parking* available here.

Features

Las Trampas is one of the district's "wilderness parks." Purists may point out that, like its fellow, Sunol, it contains too many power lines, fences, domestic animals and introduced plants to merit the designation "wilderness." However, we could hardly expect these areas so near the metropolis to have remained as they were in the 1820s. We should be grateful that the park district has preserved a few enclaves of, at least, the 1920s.

Las Trampas gets its name, "the traps," from the traps that the Indians and subsequently the early Spanish Californians set in the chaparral to catch elk. The elk are gone, but the park handout says that the area still contains—in addition to the ubiquitous deer—raccoons, foxes, opossums, bobcats, skunks, squirrels, and perhaps even a mountain lion or two. Because the EBRPD leases the park for grazing, you will probably see cattle, sheep and horses.

In addition to these live animals, you may find some fossil animals. Both the main ridges that run through the park, Las Trampas Ridge and Rocky Ridge, are composed of sedimentary rock laid down when this area was under the sea about 15 million years ago, and subsequently folded upward by earth forces. One doesn't have to have very keen eyes to find clamshells in the sandstone of these ridges of folded rock.

The short hike described here gives just a scant introduction to the many miles of trails that run through this fascinating country. Furthermore, the west side of Las Trampas park adjoins extensive EBMUD acreage containing hiking and equestrian trails. With the district's *trail permit* and map you can plan a variety of all-day trips or car-shuttle excursions through some fairly wild territory.

Facilities

Open 8 A.M.–dusk. Water, toilets, picnic tables, grills near parking lot; Little Hills Regional Recreation Area available for group picnicking by reservation (837-0821); horse rentals from Las Trampas Stables (838-7546).

Regulations

The usual for the EBRPD.

Along Las Trampas ridge

Distance   4-mile loop.
Grade   Moderate.

Features

Although this hike is fairly short and involves no excessively steep climbs, the Ridge and Nordstrom trails contain enough minor ups and downs to warrant wearing boots. Note also that there is *no water* along the route.

If you try this hike in spring and find that both the Creek and Valley trails are too deep in sticky mud for comfortable walking, return to the parking lot and take Rocky Ridge Road to the top of the ridge for a hike with a magnificent view!

Description

From the park entrance take either the Valley Trail, which runs along the east bank of Bolinger Creek, or the heavily shaded Creek Trail, which runs along the west bank for ½ mile to join the Valley Trail. The valley along Bolinger Creek is idyllically bucolic, especially

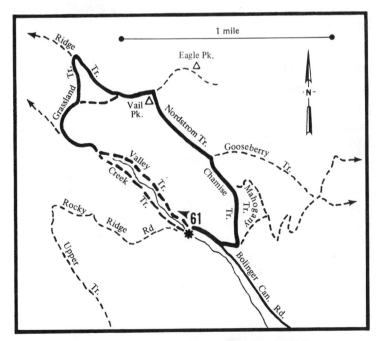

Las Trampas Wilderness Regional Park

when the grass is still green and patterned with wildflowers. Coast live oaks, maples, buckeyes and bay trees shade the trail, and the upthrust peaks of Las Trampas Ridge tower protectively over it.

Less than a mile from the trailhead, the Valley Trail comes to a junction at a saddle. Turn right here onto the Grassland Trail (sign). Climb rather steeply on it amid chamise, ceanothus and black sage. At the top of the ridge, turn right, and continue along the crest on the Nordstrom Trail. It offers views of other sandstone ridges nearby, and in spots you can look out over the valley to Mt. Diablo. The sandy patches of trail remind you that this land was once under sea. As you pass Vail Peak, the Ohlone Trail leads down and then up to nearby Eagle Peak.

Now you walk through chaparral: scrub oak, chamise, toyon and buckbrush, a white ceanothus. When the Gooseberry Trail branches left, stay on the continuation of the Nordstrom Trail, the Chamise Trail, which descends through wild cucumber, more buckbrush and the chamise of its title. The Mahogany Trail branches off to the left and comes in again toward the end of the Chamise Trail, which drops down a steep hillside to meet Bolinger Canyon Road at an enormous old oak tree. Turn right on the road and walk the short distance back to the parking lot—surveyed, perhaps, by sheep grazing above you on the hillside.

Recommended reading

Knight, Walter, *et al., The Story of Las Trampas*. Oakland: East Bay Regional Park District.

Nearby attraction

Adjoining Las Trampas Park to the east is Eugene O'Neill's Tao House, where the playwright lived from 1937 to 1944. Here in his cool, quiet "dream house" he composed some of his greatest works, including *The Iceman Cometh* and *A Long Day's Journey Into Night*. The National Park Service now administers Tao House and conducts free tours of it twice daily. *Reservations are essential* and should be made well in advance of when you plan to visit; phone 838-0249. The tours start in downtown Danville. This town itself is worth walking around. The Danville Hotel has been refurbished in 1880s style and contains a magnificent Old West bar.

Sunol Regional Wilderness

Address and phone
Box 82, Sunol 94586; 862-2244

Maps
Topo *La Costa Valley;* trail maps available at headquarters; Erickson's *Recreational Map . . . South East Section.*

How to get there
From Highway 680 exit on Calaveras Road just south of the town of Sunol. After 5 miles on Calaveras, turn left on Geary Road and follow it to its end.

Features
Sunol is a semiwilderness park that contains an astonishing variety of magnificent scenery, including a rocky gorge called Little Yosemite. East Bay residents who have never been to Sunol (and surprisingly few have) are often overwhelmed when they first view its unspoiled grandeur. "I never knew there was anything like this in Alameda County!" is a common reaction.

Sunol also contains a great deal of wildlife. You probably won't be lucky enough to see the bobcats or cougars that reportedly inhabit the park, but you may see a golden eagle or a peregrine falcon, and you will almost certainly see and hear the flamboyant yellow-billed magpies that frequent the sycamore-shaded picnic areas along Alameda Creek.

Sunol has an extensive system of trails designed to suit all tastes, from an easy self-guiding nature trail to some peaks that offer fairly stiff climbs. These are described on the park handout. In 1978 the park inaugurated a group of backcountry backpacking camps, which are described below. These camps now constitute one of the stops on the Ohlone Wilderness Trail, described on pp. 173–74.

Facilities
Open for day use 8 A.M.–dusk; water, restrooms, picnic tables, grills, some wheelchair-accessible; group picnicking by reservation (531-9043); Old Green Barn visitor center open 9 A.M.–4 P.M. weekends and holidays; extensive nature-study programs.

Camping: Family and individual camping by reservation at park headquarters, at entrance kiosk or by phone (862-2244); group camping by reservation (531-9043). For information about the backpacking facilities, see below, Chapter 63.

Regulations

Small parking fee; small additional dog fee; dogs on leash and under control; *no alcoholic beverages at all,* not even beer or wine.

Camping: Moderate overnight fee per vehicle; stay limit 14 days; campers under age 18 must be accompanied by an adult 21 or older.

At times of extreme fire hazard the park may be closed.

62   To Little Yosemite

Distance   3½-mile round trip; longer if desired.
Grade   Easy.

Features

This narrow gorge where Alameda Creek rushes over huge boulders is one of the most spectacular sights in the park and is easy to walk to.

Description

If you come to Sunol on a weekend, you may want to start out by visiting the Old Green Barn, the center of the park's nature-interpretation program. In the fall of 1986 Pleasanton Readymix Concrete Company donated six cubic yards of cement to construct a new floor for the barn. The old floor, of wooden planks over dirt, was bringing nature a little *too* close: squirrels were tunneling under it, and at least once a rattlesnake made an appearance.

The most direct route to Little Yosemite is via the graveled road that runs from the picnic area across the creek. In fact, you can cut about a half mile from the route by parking in the picnic area and starting there. The road runs gently uphill, first through and then alongside the San Francisco Water Department's lush lands. Although these are off-limits to hikers, they effectively extend the wilderness viewshed of Sunol. (For a while the water department closed the road, but in 1987 the EBRPD reached an agreement with them to reopen the road to hikers.)

A more scenic route to Little Yosemite is via the Canyon View Trail. To reach it, cross Alameda Creek on the fancy footbridge installed in the fall of 1987 upstream from the headquarters building. This bridge replaces one farther downstream that was washed away in the storms of 1982. The beginning of the Canyon View Trail is part of the Ohlone Wilderness Trail and is marked by its distinctive red marker. As you walk along the north side of the creek under spreading oaks and sycamores, you may see and hear yellow-billed magpies. When the Indian Joe Creek Trail goes off to the left, stay on the Canyon View Trail, which gently ascends a grassy slope dotted with blue oaks and valley oaks. In spring this hillside is a carpet of wildflowers. The McCorkle and Ohlone trails go off to the left. The Canyon View Trail runs along the hillside overlooking the rugged gorge of Alameda Creek. You turn right on an old ranch road to descend to the graveled road and Little Yosemite. A path leads steeply down to the creek. Here you can sit on a boulder amid the rushing water and feel almost as far from urban turmoil as if you were at Big Yosemite.

Ambitious hikers may wish to return by climbing one of the trails out of Little Yosemite that lead over the hills to magnificent view spots, such as Cerro Este. Or they may wish to continue walking upstream to explore the backpacking area. Less ambitious hikers may want to take the graveled road back.

63 Backpacking in the backcountry

Distance Minimum 3½ miles one way.
Grade The first 2¾ miles are a moderate ascent along the fire road, but it takes a bit of climbing to reach the campsites.

Features

The backpacking camps in Sunol are now a major stop on the Ohlone Wilderness Trail, but actually they pre-date the opening of that trail by several years. They were constructed in 1978 by the park staff with California Conservation Corps and CETA youth workers, plus help from Scout troops and other volunteers. There are a half dozen campsites in various kinds of terrain, some suitable for only a family, others for a large group. Park headquarters issues handouts describing and mapping them. You may want to explore the area first on a day hike.

Note: *The backpack area may be closed during fire season, June through October.*

Facilities

Water, toilets near all the campsites.

Regulations

Permits and reservations are required (phone 862-2244); sites can be reserved up to 6 months in advance; children 18 or younger must be accompanied by an adult 21 or older. There is a small nightly fee. The park leaflet lists a number of other regulations; of these, the most important to know before starting out are:

Pets are prohibited;

Alcoholic beverages are prohibited;

Open fires are prohibited; bring a camp stove or food that needs no cooking.

Description

The Ohlone Wilderness Trail approaches the backpacking area via the Canyon View and McCorkle trails. This is a scenic route, but it involves a considerable climb. Lazy backpackers and day hikers can reach the camps by taking the graveled road to Little Yosemite and continuing upstream on the road along Alameda Creek. The creek becomes gentle and fairly level above the gorge. This is an idyllic spot, where cattle graze along the meandering stream and birds nest in the oaks and sycamores. You pass the "W" tree, so named for its unusual shape. The road ascends above the creek, looking across to the steep opposite slope.

A mile from Little Yosemite, turn left on the McCorkle Trail and begin to climb the oak-studded hill. The trail levels off in a meadow (which, incidentally, seems to be home to a vast population of ground squirrels). From here with the aid of your map of the backpacking area you can explore the trails leading to the various camps, or you can find the site reserved for you.

Hikes 64–76
The Peninsula

History

Much of the old Spanish heritage lingers on in these counties. The first overland explorer here was Gaspar de Portola, who in 1769 led an expedition up what is now substantially the route of Highway 1. A series of state historical plaques mark his party's camping spots. It was this group that first mentioned the *palos colorados*, or coast redwoods. On November 2 a deer-hunting party under Jose Ortega climbed to the top of Sweeney Ridge (east of where Pacifica now is) and looked down on San Francisco Bay. Not realizing the importance of this discovery, Portola, after a brief exploration, led his hungry, sick and weary men back to San Diego.

In 1775 Juan Bautista de Anza led a colonizing party from Sonora, Mexico, and in 1776 he chose the sites of San Francisco's Presidio and Mission Dolores. The next year saw the founding of Mission Santa Clara and the pueblo of San Jose de Guadalupe, California's first civilian settlement. During the succeeding decades until the secularization of the missions, ordered in 1833, the Franciscan fathers, supervising Indian neophytes, maintained a flourishing agriculture on the Peninsula and in the Santa Clara Valley. The missions were linked by El Camino Real, "The Royal Road." (One wonders what the padres would think of this highway in its present garish incarnation.)

As elsewhere in California, recipients of Mexican land grants took over mission lands after secularization; and as elsewhere, their ranchos became the subject of complicated and exhausting litigation after the Yankee conquest. Meanwhile the Peninsula's first major industry, lumbering, had begun to boom. The Spanish had used timber in building the Presidio, the missions and the pueblo of San Jose—but sparingly, because they came from a land where wood was scarce and other materials were favored for construction. In the 1830s, however, Englishmen and Americans, many of them runaway sailors, began settling in the redwoods as commercial sawyers. Oxen dragged the logs and timbers down to Redwood Slough, whence they were rafted up to San Francisco on the tides. A town

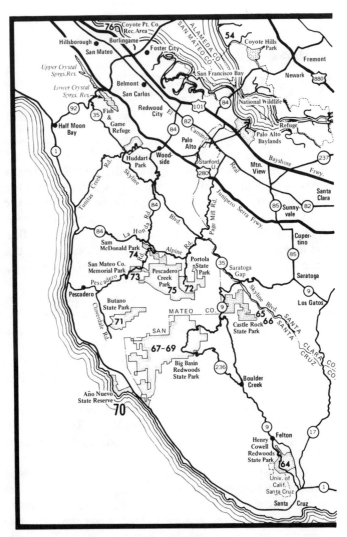

Peninsula

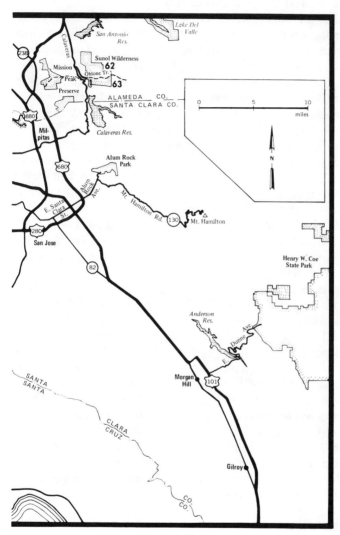

Driving Map

grew up along the slough, and in 1856 it officially became Redwood City and the seat of San Mateo County.

In 1864 the San Francisco and San Jose Railroad Company completed a line down the Peninsula, thereby ushering in an era of mansion building. Tycoons like William C. Ralston, Leland Stanford, James C. Flood and Darius Ogden Mills felt that the Peninsula's equable climate provided the ideal setting for lavish country estates. The San Francisco earthquake of 1906 stimulated a more middle-class invasion of the Peninsula, as refugees from the stricken City decided to resettle to the south. Thus began San Mateo County's career as the site of dozens of bedroom communities for commuters.

An even more explosive suburban growth took place in the Santa Clara Valley after World War II, as tract houses and asphalt rapidly covered over farms and orchards. In fact, this area has in recent years become in environmental circles an object lesson, or Horrible Example, of what *not* to do with prime agricultural land in a hungry world, and it has spurred residents of the Napa, Livermore and Petaluma valleys to take unprecedented measures to limit residential growth in their own bailiwicks.

Most recently, this area has attained worldwide fame as Silicon Valley, the birthplace of the High Tech Post-Industrial Revolution.

Meanwhile, isolated by the Santa Cruz Mountains, the coastside between Pacifica and Santa Cruz has so far remained relatively undeveloped. The major economic activities have been farming, notably of artichokes and pumpkins, and lumbering. During Prohibition the secluded coast lent itself to rumrunning. Highway 1 now runs down the coast near the route of the ill-fated Ocean Shore Railroad. Incorporated in 1905, the railroad ran tracks south from San Francisco to Tunitas and north from Santa Cruz to Swanton. The gap between Tunitas and Swanton was never closed, and passengers were carried between these points by Stanley Steamer. The railroad expired in 1920, done in by competition from autos and trucks, but some of its depots remain in various guises.

Organizations

Harold Gilliam describes the Santa Cruz mountain country as "one of the finest natural areas in any American metropolitan region." It is the site of California's oldest state park, and was the scene of the first concerted drive to "save the redwoods." These mountains inspire the same sort of fervent devotion among Peninsula dwellers that Mt. Tamalpais does among Marinites. Several organizations are dedicated to protecting them:

The Santa Cruz Mountain Trail Association
Box 1141, Los Altos 94023; 968-4509

Conducts hikes and organizes volunteers for trail building and litter clean-up.

The Santa Cruz Mountains Natural History Association
101 North Big Trees Park Road, Felton 95018; 408-335-3174

Promotes educational and interpretive activities in the state parks and publishes literature about the mountains.

The Sempervirens Fund
Drawer BE, Los Altos 94023; 968-4509

Raises money to buy land, plant trees and build trails in Big Basin and Castle Rock state parks.

The Trail Center
4898 El Camino Real, #205A, Los Altos 94022; 968-7065

Serves as a clearinghouse for information about Peninsula trails and trail activities. It also encourages volunteers to help public agencies build and maintain trails. The Trail Center has been assigned the leadership role in defining and constructing the South Bay section of the San Francisco Bay Area Ridge Trail, the proposed 350+-mile multi-use trail along the skyline of the Bay counties.

Several other groups are devoted to preserving the Peninsula's open space and promoting outdoor recreation in it. Among the more active are:

The Midpeninsula Regional Open Space District
Old Mill Office Center, Building C, Suite 135, 201 San Antonio
    Circle, Mountain View 94040; 949-5500

and, of course, the Audubon Society:

Santa Clara Valley Chapter
2253 Park Boulevard, Palo Alto 94306; 329-1811

and the Sierra Club:

Loma Prieta Chapter
2253 Park Boulevard, Palo Alto 94306: 327-8111

Hostels

Two lighthouses on Highway 1 along the San Mateo County coast have been turned into hostels ideally suited for bicyclists traveling the Bicentennial Route, as well as other visitors:

Montara Lighthouse Hostel
16th Street at Highway 1 (Box 737), Montara 94037; 728-7177

is 25 miles south of San Francisco, near Montara State Beach and Fitzgerald Marine Reserve.

Pigeon Point Lighthouse Hostel
Pigeon Point Road at Highway 1, Pescadero 94060; 879-0633

is 6 miles south of the Pescadero Road and about 6 miles from Butano State Park.

Both of the above hostels are near bus transit; for information, phone SamTrans at 761-7000.

Two other hostels are located in the foothills of the Santa Cruz Mountains:

Hidden Villa Hostel (closed June 1–August 31)
26870 Moody Road, Los Altos Hills 94022; 941-6407

Sanborn Park Hostel
15808 Sanborn Road, Saratoga 95070; 408-741-9555

All the above are under the administration of American Youth Hostels (phone 863-1444). The Hiker's Hut in Sam McDonald Park is administered by the Loma Prieta Chapter of the Sierra Club and is described below in the section on Four Parks in San Mateo County.

Public transit

For the past half century, and particularly since World War II, the Peninsula's development has been almost totally dictated by the private automobile. The region's rapid growth has led to traffic problems perhaps even more vexing than those in the rest of the Bay Area, complicated by the fact that the Peninsula's main transit link to San Francisco was traditionally the Southern Pacific Railroad. The SP—the once-mighty "Octopus" of Frank Norris's 1901 novel—now fallen upon hard times, lost money for years on its Peninsula commute service, and in 1980 fobbed it off to the state Department of Transportation, Caltrans. The resulting CalTrain gets about half its funding from the counties of Santa Clara, San Mateo and San Francisco. Highway-oriented Caltrans would like to turn CalTrain over entirely to the three counties—which object strenuously to taking full responsibility for the money-losing service.

One of CalTrain's problems is that its San Francisco terminus is the old SP yard at Fourth and Townsend streets, one mile from downtown. Vociferous CalTrain partisans want to extend its route to the Transbay Terminal at First and Mission. Meanwhile, an equally ardent group of BART fans wants to extend BART down the Peninsula, even though San Mateo County chose to stay out of BART in 1961, when it was formed. In November 1987 San Mateo County voters approved a proposition to extend BART to Millbrae. This move infuriated some residents of the East Bay who have been paying taxes for BART since 1962 but have not yet received its service to their communities.

Meanwhile . . . Santa Clara County in December 1987 opened the first 6 miles of a projected 20-mile-long light-rail system. In addition to the cost overruns and schedule delays that inevitably seem to accompany any public-transit project these days, this one was plagued by allegations of bribery and embezzlement against one of the major contractors. Furthermore, it suffered an embarrassing public-relations gaffe: the supervisors who had originally announced that the system would be called by the acronym SCAT (for Santa Clara County Area Transit) hurriedly withdrew that nickname when one of the word's dictionary definitions was pointed out to them.

Here follows a brief summary of intercity transit systems:

BART runs from the East Bay and San Francisco to Daly City. Phone 788-BART; San Bruno area, 873-BART.

CalTrain runs daily between San Francisco and San Jose. Phone 557-8661 or 800-558-8661.

Greyhound buses run daily from San Francisco to San Jose and to Santa Cruz. In San Francisco, phone 433-1500; elsewhere, look in the white pages.

Peerless Stages buses run daily from Oakland to San Jose and Santa Cruz. In Oakland, phone 444-2900; elsewhere, look in the white pages.

SamTrans (San Mateo County Transit District) provides bus service within the county and connects with AC Transit, BART, Golden Gate Transit, Greyhound, Southern Pacific and the airport. In San Francisco, phone 761-7000; elsewhere, look in the white pages.

Santa Clara County Transit buses run daily to various points in Santa Clara and Alameda counties. From the San Jose area, phone 408-287-4210; the Palo Alto area, 415-965-3100; South County, 408-683-4151. For information aboout its light-rail system, phone 408-287-4210.

Santa Cruz Metropolitan Transit District runs buses to some of the parks in that county. Phone 408-425-8600 or 408-688-8600.

Recommended reading

Jackson, Ruth A., *Combing the Coast: San Francisco to Santa Cruz*. San Francisco: Chronicle Books, 1985.

Rusmore, Jean, and Frances Spangle, *Peninsula Trails*. 2nd ed. Berkeley: Wilderness Press, 1989.

———, *South Bay Trails*. Berkeley: Wilderness Press, 1984. Because my colleagues Rusmore and Spangle have covered this area so thoroughly, I have omitted from this book the following parks which have appeared in previous editions but which they have described:

> Alum Rock
> Henry W. Coe
> Coyote Hills
> Huddart
> Mission Peak
> Palo Alto Baylands
> San Bruno Mountain
> San Francisco Bay National Wildlife Refuge

Taber, Tom, *The Expanded Santa Cruz Mountains Trail Book*. 5th ed. San Mateo: Oak Valley Press, 1988.

64   Henry Cowell Redwoods State Park

Mailing address and phone

Box 53, Felton 95018; 408-335-4598

Maps

Topo *Felton;* trail maps available at headquarters for a small price.

How to get there

By bus   Santa Cruz Transit #35 runs to Felton; from here it's about a 3-mile hike to the campground.

By car   Take Highway 9 to Felton. The park's picnic area is just south of town, on the east side of the road. To reach the camp-ground, take Mt. Hermon Road east from central Felton, and imme-diately bear right on Graham Hill Road; the entrance is about 2 miles along it.

The Rincon trailhead parking lot is located on Highway 9 south of the main entrance to the park. The Rincon Trail descends to the San Lorenzo River, fords it and ascends steeply to the Cathedral Redwoods. (This approach may be difficult if not impossible during the wet season.)

The Fall Creek unit of the park, undeveloped except for hiking trails, is reached from the Felton-Empire Road, northwest of the main entrance.

Features

This beautiful park of just over 4000 acres combines a picnic area near a magnificent redwood forest with a campground situated in an unusual stand of ponderosa pines—trees more commonly found in the Sierra foothills. Henry Cowell was a 49er from Massachusetts who struck it rich at Santa Cruz in the limestone business and became a substantial landowner. The Cowells might have been expected to become one of California's great dynasties, but as it turned out none of Henry's five children had any offspring. Paradoxically enough, this situation led to the name of Cowell becoming familiar to generations of college students in California, as the family's funds helped establish health centers at UC Berkeley, UC Davis, UC Santa Cruz, Stanford, Santa Clara and the University of the Pacific. The UC Santa Cruz campus is situated on what was once the principal Cowell ranch. Henry Cowell Redwoods State Park is yet another legacy of the Cowell family to the people of California.

Facilities

Extensive group and individual picnic areas, accessible by wheelchair; 113 campsites; coffee shop; gift shop; interpretive center with audio tour; nature trail; "fitness trail" near picnic area. The San Lorenzo River, which flows through the park, provides opportuni-

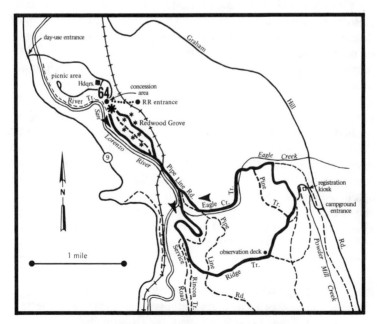

Henry Cowell Redwoods State Park

ties for swimming in summer, and fishing for steelhead and silver
salmon from mid-November through February.

Regulations

The usual for state parks.

A Redwood Grove-Campground loop

Distance   4-mile loop.
Grade   Moderate; a steady climb of about 500′ from the river to
the observation tower.

Features

The attractive campground is located in a sunny area of chaparral
and ponderosa pine that differs markedly from the lush, shady
redwood forest near the picnic area. This easy loop will give visitors
to the always-popular Redwood Grove some idea of the variety of
landscape to be found higher in the park. Campers, of course, can
take the hike in reverse.

Description

This hike begins at the Redwood Grove near the coffee shop. You
can pick up a guide to the nature trail for a small fee from the interpretive center near the trailhead, and head south. The southernmost
station on the trail, #13, is a hollow tree in which explorer John C.
Fremont allegedly took shelter for a rainy night or two in 1846.
According to Hoover and Rensch in *Historic Spots in California,*
when Fremont returned to the area later as a famous general and was
asked about the legend, he responded enigmatically, "It is a good
story; let it stand."

Just past this tree, leave the nature trail, bear slightly right to hit
the Pipe Line Road, and continue south on it under the Southern
Pacific trestle. At a Y, where a sign bears the "no horses" symbol,
bear right on the River Trail while the Pipe Line Road continues
uphill. Almost immediately you arrive at a picnic table located
above the confluence of Eagle Creek and the San Lorenzo River.
This is one of the more desirable picnic spots in northern California,
and if you happen to find it unoccupied (I never have), you may just
want to spend the day there. Otherwise, follow the trail across Eagle
Creek on a footbridge and begin switchbacking up the side of the
steep river gorge forested with redwoods and tanbark oaks. (An
alternate trail makes a shortcut uphill here and leads to a connection
between the Pipe Line Road and the Rincon Service Road.)
Continuing uphill, you reach the well-signed junction of the Rincon

Service Road and the Ridge Trail. It is possible to take a half-mile side trip here to the Cathedral Redwoods—an especially grand and somber grove—via the road or the Rincon Trail, which runs slightly above it.

Continue on the Ridge Trail, following signs toward the campground. The trail soon crosses the Pipe Line Road and becomes noticeably sandy. The vegetation changes rather abruptly, as the redwoods are replaced by live oak, Douglas fir, some chinquapin and lots of knobcone pines. As you continue to climb, ponderosa pines become prominent, standing out from the knobcones because of their much greater size.

After climbing—not too steeply—for ½ mile from the Pipe Line Road, you arrive at a tall, sturdy observation tower (water), from which you can look out over Monterey Bay. The two towers visible on clear days in the distance to the southeast are part of PG&E's Moss Landing power plant.

It was near this observation tower that the Trailside Killer of the early 1980s approached Ellen Hansen and Steve Haertle, two college students hiking along the Ridge Trail, drew his gun and ordered them into the bushes. They refused, and Hansen said, "Don't listen to him, Steve, because he's going to shoot us anyway." He did shoot them, and killed Hansen, but the wounded Haertle managed to escape. His subsequent description of the killer helped lead to a suspect's arrest, trial and conviction for two murders.

From the observation tower the Pine Trail leads north and detours around the campground to run into the Eagle Creek Trail heading back to the Redwood Grove. If instead you decide to visit the campground—which makes a good lunch spot—you can find it by following the trail where a sign carries the "no horses" symbol. From the campground you can pick up the Eagle Creek Trail from site 62 or between 82 and 84.

As the Eagle Creek Trail descends into the redwood forest, the vegetation changes just as abruptly as it did on the way up: the chaparral and pines give way to tanoak, hazel, azalea, oxalis, wild ginger and redwood violet. The Eagle Creek Trail runs into the Pipe Line Road, and from this junction you can return to the trailhead via the road or by crossing it, taking the River Trail 0.2 mile to the confluence picnic table and retracing your steps to the nature-trail loop.

Nearby attractions

Adjoining the park's picnic area are two historic railroads that make Felton a mecca for train buffs:

The Roaring Camp & Big Trees Railroad conducts a 5-mile loop trip through the redwoods on a narrow-gauge steam train. The railroad is currently running daily; special "moonlight train parties" take place on summer Saturday evenings. The R.C. & B.T. also operates a chuck-wagon barbecue. For schedules, rates and reservations, phone 408-335-4400 or 408-335-4484. The sound of the locomotive's whistle makes a charming accompaniment to hikes in the state park.

The Santa Cruz, Big Trees & Pacific Railway Company is the revival of a line that operated from 1875 until 1941, most of that time under Southern Pacific ownership. During its heyday it carried thousands of picnickers to the beach, plus such notables as John C. Fremont, Teddy Roosevelt and John D. Rockefeller. In 1985 the train resumed service between Roaring Camp and Santa Cruz. Its extraordinarily scenic route runs through the redwoods and along the San Lorenzo River gorge. For schedules, rates and reservations, phone 408-335-4400 or 408-335-4484.

65   The Skyline to the Sea Trail

Address and phone

c/o Big Basin Redwoods State Park, 21600 Big Basin Way, Boulder Creek 95006; 408-338-6132

Maps

Topos *Año Nuevo, Big Basin, Castle Rock Ridge, Cupertino, Davenport, Franklin Point* and *Mindego Hill.* The Santa Cruz Mountains Natural History Association has produced two maps covering the whole trail that are indispensable for hikers and equestrians. They are available for $1 each at state parks in the Santa Cruz Mountains or from 101 North Big Trees Road, Felton 95018.

How to get there

By bus   Santa Cruz Metropolitan Transit #37 runs to Big Basin park headquarters and #40 runs to Waddell Creek parking lot at the "sea" end of the trail. Because these buses run infrequently, it is necessary to have up-to-date schedules; phone the transit district at 408-425-8600 or 408-688-8600.

By car   The trail begins at Castle Rock State Park (see next chapter), where overnight parking is available. For overnight parking in Big Basin State Park, check with a ranger.

The "sea" end is at Waddell Beach, 15 miles north of Santa Cruz.

Features

As its name suggests, the Skyline to the Sea Trail runs mainly downhill and offers plenty of scenery: vistas over the heavily forested Santa Cruz Mountains and watershed valleys, all the way to the ocean sparkling in the distance. The trail runs through the redwoods of Big Basin and ends by following Waddell Creek to its mouth at the beach.

This trail is a monument to the hardworking members of the Sempervirens Fund and the Santa Cruz Mountain Trail Association. During one weekend in 1969 they organized more than 2500 volunteers to clear 25 miles of trail within and between Castle Rock and Big Basin state parks. Since then the clubs have acquired more land, cleared more trails and built camping facilities. The Skyline to the Sea Trail now runs 37 miles and includes a number of camps spaced at convenient intervals for backpackers of all ages and every condition. An average of 20,000 people a year use the trail for hiking, walking, jogging, marathons, and, on some parts, mountain bicycling and horseback riding.

This trail offers Bay Areans a wonderful opportunity for a leisurely outing over a long weekend in a beautiful and varied landscape, without having to face seven or eight hours of driving to a trailhead and back. And now you can even get there on the bus! Non-backpackers can sample the trail by making a day loop in Castle Rock or Big Basin park. An even easier outing is to walk or bicycle from the "sea" end to one of the trail camps for lunch. A fairly level road leads through the Rancho del Oso section of Big Basin Park for a mile to Alder Camp and another ¼ mile to Twin Redwoods Camp, both situated along Waddell Creek.

Facilities

Toilets in all the camps; water at most, but check in advance.

Regulations

Castle Rock trail camp is on a first-come, first-served basis; all the others require advance reservations, obtainable from Big Basin park headquarters at the above address or phone number, from eight weeks in advance up to the arrival date. Small camping fee per person per night. No dogs, no open fires, no firearms.

Description

Rather than attempt to describe here all of this 37-mile trail and its many additional miles of connecting trails, I urge readers to obtain the two inexpensive maps mentioned above, which are highly informative and just about essential for hiking in this area.

66 Castle Rock State Park

Address and phone

15000 Skyline Boulevard, Los Gatos 95030; 408-867-2952

Maps

Topo *Castle Rock Ridge; Skyline to the Sea Trail Map #1* (see preceding chapter); leaflet with map available at trailhead for small donation.

How to get there

From Saratoga Gap, at the junction of Highway 9 and Highway 35 (Skyline Boulevard), drive south on 35 for 2½ miles to the parking lot on the right.

Features

This hike is one of the most spectacular in the Bay Area, encompassing oak-madrone woodlands, fantastic sandstone formations, a view straight down a waterfall, and panoramic vistas across hill and forest to Monterey Bay and the ocean. The route passes near two favorite haunts of Bay Area rock climbers, where aspiring mountaineers can practice. At the same time, people who are nervous about heights can get the *illusion* of mountaineering, without the anxiety, by following (in Vibram-soled boots, of course) the well-designed trail along the face of Varian Peak.

Castle Rock Park is well worth the drive from the City, especially along scenic Skyline Boulevard on a relatively smogless day. It also provides a chance for an easy overnight backpacking trip; or it can serve as the first stop on a longer backpacking trip, since it contains the first segment of the Skyline to the Sea Trail.

Facilities

Near the trailhead, a toilet; at the camp, 2½ miles from the parking area, water, restrooms, picnic tables, shelters and primitive campsites available on a first-come, first-served basis; Danny Hanavan Nature Trail near camp. As this book goes to press, park headquarters is still located at the camp, but it is due to be relocated near Skyline Boulevard.

Regulations

No dogs, horses, motorcycles, smoking, mountain bikes, fires or firearms on the trails; parking area closed from sunset to 6 A.M.; small camping fee per person per night.

A hike to the campground and back

Distance 5½-mile loop.
Grade Moderate verging on strenuous; boots strongly recommended.

Description

The trail to the campground starts at the west side of the parking lot. This part of the Skyline to the Sea Trail has been rechristened the Saratoga Gap Trail. You can take a 0.3-mile side trip to Castle Rock beginning a few hundred feet from the trailhead. The rock—an 80-foot-high, oddly eroded sandstone formation—is worth the visit. Rock fanciers may note also the fantastic sandstone boulders on the right-hand side of the main trail near the trailhead.

The Saratoga Gap Trail gently descends under oaks and firs along the shady bank of a creek—which may be reduced to a trickle by the end of the dry season. Continue descending and soon cross the creek on a footbridge. At a little cascade over a jumble of boulders you pass the trail leading to Goat Rock, another favorite of rock climbers, which you can visit on the return trip.

At 0.8 mile from the trailhead you reach Castle Rock Falls. Here a wooden observation platform allows you to look down the

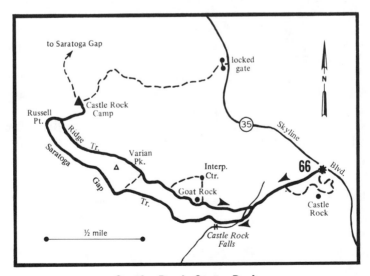

Castle Rock State Park

hundred-foot waterfall of Kings Creek and out through a canyon over the San Lorenzo River watershed to the ocean.

The trail continues along the steep, wooded hillside, passing a couple of little springs and going through some bouldery spots. In ½ mile you emerge from the trees into chaparral and can enjoy a superb view over the hills to Monterey Bay. As you continue on the trail, chaparral alternates with madrone- and oak-forested canyons. The connection with the Ridge Trail comes in at a sign.

Your trail begins gradually descending along the face of Varian Peak. This landmark was named (after the topo was printed) for the late Russell Varian, physicist and inventor, who was largely responsible for preserving the Castle Rock area for the public. As you make your way along the steep cliff, marveling at the panorama of ridges, valleys and sea, a cable railing provides a reassuring handhold for the acrophobic.

The Russell Point Overlook is a possible lunch spot, but the trail camp 0.3 mile to the east offers more facilities, including water, and presents a change of scenery. About halfway between Russell Point and the campground a sign indicates the Ridge Trail running southeast. After lunch you can return to this trail for the return journey.

The Ridge Trail ascends through bay trees, madrones and some magnificent live oaks and black oaks. A variety of pitted and hollowed boulders add a picturesque touch. About a mile from the campground, in a glade studded with black oaks, is the Emily Smith Bird Observation Point. (Miss Smith was a professor of ornithology at San Jose State College and a founder of the Santa Clara Valley Audubon Society.)

A trail loops left to the Interpretive Exhibit, dedicated in 1985. It was designed by Gordon Ashby, renowned for his work on many of the Bay Area's outstanding museums. The loop trail returns past Goat Rock, that other climbing favorite, and rejoins the Ridge Trail, which itself rejoins the Saratoga Gap Trail at a huge Douglas fir.

Big Basin Redwoods State Park

Address and phone

21600 Big Basin Way, Big Basin 95006; 408-338-6132

Maps

Topos *Año Nuevo, Big Basin, Davenport* and *Franklin Point;* trail map available at headquarters for a small price. Also available at headquarters are the *Skyline to the Sea Trail Maps #1* and *#2* and *Short Historic Tours in Big Basin Redwoods State Park.* These helpful guides are well worth their modest prices.

How to get there

By bus   Santa Cruz Metropolitan Transit #37 runs—currently two times per day—to park headquarters; #40 runs to Waddell Beach and the Rancho del Oso trailhead at the southwestern end of the park. Thus you can plan a one-way hike or backpack of 10½ or more miles from one bus stop to the other. For schedules, phone 408-425-8600 or 408-688-8600.

By car   From Saratoga Gap, at the junction of Highway 9 and Highway 35 (Skyline Boulevard), proceed downhill on 9 for 6 miles to Waterman Gap. From here, ordinary cars can branch off on Highway 236 to reach park headquarters in 8 miles. This narrow, winding road is not advisable for large campers or trailers: they should follow Highway 9 to Boulder Creek and take the lower end of 236 into the park.

The parking lot for Waddell Beach and Rancho del Oso is on Highway 1, 15 miles north of Santa Cruz and just south of the San Mateo County line. (However, backpackers should not park overnight at Waddell Beach but should arrange for parking with the Rancho del Oso ranger.)

Features

Big Basin is the oldest of California's state parks, one of the largest (over 15,000 acres) and one of the most popular. Its ancient groves of towering redwoods and its sparkling waterfalls tucked away in fern-bordered niches and canyons attract visitors all year round.

History

Indians camped in the coastal areas near the present park, but they probably avoided the dense redwood forest of the basin—not only because of their religious beliefs but also because grizzly bears were numerous there. Spanish explorers on their way up the coast skirted the area and marveled at the trees. However, the Spaniards never undertook lumbering operations in Big Basin. The first commercial lumberman in the area was a pioneer from Kentucky, William W. Waddell, who in 1862 built a sawmill and established his home near the confluence of the east and west forks of the creek that still bears his name. Waddell also built a wharf near Año Nuevo Point for shipping his lumber. His flourishing business foundered after he was fatally mauled by a grizzly in 1875.

After Waddell's death, other settlers filtered into the area and staked their claims to timberland. The big trees might have been logged off early in the 20th century except for the determination of one man, artist Andrew P. Hill, who started a movement to save redwoods even before William Kent bought the land that is now Muir Woods. In 1899 Hill was trying to photograph some redwood trees for a London newspaper when an irate property owner ordered him off. This contretemps stimulated Hill to gather a group of prominent citizens together to preserve at least some of the forest for the public. In May 1900 they camped in the Big Basin redwoods and met at Slippery Rock to form the Sempervirens Club, devoted to urging the state to purchase and save this area. Their intense politicking was rewarded in 1902 when the legislature established what was then called California Redwood Park.

The park was not yet out of the woods, however. In 1904 a disastrous fire burned over much of it, sparing only the headquarters area. A few years later the park was exploited in a secret collusion between corrupt state officials and a lumber company. The era of graft came to an end in 1910, when reformer Hiram Johnson became governor. The park, which was renamed Big Basin in 1927, went on to become immensely popular. During the '20s it was much more urbanized than it is now: it contained an inn, a dance floor, tennis courts, a swimming pool, boating facilities and a drive-in tree!

During the Great Depression of the 1930s a Civilian Conservation Corps group was stationed at Big Basin to do maintenance work and construct trails, campgrounds and buildings. The present headquarters building and nature lodge are among the CCC's legacies to the park.

Even as early as 1929, planners had begun to worry about the adverse effects of too many people arriving at the park by automobile. In the 1940s the State Park System began phasing out some of the non-natural tourist attractions.

The Sempervirens Club was reincarnated in 1968 as the Sempervirens Fund, dedicated to acquiring land for Big Basin and Castle Rock parks. Thanks largely to their diligent efforts, Big Basin was able in 1978 to obtain the historic land of Rancho del Oso—Ranch of the (Grizzly) Bear—running south along Waddell Creek to the beach. This acquisition allowed the Skyline to the Sea Trail to be completed and trail camps to be built along the creek. The trail now ends at the spot where the Portola expedition camped for three days on the way up the coast in October 1769.

Both the snows of 1973–74 and the storms of 1982 and 1983 damaged the steep-sided, heavily wooded basin. In January of 1983 a giant tree that came crashing down near the campfire center partly destroyed the old Redwood Inn and a ranger's residence. Fortunately the ranger was elsewhere at the time. As so often in the past, the Santa Cruz Mountains' protective, dedicated volunteers sprang into action to help the park staff clear trails and repair campsites.

Activities for hikers and campers

The park maintains a museum of history and natural history where you can study the geology, flora and fauna of the region. The rangers conduct extensive interpretive programs during summer. There are enough hiking opportunities in and around Big Basin to keep anyone busy for at least a week's vacation. As befits such a popular, crowded park, all the trails near headquarters are well maintained and well signed. The maps described above contain suggestions for outings of all kinds, plus a lot of other useful information.

Most newcomers to the park, especially families with small children, will want to start with the easy, self-guiding Redwood Loop Trail near headquarters. At the beginning of the trail is a mysterious-looking Time Capsule which was placed here in 1978 to celebrate the 50th anniversary of the State Park System. Various persons and organizations deposited items in the capsule, and in 2028, when it is opened, we will find out what they are!

Facilities

158 picnic sites, 188 campsites (including one for the disabled), 5 group campsites; reservations necessary for group camping and desirable for individual camping during summer and weekends. During summer, nature programs, snack bar, grocery store and gas station. (One of my companions, gazing around at the campfire circle, christened this place "the poor man's Bohemian Grove"!)

At Rancho del Oso: Nature and History Center open weekends; phone 408-427-2288.

Regulations

The usual for state parks. Campsites along the Skyline to the Sea Trail must be reserved in advance from park headquarters; small fee per person per night.

Recommended reading

Cooney-Lazaneo, Mary Beth, and Kathleen Lyons, *Plants of Big Basin Redwoods State Park and the North Coastal Mountains of Northern California.* Missoula: Mountain Press, 1981. The excellent photos by Howard King make this guide helpful for the whole northern California coastal region.

67 The Creeping Forest Trail

Distance   2½ mile loop.
Grade   Easy.

Features

The first time I set off on this trail, I found myself inadvertently accompanying some children who had picked it because they thought the sign said "Creepy Forest." They were not disappointed. Any redwood forest can be a bit scary, especially in the late afternoon of a cloudy day. This one, full of oddly slanted trees and dense undergrowth, suggests all sorts of possibilities to confirmed watchers of the late-night TV movie: it seems a logical place for bandits, Bigfoot or extraterrestrial visitors to hang out. Furthermore, the fact that it connects with the Dool Trail may subliminally suggest the word *ghoul*. Actually that trail is named for William H. Dool, the popular warden of the park from 1911 to 1928, who originated campfire programs here. And there is a natural explanation for the Creeping Forest: it results from a 1952 landslide that pushed the trees off perpendicular.

This trail is still a good one for introducing children to the redwoods. More ambitious hikers can continue on Middle Ridge Fire Road, described in *Short Historic Tours* (see "Maps" above).

Description

From headquarters, go west past the campfire circle and cross Opal Creek to reach the Skyline to the Sea Trail, amply signed. Turn right on it and walk along the west bank of Opal Creek. You will pass the Dool and Sunset trails branching left. Continue along the west bank of the creek, crossing the Gazos Creek Road and traversing the picnic area, to a sign indicating the start of the Creeping Forest Trail.

The trail ascends through thick huckleberry, under redwoods. After a half mile it nears the Gazos Creek Road and continues through a multitude of young Douglas firs, older firs and redwoods. At one point it goes through the roots of a giant fallen tree and along its trunk. Some groves along the trail are specially named: the Sempervirens Fund makes it possible to dedicate a tree or a grove to a person, family, organization or event.

When the trail approaches the Gazos Creek Road again, you can continue west on either the road or a parallel trail. Both routes soon arrive at the Dool Trail, which will return you to headquarters in less than a mile.

68 The ascent of Pine Mountain

Distance 5–6-mile round trip.
Grade Moderately strenuous; an ascent of 1000'; rocky sections make boots desirable.

Features

In 1982 Big Basin celebrated its 80th birthday by acquiring—with the aid of the Sempervirens Fund—a parcel of land that included a section of the Pine Mountain Trail. Hikers had actually been climbing up Pine Mountain for years, but part of their route went through privately owned land.

The climb to the summit goes through several diverse plant communities and provides splendid views.

Facilities

No water or restrooms on much of the route.

Description

From headquarters, go west past the campfire center and cross Opal Creek to reach the Skyline to the Sea Trail. Turn left on it to walk along the creek through redwoods, tanbark oaks, huckleberries and azaleas. You will pass the trail branching right that leads to the Middle Ridge Road. Continuing along the west bank of Opal Creek past a waterfall, you soon come to the Hihn-Hammond Road. Turn left on it to cross Opal Creek, immediately turn right to cross Blooms Creek, and head southeast on the East Ridge Trail to its junction with the Pine Mountain Trail. (This sounds complicated, but the trails are so abundantly signed that hikers will have no problems.)

As the trail ascends, joining Pine Mountain Road for a few yards, there are fewer redwoods and more tanbark oaks. Soon these trees give way to Douglas firs, knobcone pines and madrones. As you continue to climb, manzanita, ceanothus, chamise, chinquapin and other chaparral plants become prevalent.

After hiking for 2½ miles you reach a trail going left, at an acute angle, to Buzzards Roost, a craggy, weathered sandstone formation. You can continue ½ mile to the summit of Pine Mountain if you like, but you won't get much from the trip except perhaps a righteous feeling of accomplishment, because a dense stand of spindly knobcone pines on the summit obliterates the view. A forest fire swept over Pine Mountain during the Labor Day weekend of 1948 and destroyed 20,000 acres of brush and timber. The heat of a fire, however, causes the closed cones of the knobcone pine to open and its seedlings to disperse, thus ensuring the survival of the species.

To look out over the countryside, climb instead to the top of Buzzards Roost. To the south and west is the Pacific, except where Pine Mountain obscures the view. Also to the west is Chalk Mountain Lookout. To the north you look out over the Big Basin forest. To the northeast is the ridge running southeast from Saratoga Gap. Due east, not far away, is Eagle Peak Lookout. To the south are Lockheed's white domes.

You can add a little variety to your return trip by making a scenic detour along Blooms Creek.

69   Some longer trails

Three trails running west from headquarters offer the strong hiker or leisurely backpacker an opportunity to make a daylong loop trip or to hike or backpack 10+ miles to Waddell Beach:

The Sunset Trail and the former Berry Creek Falls Trail, which is now a segment of the Skyline to the Sea Trail, have long formed a favorite 10-mile loop route up and down through lush forest and across creeks to spectacular waterfalls.

A newer trail is the one named for Howard King. Photographer King, who has attained virtually the status of a legend in Big Basin within his lifetime, began hiking in the park more than two decades ago, when he was a technician at Hewlett-Packard. Since his retirement in 1971 he has devoted his full time to volunteer work in the park. He laid out the trail named for him as a scenic and more pleasant alternative to the Hihn-Hammond Road. Youth Conservation Corps workers and Sempervirens Fund volunteers helped him build it.

70 Año Nuevo State Reserve

Address and phone

New Years Creek Road, Pescadero 94060; 879-0595

Map

Topo *Año Nuevo;* trail map available at Visitor Center.

How to get there

By bus SamTrans runs the Elephant Seal Special from San Mateo to Año Nuevo and back during winter months. Reservations are necessary: phone 348-SEAL or write SamTrans, 400 South El Camino, San Mateo 94402.

Santa Cruz Metropolitan Transit District #40 runs to Año Nuevo, currently 5 times a day. For schedules phone 408-425-8600 or 408-688-8600.

By car On Highway 1 drive 7 miles south of Pigeon Point and turn west on New Years Creek Road to reach the parking lot.

Features

Año Nuevo Point was frequented by Costanoan Indians, as evidenced by the shell mounds that archeologists have discovered under its sand dunes. Explorer Sebastian Vizcaino named it: as he sailed north up the coast in January 1603, this was the first headland he sighted. From 1890 to 1948 the U.S. government maintained a lighthouse on Año Nuevo Island, ½ mile from the point. Nevertheless, the area was the scene of several shipwrecks. If you visit here on a foggy day, you will readily understand why.

The state established a wildlife reserve here, but few people visited it until the 1970s, when word spread that elephant seals were coming to the island each year in ever-increasing numbers. These animals had been slaughtered by the hundreds of thousands during the 19th century, and by 1892 they were nearly extinct. When the Mexican government in 1922, and later the U.S. government, put the species under protection, the seals began to make a comeback. They were first sighted again on Año Nuevo Island in 1955, and first began breeding here again in 1961. They are slowly extending their range northward: in the 1970s a small breeding colony reached the Farallones and in the early 1980s one reached Drakes Estero in Point Reyes National Seashore.

The huge, grotesque-looking males arrive on the island in December and begin battling to see who will end up with harems of females; the losers retreat to the mainland beach. The females arrive on the island in January, give birth to young conceived the previous year, and mate with the dominant males. The adults leave Año Nuevo in March, and the pups in April. They return during the summer to molt: females and juveniles from April to May, sub-adult males from June to July, and adult males from August to September.

When the return of the seals became publicized, hundreds of people began visiting Año Nuevo every weekend during the breeding season, and some of them treated the two-ton bulls with alarming disrespect. Consequently, the rangers limited the number of visitors allowed at any one time and set up guided tours to the beach. Even more crowds arrived in early 1975 when the papers reported that a female, for the first time in recent history, had swum to Loser's Beach to give birth to a pup and subsequently mate with an erstwhile loser.

The oceanic storms of January 1983 were devastating to the island seal rookery. Huge waves flooded the nurseries, carrying pups out to sea or separating them from their mothers. Burney J. Le Boeuf and Richard S. Condit, writing in the California Academy of Science's *Pacific Discovery* of July–September 1983, called this "the greatest tragedy to befall these animals since their near extermination by commercial hunters in the last century," and estimated that pup mortality on the island was as high at 70 per cent. Although the mainland beach was also buffeted by the waves, the seal colony was less crowded there, and many of the mothers were able to move inland with their pups, so that the pup mortality rate was only slightly higher than usual. Le Boeuf and Condit expect that the mainland colony will become larger than the more vulnerable island colony.

Nowadays if you come to Año Nuevo from December through April you should have an advance reservation for the escorted tour of the beach where the elephant seals are in residence. At other times, however, you may obtain a permit from the Visitor Center to wander over one of the most beautiful spots on the San Mateo coast, and you may see and hear other species of seals and sea lions.

Facilities
Water, restrooms, picnic tables, phone near parking lot. Visitor Center with bookstore and museum open daily 9:15 A.M.–5 P.M.. Wheelchair-accessible trail and guided walks for the disabled; phone 879-0454.

Regulations

During elephant-seal breeding season (December through April) admission to the reserve is possible only by previous reservation through Ticketron or by one of the bus tours mentioned above. Small parking fee; moderate fee for elephant-seal tour; no dogs, horses, motor vehicles, fires or firearms.

Description

If you arrive during the breeding season, you will of necessity take one of the scheduled, guided tours of the reserve. These well-organized walks are led by rangers and enthusiastic students from UC Santa Cruz. The tour takes about 2½ hours and covers about 3 miles. Under the leader's guidance, you may approach the bulls surprisingly closely.

At other times of the year, you can walk along the beaches or through the sand dunes after getting a permit from the Visitor Center. The area is often foggy or windy. Walking toward the island is a spooky experience when seals and sea lions are honking and barking noisily from it but it's completely hidden in fog.

If the weather is fairly clear, you'll be able to see the island and its abandoned lighthouse, plus (with binoculars) whatever pinnipeds are sporting on it. These may include tawny brown Steller's sea lions, dark brown California sea lions and smaller, mottled harbor seals. (Don't even think of going to the island. It's not only illegal but extremely dangerous.)

On the trip back you can explore sand dunes or sheltered beaches that you missed on the way out. You may see cormorants perching on the rugged offshore sea stacks. The backdrop to the changing vistas is the range of blue-green mountains rising steeply on the east.

Recommended reading

Le Boeuf, Burney J., and Stephanie Kaza, eds. *The Natural History of Año Nuevo*. Pacific Grove: Boxwood Press, 1981.

Butano State Park

Mailing address and phone

Box 9, Pescadero 94060; 879-0173

Maps

Topo *Franklin Point;* trail map available from park contact station for a small price, and one posted near the restrooms in the campground.

How to get there

From Highway 1 southbound, go 2½ miles east on Pescadero Road and 4½ miles south on Cloverdale Road to Butano State Park Road. From Highway 1 northbound, go north on Gazos Creek Road and bear left on Cloverdale Road; total distance to the park on these roads is about 5 miles.

The road to the campground is not suitable for large trailers.

Features

Most of this park, including the campground, is densely forested with redwood and Douglas fir. The narrow canyon of Little Butano Creek, which runs through the park, supports a virtual rainforest of lush ferns, shrubs and trees. The shady, secluded campground provides a welcome refuge to the frazzled city-dweller seeking solitude in nature.

Incidentally, although the name "Butano" sounds Spanish, it is probably of Indian origin; according to Gudde, it may refer to a drinking cup made of an animal horn. The accent is on the first syllable.

Facilities

35 campsites reservable through Mistix, of which 14 require a short pack-in; nature programs in summer. Butano Trail Camp, near the upper reaches of Little Butano Canyon, can be reached by hiking in about 5 miles, with an elevation gain of 1400'; campsites must be reserved in advance by phoning or writing the park.

Regulations

The usual for state parks. To maintain a quiet atmosphere, no areas for organized games are provided.

A hike around the Campground

Distance 5-mile loop.
Grade Moderate.

Features

This route provides an introduction to the park, and the ascent of about 800′ is more gradual than the steep descent from the Año Nuevo lookout to the contact station.

Facilities

No water or restrooms on most of the route.

Description

From a locked gate at the east end of the campground, take a fire road, which ascends gently through redwood forest. Pass an unmarked, unmapped road going back to camp at an acute angle on the right. In a short half mile, turn right on the Goat Hill Trail (sign). It climbs, not steeply, under redwoods and Douglas firs for another short half mile to arrive at a clearing that looks like a natural amphitheater. The Goat Hill Trail passes the Doe Ridge Trail and skirts the shallow bowl of the clearing, which must have once been the site of a ranch, to judge by the occasional old fruit and nut trees. Continue on the Goat Hill Trail past the sign OLMO FIRE TRAIL CONNECTION. Where the Goat Hill Trail forks right to return to the park access road, bear left, re-enter forest, and soon arrive at the

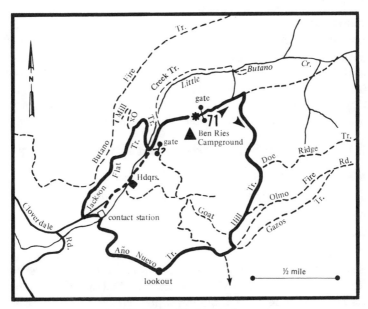

Butano State Park

Olmo Fire Road and the Gazos Trail. Turn right on the fire road and soon pass an unsigned trail on the left. Not far beyond, bear left on the Año Nuevo Trail (sign). It runs through a Douglas-fir forest with a profuse undergrowth of blackberry bushes, to arrive in ½ mile at the Año Nuevo overlook, a small clearing among lichen-covered firs. From here you can look south to Año Nuevo Island when visibility permits. (On one of my visits, a gaggle of frustrated Asian tourists with expensive cameras were photographing a sea of fog through the trees where the park brochure advertised a "panoramic view" of the island.)

The trail now descends, sometimes steeply and sometimes by switchbacking, through more firs and more blackberries. After about a mile it levels off in a thicket of willows and crosses a streamlet on a footbridge to arrive at the park contact station.

From here you can, of course, walk the mile back to camp on the road, but a somewhat more interesting route is via the Jackson Flat Trail, which begins a few hundred feet west of the contact station, at a sign. It goes uphill and soon curves northeast into a woods of live oak, Douglas fir and eventually redwoods. In less than a mile the Jackson Flat Trail reaches a junction with the Mill Ox Trail, which descends to Little Butano Creek and the access road leading back to the campground.

Nearby attractions

Both Pescadero State Beach and Pescadero Marsh are popular with birders, especially during the fall migrations. The town of Pescadero itself has a lot of old-fashioned charm. Its 19th century Portuguese heritage is apparent in the annual Chamarita, or Festival of the Holy Ghost, which takes place on the sixth Sunday after Easter. A newer tradition is the Labor Day Artichoke Festival, first held in 1980.

Four parks in San Mateo County

Maps

Topos *La Honda, Mindego Hill* and *Big Basin;* trail maps available at the various headquarters.

How to get there

From Highway 35 (Skyline Boulevard): To reach Portola, go south on Alpine Road for 3 miles and south again on Portola State Park Road to its end. To reach Memorial and Sam McDonald, go south on 84 (La Honda Road) for 6½ miles and left on Pescadero Road. Pescadero Creek Park is reached via Sam McDonald or Memorial.

Features

Nestled on the western slope of the Santa Cruz Mountains, in the southern part of San Mateo County, are one state park and three county parks. All four parks are close enough together that if you are camping at one, you can easily explore the others. All of them feature similar redwood-forest ambience. They are linked by a system of hiking trails.

Below are capsule descriptions of these parks and their facilities. For further information about the three county parks, consult the Department of Parks and Recreation, County Government Center, Redwood City 94063; phone 363-4020.

72 Portola State Park

Address and phone   Star Route 2, La Honda 94020; 948-9098

Features   This park is in a deep canyon traversed by Peters Creek and Pescadero Creek. Trails lead along the creeks and up the ridges through second-growth redwood and Douglas fir.

Facilities   52 campsites reservable through Mistix; 5 backpack campsites reservable through the park; hot showers and laundry tubs; group picnicking and camping by advance reservation; trout fishing; self-guiding nature trail; naturalist programs in summer.

Regulations   The usual for state parks.

73 Memorial County Park

Address and phone   9500 Pescadero Road, La Honda 94020; 879-0212

Features   Memorial has the most beautiful redwoods of any of these four parks. The county acquired the land in 1924, just one jump ahead of the loggers, who had cut over most of the surrounding territory. The WPA constructed many of the park facilities in the 1930s. Campsites are attractively dispersed under the big trees. It is understandable why families flock to this park every summer.

Facilities   140 campsites available on a first-come, first-served basis; group picnicking and camping available by advance reservation (phone 363-4021); fishing, swimming; naturalist programs in summer; nature trail accessible to the physically limited.

Regulations   Moderate camping fee per night; small day-use fee. The park brochure lists a number of rules regarding fires, noise, etc.; of these, the most important to know in advance are that pets are not permitted and that adult supervision is required for overnight campers under 18.

74   Sam McDonald Park

Address and phone   13435 Pescadero Road, La Honda 94020; for information, 747-0403; for reservations, 363-4021

Features   Sam McDonald, a descendant of slaves, worked at Stanford University for over 50 years, beginning as a janitor. He started to acquire this land in 1917, and when he died 40 years later he left his 400 acres to Stanford, specifying that it be used as a park for the benefit of young people. The county subsequently acquired it from the university.

An unusual feature of this park is the Hiker's Hut located 1½ pedestrian miles from headquarters. "Hut" is not quite an adequate word for this A-frame structure which came prefabricated in one box from Denmark, and subsequently added recycling privies to its facilities. The hut was a project of the Loma Prieta Chapter of the Sierra Club, which maintains it for the use of the public as well as club members.

Facilities   Water, restrooms, picnic tables, phone at headquarters; youth group camping by reservation; horse camp by reservation. For Hiker's Hut information and reservations phone 327-8111 1–5 p.m. weekdays.

Regulations   Both the park and the Hiker's Hut have a number of rules regarding fires, noise, etc.; of these, the most important to know in advance are that pets are not permitted and that adult supervision is required for overnight campers under 18. The Hut charges a moderate overnight fee.

75   Pescadero Creek Park

Address and phone   Same as Sam McDonald

Features   The county acquired these 6000 acres of Pescadero Creek watershed from a lumber company. Extensive logging took place here for decades; now old logging roads and trails lead hikers and backpackers through second-growth forest. A few of the trails are open to mountain bikes. Ray Hosler of the *Chronicle*'s "Cycling" column has recommended the Old Haul Road.

Facilities   Two hike-in backpacking camps; for permit, check in at Memorial.

Regulations   No pets.

76   Coyote Point Recreation Area and Museum

Address and phone

Coyote Point, San Mateo 94401; Recreation Area 573-2592; Museum 342-7755

Maps

Topo *San Mateo;* park map available at entrance kiosk.

How to get there

From Highway 101 southbound   Exit at Poplar Avenue, go west to Humboldt (following signs to Coyote Point), take Humboldt north to Peninsula, go east on Peninsula to North Bayshore Boulevard, and take North Bayshore Boulevard south to Coyote Point Drive, which runs into the park.

From Highway 101 northbound   Exit at Peninsula Avenue, loop around under overpass on North Bayshore Boulevard and turn left onto Coyote Point Drive.

Features

> The Coyote Point Museum is prime evidence of the ongoing revolution in ideas about the human role on this planet, a revolution that is likely to change our lives even more radically than the micro-processing revolution based in Silicon Valley.
>
> —Harold Gilliam, San Francisco
> *Exonicle,* October 4, 1981.

For many years Coyote Point has been a San Mateo County bayside park popular among Peninsula dwellers for family fun. The opening of the unique and spectacular Coyote Point Museum for Environmental Education in 1981 has made it a magnet for people from the entire Bay Area. This is not just a natural-history museum in the traditional mold, full of stuffed animals and pedantic labels. Its designer, Gordon Ashby, has frankly stated that it is a place with a purpose—and that purpose is "to save the world." It differs from other museums, furthermore, in that—although children love it and find it enthralling—the designer intended it to appeal to all ages, and especially to adult decision-makers. Like the Oakland Museum, also designed by Ashby, the Coyote Point Museum is a Bay Area treasure that all of us who live here should make a point of exploring and showing off to visitors from elsewhere.

Facilities

Recreation Area   Open 8 A.M.–dark. Extensive family picnic areas; playgrounds; group picnic areas for 25 or more available by reservation (363-4021); bicycle path; beach with restrooms, showers and lifeguard in summer; Live Animal Center; marina; rifle range; Castaway Restaurant (347-1027)—fairly elegant.

Extensive facilities for the disabled include restrooms, showers and group picnic areas; also barrier-free access to the beach and the breakwater fishing area.

Museum   Open 10 A.M.–5 P.M. Wednesday through Friday, 1–5 P.M. weekends. Wheelchair-accessible; museum store; extensive naturalist program. Current exhibits are listed under "Exhibits" in the pink section of the Sunday *Exonicle*.

Regulations

Recreation area   Moderate parking fee except for the disabled; no pets; beer and wine only; no overnight camping.

Museum   Small fee, except free on Fridays and free to members of the Coyote Point Museum Association.

Description

As the list of Facilities indicates, this 670-acre park offers lots to do and see. You may want to start out with a picnic at one of the many sites scattered about, some near the beach, others under the eucalyptus trees on the bluffs. Or you may want to walk around the point and enjoy the views over the marina toward the East Bay and north to the busy airport, the City and San Bruno Mountain. Children may want to visit the Live Animal Center, which is open the same hours as the museum.

The main attraction, however, is the splendid Museum for Environmental Education. The building, designed by Palo Alto's Spencer Associates, is of Douglas fir. It contains some of the latest developments in ecologically sound construction, such as a domestic solar hot-water system, double-glazed thermopane windows and a natural cooling system.

The Gordon Ashby interior design symbolizes a journey across San Mateo County—or, more precisely, the journey of a drop of water across the county. Although this plan might at first sound somewhat limited, actually San Mateo County contains six of California's eight biotic communities: broadleaf forest, coniferous forest, chaparral, grassland, baylands and seacoast; only Sierra and desert are lacking.

As you stroll down the ramps dedicated to each of these communities, you pass such attention-grabbers as an ant colony, a working beehive, a 13-foot-high sculptured food-chain pyramid with a red-tailed hawk at its apex, a glassed-over marshland, and a vast assortment of computer games.

After you finally tear yourself away from this stunning place, you will look around you with a new awareness of just how *Homo sapiens* is affecting Spaceship Earth.

Mallette Dean

Hikes 77–80
San Francisco

One thing is certain: if you want to walk in San Francisco, you need never walk alone. A study of the pink section of one Sunday's *Exonicle* under "Events" revealed the walking tours listed below, all of them free or very inexpensive. Of course these schedules and phone numbers are subject to change, but this list gives some idea of the immense variety of walking tours taking place in the City every week.

City Guides (sponsored by Friends of the San Francisco Public Library, 558-3981); tours of Civic Center, the Gold Rush City, Historic Market Street, and many of San Francisco's neighborhoods; every weekend and some weekdays; free.

Golden Gate National Recreation Area (556-8642, 556-0560); tours of Sutro Heights, Sutro Baths, Lands End and other parts of the GGNRA; every weekend; free.

Golden Gate Park Tours (sponsored by Friends of Recreation and Parks, 221-1310, 221-1311); every weekend from May through October; free.

Heritage Tours (sponsored by the Foundation for San Francisco's Architectural Heritage, 441-3000); tours of Pacific Heights architecture every Sunday; small fee.

A few more-specialized tours:

Murals of the Mission District (sponsored by Precita Eyes Muralists, 285-2287); every other Saturday; moderate fee.

The Performing Arts Center (552-8338); every Monday, Wednesday and Saturday; small fee.

The University of California at San Francisco—that is, the UC Medical Center (476-4394); every Tuesday; free.

And finally, only in San Francisco:

The Dashiell Hammett Tour (Don Herron, 564-7021); every Saturday, May through August, moderate fee; groups by appointment. This tour begins at noon on the front steps of the Main Library, Larkin and McAllister streets, and follows in the footsteps of Sam Spade for about 3 miles in about 3 hours.

Public transit

San Francisco's Municipal Railway, like most big-city transit systems, chronically runs a deficit, and suffers accordingly from decrepit, vandalized vehicles and insufficient scheduling, erratically observed.

Despite all the griping about the Muni from passengers, taxpayers and newspaper columnists, it remains by far the cheapest and most convenient way to get downtown and to other crowded areas where parking is expensive or nonexistent. For information about routes and schedules, phone 673-MUNI (673-6864).

BART currently runs between the financial district and Daly City. In San Francisco, phone 788-BART.

Golden Gate Transit (332-6600) will take you from any of its San Francisco pickup points to the bridge toll plaza. That is the only destination in San Francisco where GGT is allowed to deliver you.

The Red & White Fleet (546-2810) runs daily sightseeing cruises of the Bay. It also provides ferry service to Angel Island and Tiburon, as noted in the Marin County section of this book, and to Alcatraz Island, which is part of the GGNRA. Reservations for the Alcatraz tour should be made well in advance.

Golden Gate Transit (332-6600) runs ferries from San Francisco's Ferry Building to Sausalito and Larkspur.

Recommended reading

Many of the books listed on pp. 36–37 devote extensive sections to the City. Gentry and Horton's *Dolphin Guide to San Francisco and the Bay Area* contains detailed historical walking tours of the City's best-known neighborhoods.

The following deal exclusively or almost so with San Francisco:

Bakalinsky, Adah, *Staircase Walks in San Francisco*. San Francisco: Lexikos, 1984.

Doss, Margot Patterson, *San Francisco at Your Feet: The Great Walks in a Walker's Town*. 2nd revised and updated edition. New York: Grove Press, 1980. This paperback is almost indispensable for San Francisco residents. It contains more than 80 walks, arranged geographically, including maps and public-transit information.

San Francisco *Bay Guardian* staff, *San Francisco Free and Easy: The Native's Handbook*. 2nd edition. San Francisco: Downwind Publications, 1980. Just the sort of candid, unconventional guide you'd expect from the muckraking *Guardian,* it will be popular with hip tourists as well as natives. What other book tells you where to rent a cobweb machine, how to locate a dog-hair spinner, or where to get an X-rated cake?

Emphasis on architecture:

Delehanty, Randolph, *San Francisco: Walks and Tours in the Golden Gate City.* New York: Dial Press, 1980. The author was historian of the Foundation for San Francisco's Architectural Heritage for five years and led many of their walking tours. (Out of print)

Woodbridge, Sally B. and John M., *Architecture San Francisco: The Guide.* San Francisco: 101 Productions, 1982.

For more background material on what you're seeing on your travels, try the following:

Gilliam, Harold, and Michael Bry, *The Natural World of San Francisco.* Garden City, New York: Doubleday, 1967. Hardbound. Gilliam wrote the text, Bry took the photographs. Gilliam has

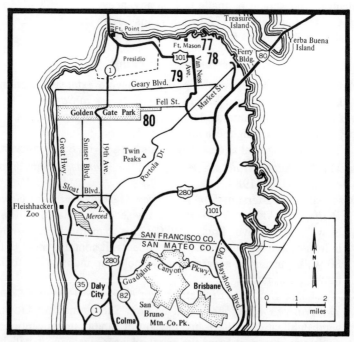

San Francisco driving map

written many books on the Bay Area, all of them well worth
reading. (Out of print)

Lewis, Oscar, *San Francisco: Mission to Metropolis*. 2nd edition.
Berkeley: Howell-North, 1980. Lewis has also written books on
more specialized aspects of the City's history, such as *The Big
Four* and, with Carroll D. Hall, *Bonanza Inn*, an account of the
Palace Hotel.

McGloin, John B., S. J., *San Francisco: The Story of a City*. San
Rafael and London: Presidio Press, 1978. (Out of print)

For up-to-date, free information, don't forget the San Francisco
Convention and Visitors Bureau and the Redwood Empire Association (see p. 36).

Mailette Dean

The Golden Gate National Recreation Area in San Francisco

Address and phone

GGNRA Headquarters, Building 201, Fort Mason, San Francisco 94123; 556-0560

Maps

Topo *San Francisco North;* free map of GGNRA available from just inside headquarters when it's open or from box on the front porch when it's closed, or from Fort Point.

Features

The unique urban playground that is the GGNRA is described on pages 20–22, and some of its Marin County holdings have been featured in that section. Space permits only a brief introduction here to the immense variety of its far-flung territories in San Francisco. A good way to explore them is by going on the free walks that park rangers conduct every weekend, just as their colleagues do in the Marin headlands. A typical weekend schedule, for example, features walks around Sutro Heights, Sutro Baths and Lands End. To find out about these, phone headquarters or look in the pink section of the Sunday *Exonicle.*

Recommended reading

Liberatore, Karen, *The Complete Guide to the GGNRA.* San Francisco: Chronicle Books, 1982. This book is especially detailed on the San Francisco holdings of the park.

77 Fort Mason and Fort Mason Center

How to get there

By bus Muni #30, #42, #47 and #49 go near the main entrance; #28 goes to the pier parking lot.

By car To GGNRA headquarters and the upper fort: Drive to the north end of Franklin Street.

To Fort Mason Center: Drive north on Laguna Street, turn left on Bay Street, and in 1 block turn sharp right at the sign.

Features

The Army and the NPS are peacefully coexisting in the upper part of the old fort, along with a hostel and a prize-winning community garden. In the pier area, a host of non-profit artistic, cultural, educational and environmental organizations are now occupying the former Army buildings. Fort Mason is certainly an example of recycling on a grand scale! It draws over 1½ million visitors a year.

The fort was used as a debarkation point for American soldiers from the Spanish-American War to the Korean War. During World War II, 1½ million servicemen shipped out from here (or as many people as now visit peacefully each year!). On the weekend of Veterans Day 1985 the fort observed a "40 Years Later" celebration and was dedicated as a National Historic Landmark. You can explore much of its history by walking north from GGNRA headquarters, as described below.

Facilities

In the upper part, water, restrooms, picnic tables, a few grills (charcoal only); GGNRA headquarters open weekdays 8:30 A.M.–5 P.M.; in Fort Mason Center, water, restrooms, picnic tables and a mind-boggling array of activities.

Regulations

Dogs must be leashed.

Description

The logical place to begin is at GGNRA headquarters, where you can pick up the park's excellent leaflet with map. Behind headquarters are the community gardens and, in Building 240, which dates back to the Civil War period, the San Francisco International Youth Hostel (771-7277).

The Great Meadow to the west of headquarters is the site of a "conversation pace" exercise gamefield designed for people over forty. Eventually a statue of the late Congressman Phillip Burton, to whom the GGNRA was dedicated in 1983, will be placed in the meadow.

To explore the historic part of the fort, walk north on Franklin Street. The Spanish placed cannon overlooking the Bay from what is now Fort Mason in 1797, three years after they built fortified Castillo de San Joaquin above what is now Fort Point to the west. The guns here, like those at Fort Point, never fired a shot in anger; in fact, the Spanish allowed them to fall into neglect. The Americans called the promontory Black Point, probably because it was then covered with dense laurel, which appeared dark from the Bay. (Most of the trees on the fort now are exotics that have been introduced over the past century and a quarter—some of them by John McLaren; those on the promontory are mainly Monterey cypress, toyon and eucalyptus.)

In 1850 President Millard Fillmore officially set the area aside for military use. However, the Army did not occupy it for several years, and meanwhile a number of squatters settled here, of whom the most prominent was General John C. Fremont. In the 1860s Colonel Richard Barnes Mason succeeded in dispossessing the squatters, and later the fort was named for him. (Fremont first challenged Mason to a duel, but later, instead, took the matter to court—where his side lost.)

Fortunately, four of the squatters' houses that date from 1855 remain today, albeit considerably modified, and they are still occupied by Army personnel. The southernmost one, which was extensively remodeled in the 1880s, now serves as the Officers' Club. As you walk north on Franklin Street, historic plaques describe these handsome houses, including the one where Senator David C. Broderick died after his duel with Judge David S. Terry.

On the west side of Franklin Street are several houses which the Army constructed between 1863 and 1890 to serve as enlisted men's quarters. Note that architecturally these houses are exactly what the Army was building during this period in the eastern United States: they show no trace of Spanish influence, nor any acknowledgment that the climate of California might be different from that of, say, Massachusetts—their steeply pitched roofs are ideally designed for shedding several feet of snow! Note also the expanse of greenery around the houses: in land-poor San Francisco, only the military can afford such spaciousness! and so the sergeant at Fort Mason has a bigger lawn than the millionaire on Pacific Heights. (These two phenomena appear on a grander scale in the Presidio.)

At the north end of the fort, you can pause to picnic or just enjoy the superb view of the Bay and its shipping. It is easy to understand why Fremont was so eager to defend his claim to this property.

In 1982, while clearing the way for a larger picnic ground at Black Point, workers uncovered the brickwork of a gun battery built during the Civil War as part of San Francisco's plan to protect the Bay from Confederate attack. Under the sponsorship of the Golden Gate National Park Association, a youth group, the San Francisco Conservation Corps, excavated and restored the artillery emplacement to its original appearance. The result is a truly unique picnic spot (tables, water, grills; closes at sunset.)

From here you can take the stairway that leads down the eastern slope of the fort to Aquatic Park and thence continue to the manifold attractions nearby, such as the Maritime Museum, Ghirardelli Square and the Cannery. Or you can head west, down to the piers that now house Fort Mason Center. For decades these were Army transport docks, and, as noted above, during World War II more than 1½ million soldiers debarked from them. As one of the more innovative aspects of this innovative park, the pier area and its huge sheds now house a host of nonprofit organizations and activities. The Fort Mason Foundation (Building A; 441-5706) administers the center in cooperation with the NPS.

A kiosk in the parking area contains a directory of the residents and a program of what's happening in the center's various classrooms, galleries and theaters—and there's always *something* happening. The giant piers have been the scene of the Chinese Trade Exhibit, the Dickens Christmas Fair and innumerable ethnic festivals and crafts fairs. Among the more than 50 resident organizations are the Magic Theater, the Mexican Museum, the Oceanic Society and Greens—a vegetarian restaurant operated by the Zen Center which has become so popular that reservations are almost always necessary days or even weeks in advance (771-6222).

One of the main attractions at Fort Mason Center is the S.S. *Jeremiah O'Brien,* berthed at Pier 3, the last unaltered Liberty Ship in operating condition. Built in 1943, the *O'Brien* carried food and ammunition to Great Britain and ferried troops and supplies to the Normandy beachheads. After an honorable retirement of many years with the Mothball Fleet in Suisun Bay, the *O'Brien* was selected to represent all 2750 Liberty Ships as a memorial "to the millions of men and women who built, sailed, defended, repaired and supplied" them during World War II. A group of dedicated volunteers—some of them old salts, some of them not even born until well after the war—have spent thousands of hours restoring the *O'Brien*. The ship is now open to the public daily, 9 A.M.–3 P.M., and once a month an Open Ship weekend (small donation) features the running of the triple expansion engine and the operation of the coalstove galley. Twice a year, in May, the ship makes a 5-hour cruise around the Bay. For schedules and information, phone 441-3101.

If you want a scenic, breezy hike after exploring the Fort Mason Center, continue west on the Golden Gate Promenade, described in the next chapter.

78 The Golden Gate Promenade

Distance   3½ miles one way.
Grade   Easy.

How to get there

By bus   Muni #28 roughly parallels the route and stops at both termini, Fort Mason and the Golden Gate Bridge toll plaza, thus providing an easy means of making a one-way hike. Muni #30, #42, #47 and #49 run near Fort Mason.

By car   Park at Fort Mason (see preceding chapter), along the Marina Green, or at Fort Point.

Features

This route along San Francisco's northern waterfront presents extraordinary diversity in its 3½ miles: magnificent vistas of the Bay and the Marin headlands; military structures spanning 125 years; upper-middle-class dwellings; beach, greensward, yacht harbors and fishing piers.

The promenade route, which is marked by blue-and-white sailboat signs, runs between Fort Point and Aquatic Park, and if you take it in that direction—i.e., eastward—you will be starting at the oldest building and ending among some of the newest, in Ghirardelli Square and the Cannery; furthermore, you won't have to walk uphill at the end. On the other hand, if you start at Fort Mason you can pick up the free leaflet and map of the GGNRA at headquarters. I've arbitrarily chosen to describe it starting there and heading west. To get maximum enjoyment of the superb scenery, you can of course make it a round trip.

The Golden Gate Promenade is popular with bicyclists and enormously popular with joggers.

Facilities

Water, restrooms, picnic tables at beginning and end and various places along the route.

Regulations

Dogs on leash. On the Marina Green: no overnight camping; no football, rugby, soccer or lacrosse.

Description

From GGNRA headquarters, head west through Fort Mason to Gashouse Cove at the foot of Laguna Street. (The enormous gas-storage tank that used to dominate this site has given way to apartment buildings.) Here begins San Francisco's yacht harbor. Two blocks northwest begins a Parcourse designed to test and improve one's physical fitness. Along its 2½-mile loop the Parcourse contains 18 stations with equipment for a variety of conditioning exercises. In recent years similar exercise gamefields have sprung up like mushrooms all over the Bay Area, but this was one of the first.

The Golden Gate Promenade and the Parcourse route continue on the seawall bordering the Marina Green. As you walk or jog along it, you can look out over the yachts to the bridge, the Marin headlands, Mt. Tamalpais, and Angel and Alcatraz islands. The Marina Green itself, like most of the district, is Bay fill dating from the 1915 Panama Pacific International Exposition. For several years it was used as an aircraft landing field, until nearby residents complained of the danger. In an early example of recycling, the seawalls along the Green and the yacht harbor were constructed of blocks and cobbles uprooted during San Francisco's street-rebuilding programs, and may originally have come to the City as ballast for sailing ships in the 19th century.

During recent decades the Marina Green has been a place where San Franciscans have flocked to engage in sunbathing, kite flying, boat watching, Frisbee throwing, running and jogging. The Park Service wisely recognized that these activities were indeed this area's highest and best uses, and chose to leave it as it was, except for the additions of the Parcourse and a new jogging track. Note, near the middle of the north side of the Green, Haig Patigian's sculptured monument to financier William C. Ralston, who swam to his death from today's Aquatic Park, a mile east of here, the day after his Bank of California failed.

Where the yacht harbor interrupts the Marina Green, the Golden Gate Promenade and the Parcourse continue along the old Belt Line railroad. On either side of you are symbols of the Good Life—fancy Mediterranean-style villas on your left and two yacht clubs plus some of the harbor's more opulent boats on your right. You can make a side trip here at the Lyon Street signal to the Palace of Fine Arts, Bernard Maybeck's masterpiece and the one building remaining from the 1915 fair. It now houses the Exploratorium, a fascinating science museum full of do-it-yourself exhibits (open Wednesday through Sunday; hours vary seasonally; small fee; wheelchair-accessible; phone 563-3200). The Exploratorium is the creation of the late physicist Dr. Frank Oppenheimer.

The Golden Gate Promenade turns north toward the Bay across the continuation of the Marina Green, the part most popular with

sunbathers, past a windowless concrete storm-water-overflow building to some broad concrete stairs leading down to the Bay. Before
taking these stairs you can, if you like, make another side trip to "the
world's first underwater pipe organ." To do so, you go east on the
breakwater past the St. Francis Yacht Club, the lighthouse and the
Golden Gate Yacht Club, all the way to the end. The Wave Organ
was the brainchild of Peter Richards, co-director of the Exploratorium's artist-in-residence program. In June of 1986 the organ was
dedicated to Dr. Oppenheimer, who had died the previous year. One
of San Francisco's weirder monuments, it consists of a number of
polyvinyl chloride pipes of various lengths set among a jumble of old
paving blocks and headstones from Laurel Heights cemetery. The
pipes go into the Bay and resonate to the motion of the waves.
Actually, the Wave Organ is pretty quiet, especially at low tide, but
one certainly can't complain about the view from it!

The next mile of the promenade runs along the shore edge of the
Presidio and Crissy Field, which formerly accommodated planes
and now accommodates helicopters. This portion of the route has to
be one of the most unusual walks in the world, combining a wild
variety of disparate features. On your right are a rough breakwater
of jumbled concrete blocks, a sandy beach and the ever-changing
vista of Bay, ships and bridge. To your left, behind a fence, is an
Army parking lot; as you walk along you see Presidio buildings of
diverse ages and styles, the freeway running over them, the rotunda
of Maybeck's Palace, the mansions of Pacific Heights and the
Presidio's forest in the background—and, of course, that unique
landmark, the Mt. Sutro television tower. And under your feet are
plentiful specimens of the state flower, California poppy. (Indeed,
botanists have designated the Presidio as the type locality for this
plant.)

Crissy Field is in a state of transition as the Army, the NPS and
the City try to plan for its future development, with the aid of public
input via the GGNRA Citizen's Advisory Commission. In addition
to the governmental bodies, various traditional user groups have
strong opinions about what should be done with the place: The
windsurfers want parking close to the beach (the Bay off Crissy Field
is a world-class windsurfing area). The bicyclists want a good bike
path. The native-plant lovers want to preserve the vegetation on the
coastal dunes. A number of peace organizations want to designate
Crissy Field a Peace Park. As Greg Moore of the Golden Gate
National Park Association remarked at an Advisory Commission
meeting, ". . . the Crissy Field area has groups of loyal fans with

specific but diverse and sometimes conflicting views about the area's future character."

You pass the Coast Guard station, a charming enclave of New England Victoriana (except for the palm trees) amidst its utilitarian Army surroundings. The Coast Guard is eventually scheduled to move across the Bay to East Fort Baker. The Golden Gate Promenade jogs around a jeep/truck parking lot and arrives at an always-popular pier where anglers fish for perch and crabs. Just beyond are two recycled, repainted Army buildings which the Park Service is using for office and classroom space. The last few hundred yards are along a seawall where on windy days ocean spray blows into walkers' faces. The cliffs above Fort Point and the southern end of the Golden Gate Bridge contain large quantities of serpentine, the official state rock. Amateur botanists can find a wide variety of plants, both native and introduced, on these cliffs.

Fort Point was built during 1853 to 1861 in a style similar to Fort Sumter in South Carolina, whose fall to the Confederates began the Civil War. Like so many other military artifacts, it became obsolete almost as soon as it was built. Never a shot was fired in anger from the fort; the main enemy of the soldiers stationed here was boredom. The old brick fort is now a National Historic Site and is open free daily from 10 A.M. to 5 P.M. The rangers, clad in Civil War uniforms, will give you a historical leaflet about the building, and you can take a guided tour around it; it also contains a small store and an interesting museum.

Now you can retrace your steps along the promenade, appreciating on your eastward trip the views of Fort Baker, Tiburon, Angel Island, Alcatraz, the Berkeley Hills, Mt. Diablo, the Bay Bridge and the San Francisco skyline. Or you can reach the bus by taking the paved path that starts at the marked pedestrian crossing and leads uphill. When you near the top, head for the gate in the green fence. It will bring you out behind the statue of Joseph Strauss, the engineering genius who managed to convince the people of San Francisco and the North Bay that the Golden Gate Bridge could and should be built. The Muni #28 stops across the road just a few yards south of the statue. Note that both the #28 buses going to Fort Mason and the ones going to Daly City currently stop at the same place: on the *north,* or Bridge, side of the road coming out of the tunnel.

Alternate route Just before you reach the gate to the fort, some stairs go uphill to the left and lead to a trail that runs uphill through ivy, nasturtiums and calla lilies. At a swale, turn right and walk uphill on wide-spaced stairs. Turn right again to pass some 19th-century brick powder magazines. A raised platform on the right contains a plaque describing the history of these fortifications. Next the trail leads through a small tunnel to a picnic area with a grand view of the Golden Gate. From here the trail continues uphill to join the trail coming up from the fort. It's possible to combine these two trails to make a scenic loop.

79   An Architectural Walking Tour with Emphasis on Victoriana: Pacific Heights and Cow Hollow

Distance   About 30 blocks one way; return by bus or by walking uphill 5 more blocks.
Grade   Moderate.

Maps

Topo *San Francisco North* or any street map—although you don't really need a map for this city walk.

How to get there

By bus   Muni #3, #22, #24 or #83 to Jackson and Fillmore streets.
By car   Drive to Jackson and Fillmore streets.

Features

Most of San Francisco's 19th-century architecture is west of Van Ness Avenue. After the quake and fire of 1906 had destroyed much of the downtown area, the Army dynamited buildings along Van Ness in a desperate gamble to keep the flames from spreading across it. The gamble paid off, and as a result scores of century-old houses remain today in the Mission District, the Western Addition and Pacific Heights; among them are many elegant Victorians.

Although Pacific Heights contained a number of mansions by the end of the 19th century, it was by no means completely built up. Enough open space remained to permit succeeding generations of architects to display their talents there. Consequently, today the area is a living museum of fashionable residential architecture since the 1860s. Interspersed with the Victorian buildings are works by early 20th-century architects, such as Willis Polk and Bernard Maybeck, and by modern masters, such as William Wurster.

The Victorians, once dismissed as hopelessly old-fashioned, have in recent years become the most sought-after houses in the City. It takes a lot of money or a lot of time or both to renovate a dilapidated Victorian dwelling, but many people feel that the spaciousness and charm of these buildings make it well worth the effort. Purists may complain that some new owners have been a bit overexuberant with their paint jobs: originally most of these houses were painted in more-muted colors, and the natural play of light and shadow was expected to show off the elaborate ornamental wood carving. However, as you walk past some of these newly gaudy houses, remember that a lavender Victorian with crimson trim is preferable to a gray concrete box supplanting a *razed* Victorian.

In any case, authenticity is a notion that is not particularly relevant to San Francisco's Victorian architecture, which is, above all, eclectic. Many of the men who designed these houses were not trained architects but skilled carpenters using builders' copybooks. They picked individual features from the entire architectural past, combining classical pilasters with medieval turrets according to their fancy (or their patrons' fancy) and imitating European stone or masonry forms in California's abundant pine and redwood. The results may be flamboyant—may, in some instances, reek of *nouvelle richesse*—but they are seldom dull.

If you want to see the insides of some of these restored Victorians, watch the newspapers for house tours sponsored by historical societies and architecture-preservation groups (a few such groups are listed in the back of the book).

On architecture tours and in architecture books, some stylistic terms that may baffle the uninitiated frequently recur. Even professionals are sometimes vague about defining them—perhaps because many 19th-century Bay Area buildings incorporate characteristics of all these styles, plus elements from the Roman, the Gothic, the Tudor or whatever else happened to catch the builder's fancy. A hint to the neophyte: check the bay windows. The bay window was so popular as to be almost ubiquitous in 19th-century San Francisco architecture, because in this fog-ridden City it let in more light than did the conventional flat window. It took different forms as architectural styles succeeded one another.

Here is a highly oversimplified glossary:

Italianate: Popular in the late 1850s and 1860s; characterized by slanted bay windows, general symmetry, a flat facade and often a false front.

Stick: Popular in the 1870s; characterized by boxy, rectangular bay windows, vertical wood stripping on the corners and sometimes pointed towers.

Eastlake: Frequently associated with the Stick style, this term refers to Sir Charles Eastlake, an English furniture designer who advocated a straightforward use of wood, decorated with incised designs in geometric or botanical patterns. Bay Area builders enthusiastically incorporated their own adaptations of Eastlake's ideas into the exteriors of houses; he subsequently disavowed such usage, but the builders paid no attention.

Queen Anne: A hodgepodge style popular from the 1880s until the end of the century; characterized by rounded bay windows, asymmetry, and frequently a round tower on one corner.

In the course of the Description below, I occasionally refer to the books listed on p. 37 and p. 276 that discuss these buildings.

Description

From the intersection of Jackson and Fillmore streets, walk 1 block north on Fillmore. Much of the west side of the street is occupied by Calvary Presbyterian Church (1901), which *Here Today* describes as "a rather attenuated version of Classic Revival." The adjoining school building was originally in the same style as the church, and when the elders decided to replace it as being unusable and unsafe, some diehard preservationists protested and actually succeeded in having it put on the National Register of Historic Places. The City's Board of Permit Appeals voted 3-2 to let the wreckers proceed, because the structure violated several building and safety codes. The new school is in sharp contrast to both the original church and the three Victorians that complete the block.

Turn left on Pacific Avenue to walk through what may be San Francisco's most elegant residential neighborhood. The Leale House, #2475, is one of the oldest houses in Pacific Heights, built around 1855. (The Italianate facade, however, probably dates from the 1880s.) Larger than it appears from the street, it was once a farmhouse when nearby Cow Hollow, down the hill to the north, was dairy country. Continue west on Pacific. The houses here exhibit a pleasant diversity of style. The 2800 block contains some especially grand mansions. Toward the end of the block you can make a short side trip into Raycliff Terrace, where you can glimpse portions of some houses designed in the 1950s—quite a contrast to the monuments on Pacific.

Turn left, downhill, on Broderick. At Jackson, walk (or just look) west to #2944, at the middle of the north side of the street, designed in 1939 by H. T. Howard, which Gebhard *et al.* call "one of the best examples of the Streamlined Moderne style in the city." Continue south on Broderick. The 2200 block contains several Stick-style houses from the 1880s.

Turn right on Washington. This block contains a number of delightful Victorians. #3022 is obviously an old firehouse (1893) cunningly remodeled to serve as a private residence. Across the street, #3021, a well-preserved Stick house dating from 1890, takes on a more sinister aspect when you learn that the German-American Bund occupied it before World War II.

When you reach Lyon Street, cross it to enter the Swedenborgian Church of the New Jerusalem (closed Mondays). Completed in 1895, this church building was a collaborative effort of its pastor, Rev. Joseph Worcester, artist Bruce Porter, and architects A. Page Brown and the young Bernard Maybeck, who was then in Brown's employ. The charming walled garden contains plants from around the world, each chosen for its symbolic meaning. The church building is an early example of the California architectural practice of using natural materials in a simple, direct manner. Bay Area hikers will immediately recognize the pillars supporting the tiled roof as madrone logs with the bark still on. The handmade maple chairs have seats woven of tule reeds from the Delta. On the north wall are landscape paintings by William Keith. The stained-glass windows are by Bruce Porter. It's obvious why this attractive church is extremely popular for weddings.

When you leave the calm of the church and garden, walk north on Lyon 1 block and turn left on Jackson. At #3157 is a small funicular. Turn right on Presidio Avenue. #21-23 is a double house built in 1900 and remodeled by Bruce Porter in 1915. Presidio Avenue crosses Pacific Avenue here to enter the pine-and-cypress woods of the Presidio. From the hilly intersection of the two avenues you can overlook part of the Julius Kahn Playground to the west.

Now go left, steeply downhill, on the 3200 block of Pacific, to enjoy a group of brown-shingled houses that exemplify early-20th-century Bay Area residential architecture at its finest. The challenge presented by the steep hill and the north side's irregularly shaped lots apparently inspired architects to do some of their best work. If you walk down the south side and back up the north side, you will pass #3203 (E. T. Sheppard, 1902; remodeled by Willis Polk); #3233 (Bernard Maybeck, 1909); #3235 (William F. Knowles, c. 1908); #3255 (remodeled by Willis Polk, 1910); #3277 (Willis

Polk, 1913); #3240 and #3236 (William F. Knowles); #3234 and
#3232 (Ernest Coxhead, 1902).

Now walk east on Pacific. The 3100 block, though not as
elegantly harmonious as the 3200 block, has some pleasant houses
that further demonstrate how architects have coped with San Francisco's steep hills. Ernest Coxhead designed #3153 and #3151 in
1912.

Turn left on Lyon and walk downhill 1 block to Broadway. You
can pause and rest at the Lyon steps to enjoy the magnificent view.
Prominent at the foot of steep Lyon is the Palace of Fine Arts,
Bernard Maybeck's majestic contribution to the Panama-Pacific
Exposition of 1915. Its gray-green rotunda and buff and ochre
Corinthian columns contrast strikingly with the blue Bay beyond it.
The palace was moldering quietly away until 1962, when philanthro-
pist Walter Johnson contributed over $4 million toward its res-
toration.

If you're tired of looking at houses, you can cut straight down
Lyon to the palace and end your excursion with a visit to the
Exploratorium, a museum full of do-it-yourself scientific exhibits
that now occupies part of the building (described in the preceding
chapter). Otherwise, walk east on Broadway. The ensuing 3 blocks
incorporate architectural elements from the last 2½ millennia, and
perhaps the next one also. Willis Polk designed #2960, #2880 and
#2801. Of #2901, Woodbridge and Woodbridge comment: "An
example of determined neo-classicism prevailing over all odds. This
Renaissance palace is perched on a cliff and is approached by a
complicated ramp from below." In stark contrast to their eclectic,
backward-looking neighbors are solar-panelled #2776 and neo-
Streamlined Moderne #2725.

When you reach Divisadero, go right, uphill, far enough to see
the cleverly disguised garage doors of #2555. Delancey Street, a
self-help rehabilitation group, occupies #2563. Across the street,
#2560, designed by William Wurster in 1939, shows how a modern
architect made use of one of San Francisco's most advantageous
view spots.

Now turn around and go downhill on Divisadero. Another
striking modern house is boxy #2660, designed by John E.
Dinwiddie in 1938. Woodbridge and Woodbridge call this: "A lone
example in San Francisco of the residential work of this prominent
local Modernist. The canted, boxed view window was so much
imitated by tract builders as to become a cliche'." This house contrasts vividly with the houses on the other three corners of this

intersection, especially the baroque mansion at 2700 Vallejo, designed by Henry Smith in 1915. After studying its exterior you will not be surprised to learn that the client who commissioned it was the descendant of a marble importer.

Go downhill on Divisadero another block and turn right on pleasant, tree-shaded Green. Ernest Coxhead designed #2421 (his own house) and #2423 in the 1890s. As you walk down the steep 2400 block, the brick-red spire of St. Vincent de Paul Roman Catholic Church (Shea & Lofquist, 1916) is prominent two blocks ahead.

Turn right on Pierce for a side trip to #2727, the *pièce de résistance* of this walk: the Casebolt House. Built in 1865-66, this elaborate Italianate mansion once stood alone, surrounded by extensive farm and pasture land. Newly painted white, it has been beautifully maintained. Elaborate landscaping sets off its magnificence.

Retrace your steps to Green and continue north on Pierce to Union. A side trip of ½ block west (left) brings you to #2460, a well-maintained mansard-roofed house dating from about 1872. Return to Pierce and continue east on Union. On the southwest corner of Union and Steiner is the Episcopal Church of St. Mary the Virgin, a pleasant, unpretentious shingled structure built in 1891 and remodeled by Warren Perry in 1953. In the courtyard are murals by Lucienne Bloch and a fountain fed by an old artesian spring which reputedly has curative powers.

If you feel the need for something stronger than artesian-spring water, you can drop in to one of the many cafes and saloons along Union, currently San Francisco's trendiest street. Some handsome Victorians on Union that date from the 1870s have been renovated to accommodate shops and galleries. One of them, #1836–1850, was home to Boss Abe Ruef early in his career.

You can finish this walk with a visit to one or both of two architectural landmarks: the Vedanta Society's Old Temple and the Octagon House. The temple, at Webster and Filbert, was designed in 1905 by Swami Trigunatitananda and architect Joseph A. Leonard. The upper stories attempt to incorporate architectural features from the world's leading religions; the ecumenical result must be seen to be believed. *Here Today* calls it "perhaps the most unusual building in San Francisco." The Octagon House, at Union and Gough, dates from 1861 and is one of two octagonal houses remaining in the City. It belongs to the Colonial Dames of America, who maintain it as a museum (open 1–4 P.M. the first Sunday and the second and fourth Thursdays of the month).

If you don't want to walk back to your starting place, you can take the #22 from the northwest corner of Fillmore and Union. (The bus jogs west on Union 1 block to climb Steiner instead of ultrasteep Fillmore.) To go downtown, take the #45 running east on Union. To go to North Beach, take the #41 running east on Union. The #41 continues to within a block of the East Bay Terminal.

Nearby attraction   In 1981 the 2200 block of Webster Street and the north side of the 2300 block (between Washington and Jackson) were designated San Francisco's first Residential Historic District. Most of the houses in the district are one- and two-family homes built between 1878 and 1880 in the Italianate style. Difficult though it may be to believe now, the original owners of these homes were middle-class folks, not the City's elite.

80   Golden Gate Park

Address and phone

McLaren Lodge, Fell and Stanyan Streets, San Francisco 94118; 558-3706

Maps

Topo *San Francisco North;* map available for a small price at McLaren Lodge (open weekdays 8 A.M.–5 P.M.).

How to get there

By bus   Muni #7 and #33 run to the southeast corner; #71 and #72 run along much of the south side; #21 runs a block from the Panhandle and along part of the northeast portion of the park; #5 runs along the full length of the north side; #16X runs along the Panhandle and part of the south side; #44 runs through the Music Concourse area; #28 and #29 run through the park on Cross-Over Drive; #18 runs along the west end. (Note that Muni routes are subject to change with very short notice; if in doubt, phone 673-MUNI.)

By car   From the Bay Bridge and Highway 101 exit on Fell Street and continue on it into the park. From the Golden Gate Bridge exit on 19th Avenue-Highway 1 soon after leaving the toll plaza and continue on it into the park. From Highway 280 northbound exit north on 19th Avenue-Highway 1-Golden Gate Bridge when 280 turns east, and continue on it into the park.

Features

Most Bay Areans—and even most tourists—are familiar with Stein-hart Aquarium, the de Young Museum and the Japanese Tea

Garden; and many of them have a mental picture of crusty old "Uncle John" McLaren planting grass to tame the sand dunes or brandishing his fist at the statues that bureaucrats insisted on placing in his park. Yet I am constantly amazed at the number of people who have lived in San Francisco for decades and have never visited Strybing Arboretum or Spreckels Lake or heard of William Hammond Hall. It shouldn't take a gas shortage to prompt Bay Areans to become acquainted with one of the world's great urban parks, a place of infinite variety, beauty and entertainment.

History

In 1868 San Francisco acquired title to some 1000 acres of "outside lands," a half-mile-wide stretch running east from the ocean. Although the area consisted mainly of windblown sand dunes, the city fathers enthusiastically decreed that it should become the site of a great park. In 1871 an engineer, William Hammond Hall, was appointed superintendent. In many important respects Hall, who was an admirer of the great landscape architect Frederick Law Olmsted, shaped the subsequent development of Golden Gate Park: He planned it to be a rustic, natural place instead of an elaborate, formal one. He laid out the basic road system, using a curving pattern for protection from wind. And he began the conquest of the dunes, by planting them in succession with barley and beach grass, then lupine, and finally hardy trees such as eucalyptus and Monterey pine and cypress.

Hall soon ran into conflicts with the politicians—as might be expected of a superintendent who proclaimed: "The value of a park consists of its being a park, and not a catch-all for almost anything which misguided people may wish upon it." In 1876 his opponents succeeded in getting the park's budget reduced to practically nothing, whereupon Hall angrily resigned. He subsequently went on to a distinguished engineering career, and in his capacity as state engineer he was instrumental in choosing John McLaren, a Scottish gardener then employed on a San Mateo estate, to become park superintendent in 1890. McLaren dedicated himself to the job until his death in 1943 at the age of 96, becoming along the way one of San Francisco's great folk heroes and the subject of innumerable stories and legends.

McLaren shared Hall's fundamental view of what an urban park should be: a natural, sylvan oasis for the frazzled city-dweller. However, being somewhat more of a pragmatist than Hall, he allowed—albeit reluctantly—bureaucrats and wealthy benefactors to place buildings, playgrounds, race tracks and statues in his domain. (The statues, which he called "stookies," he tried to hide with shrubbery.) McLaren completed planting the dunes to the park's west boundary, discovering by experiment which species would withstand the blowing sand. He obtained seeds from botanists all over the world, and found that San Francisco's temperate climate would support an amazing variety of plants—if they were irrigated. He had wells dug in the park and found abundant fresh water, which for many years was pumped by the windmills at the west end. Because of McLaren's tireless efforts, Golden Gate Park now contains a great horticultural collection.

One of the first invasions of the park that McLaren unsuccessfully tried to repel was the Midwinter Fair of 1894. The brainchild of several prominent businessmen led by M. H. de Young, it was designed both to stimulate recovery from the depression of 1893 and to publicize San Francisco's equable climate (hence "Midwinter" was an essential part of its name). The fair was centered on the Music Concourse; the chief remnant of it today is the ever-popular Japanese Tea Garden. Unlike most world fairs, the Midwinter Fair made a profit, some of which went to help found the de Young Museum of Art.

McLaren and his successors have had to suffer several other intrusions on their turf, the most conspicuous being Kezar Stadium

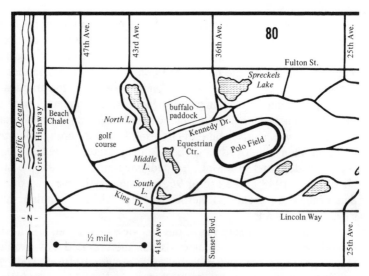

Golden Gate

in 1924-25. The issue of construction in the park is far from dead: more than half a century after McLaren lost the battle of Kezar, some citizens are still proposing new buildings and additions to old ones, while other citizens continue to echo Hall's protestation that a park should be a park and not a catch-all.

One such controversy revolved around a Bicentennial gift from San Francisco's sister city Taipei, the Kinmen Pavilion. After five years of protest from park preservationists proved futile, Harold Gilliam expressed himself forcefully in the San Francisco *Chronicle:* "The idiotic notion of building a Chinese pavilion on the shore of Stow Lake in Golden Gate Park was scarcely believable when it was first proposed, but there it now stands, marking the latest chapter in the long sad saga that might be titled the clobbering of Golden Gate Park. . . . In a park that was supposed to be a leafy enclave from the urban pavements and pressures, there are now 28 acres of buildings."

Golden Gate Park has suffered, as have so many other municipal amenities and services, from post-Proposition 13 budget cutbacks, as the maintenance staff has been considerably reduced. Many of the trees planted by Hall and McLaren are nearing the end of their lives, but funds for reforestation are meager.

Having weathered the be-ins and love-ins of the hippies in the 1960s, Golden Gate—like other urban parks—has had to contend

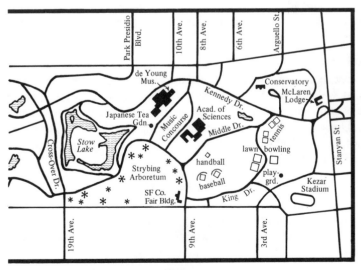

Park

with the more depressing live-ins of the homeless during the 1980s. No one knows exactly how many people have taken up residence in the park's leafy groves and glens, but many panhandlers are visible around the Panhandle and the Stanyan Street area of the park. Coping with these unauthorized residents has added to the burdens of an already-pressured park staff.

Facilities

Golden Gate Park has almost every amenity that any civilized person could wish for in an urban park, except an elegant restaurant—which some San Franciscans feel would be a desirable addition (but John McLaren probably wouldn't). At present the only places to buy food are a few snack bars in the most popular areas; the Japanese Tea Garden, which has an extremely limited menu; and cafeterias in the California Academy of Sciences and the de Young Museum. The park has so many beautiful picnic spots that you may prefer to bring your own bread, cheese and salami for lunch at a place of your choosing. To reserve a group picnic area, phone 558-4728.

You can rent bicycles at several places on the park's periphery, notably Stanyan Street. For information about the wide variety of other athletic facilities available, consult the map and leaflet issued by McLaren Lodge.

One reason Golden Gate Park has such flourishing vegetation is that it's frequently bathed in fog. Even if the rest of the Bay Area, including downtown San Francisco, is sweltering in a heat wave, take a sweater to the park.

Regulations

The east section of the park is closed to automobiles every Sunday, so that walkers and bicyclists can wander freely. In recent years rollerskating has become extremely—perhaps excessively—popular here. Dogs on leash are permitted in most parts of the park. Dogs are permitted to run off-leash in a few areas; for information, inquire at McLaren Lodge.

Recommended reading

Clary, Raymond H., *The Making of Golden Gate Park—The Early Years: 1865–1906.* San Francisco: Lexikos, 1985.

_____ , *The Making of Golden Gate Park—The Growing Years: 1906–1950.* San Francisco: Lexikos, 1986.

The author, a retired watchmaker and state government worker, has been fighting for most of his life to maintain the park as Hall and McLaren envisioned it.

Doss, Margot Patterson, *Golden Gate Park at Your Feet*. San Rafael: Presidio Press, 1978.

A few things to do in the park:

1. One excellent way to become acquainted with the park is by going on one of the free guided tours offered by Friends of Recreation and Parks on weekends from May through October. For schedules, phone 221-1311 or check the pink section of the *Exonicle*. Or join Golden Gate Audubon Society on one of their frequent birding trips around the Chain of Lakes.

2. Take a picnic lunch, including tidbits for the squirrels, to Strybing Arboretum (open weekdays 8 A.M.–4:30 P.M., weekends and holidays 10 A.M.–5 P.M.; no dogs except seeing-eye dogs; phone 661-1316). Enter by its main gate, next to the San Francisco County Fair Building (formerly the Hall of Flowers), which is near Ninth Avenue and Lincoln Way. The #71 bus and the Muni Metro N car run close to this entrance. Check the bookstore to see if you want to buy one of their many inexpensive guides to the arboretum.

North of the County Fair Building is the Garden of Fragrance designed for both sighted and visually handicapped visitors and including labels in Braille. It was re-landscaped in 1983 and a tour of it taped on cassettes. For more information phone the Helen Crocker Russell Library of Horticulture at 661-1514 (open daily except official holidays 10 A.M.–4 P.M.).

The arboretum conducts free tours every afternoon at 1:30 and weekend mornings at 10:30.

If you want to learn to recognize California native plants, the arboretum is a fine place to start. Hundreds of species are labeled, and you can examine them during every season of the year—much more effective than just studying pictures in a book. Many of the natives are in the southwest part of the arboretum, in the Arthur Menzies Garden of Native Plants and the Redwood Trail. These areas contain benches, groves and greenswards eminently suitable for picnicking. If you're alone, you may soon be joined by a fellow creature, of your own species or another.

3. If you want to get thoroughly acquainted with the park, try walking it from Stanyan Street to the ocean, successively through the north, the center and the south segments. Although each of these journeys is only a little over 3 miles long, each may take you a full day, or at least a long afternoon, because of the many distractions en route: flowers, birds, animals, museums, people playing games, and so forth. You can add to the enjoyment of these walks if you take along Doss' book and read about what you are seeing.

Appendix I

Some organizations that sponsor local outdoor activities: In the
Introduction I listed some of the advantages of going outdoors with
organized groups, and from time to time in the text I have mentioned a few. Some of the most active ones are listed here.

American Youth Hostels
Golden Gate Council
425 Divisadero Street, Suite 306
San Francisco, CA 94117
863-9939

California Academy of Sciences
Golden Gate Park
San Francisco, CA 94118

California Native Plant Society
909 - 12th Street, Suite 116
Sacramento, CA 95814

Foundation for San Francisco's Architectural Heritage
2007 Franklin Street
San Francisco, CA 94109

The Nature Conservancy
785 Market Street, 3rd Floor
San Francisco, CA 94103
777-0487

Santa Cruz Mountain Trail Association
Box 1141
Los Altos, CA 94023
968-4509

Sierra Club
730 Polk Street
San Francisco, CA 94109
   Loma Prieta Chapter
   2253 Park Boulevard
   Palo Alto, CA 94306

   San Francisco Bay Chapter
   6014 College Avenue
   Oakland, CA 94618

National Audubon Society
950 Third Avenue
New York, NY 10022

Audubon has several active local groups in the Bay Area. Among the
most active are:

   Golden Gate Audubon Society
   1550 Shattuck Avenue, #204
   Berkeley, CA 94709
   843-2222

Marin Audubon Society
Box 599
Mill Valley, CA 94942-0599

Bicycle groups (these are just two among many):

Bicycle Trails Council of Marin
Box 13842
San Rafael, CA 94913-3842

East Bay Bicycle Coalition
Box 1736
Oakland, CA 94604

Appendix II

Facilities for the disabled: The following places mentioned in this book are wheelchair-accessible or otherwise designed to accommodate disabled visitors. This list is probably not complete, because the number of such facilities is rapidly increasing.

Camping Areas: Big Basin, 259; Bothe-Napa Valley Park, 163; Marin Headlands, 46; Taylor Park, 124; Steep Ravine, 80;

Fishing piers: Garin Park, 216; Point Pinole, 178.

Picnicking areas: Armstrong Redwoods, 144; Audubon Canyon, 120; Briones Park, 223; Cowell Park, 249; Coyote Point, 272; Garin Park, 216; Lake Chabot, 207; Point Pinole, 178; Redwood Park, 203; Sunol Park, 237.

Museums, nature programs, visitor centers: Año Nuevo, 264; Audubon Canyon, 120; Coyote Point Museum, 272; EBRPD general, 168; EBRPD Botanic Garden, 188; Exploratorium, 283; Fort Cronkhite, 46; Fort Ross, 142; Muir Woods, 65; Oakland Museum, 191; Old Bale Mill, 164; Point Reyes, 132; Rodeo Beach, 50; Sonoma State Historic Park, 156; Sunol Park, 237; Tilden Park Environmental Education Center, 185.

Nature trails: Año Nuevo, 264; Memorial Park, 269; Mt. Diablo, 230; Point Reyes Earthquake Trail, 132; for the visually handicapped: braille markers, Muir Woods, 65; Strybing Arboretum, 297.

Appendix III

Since I have been writing outdoor guides, friends and acquaintances have frequently asked me for my personal favorites among all the places I've visited and described. Here follows a brief list of the ones that I automatically gravitate to:

Favorite park for hiking without having to cross a major bridge (I live in the East Bay): Redwood Regional Park. Redwood has a lot of variety in vegetation and scenery, and offers the possibility for loop hikes of almost any length.

Favorite Peninsula hike: Saratoga Gap Trail in Castle Rock State Park.

Favorite Point Reyes hike: Bear Valley-Old Pine Trail-Sky Trail loop.

Favorite beach: Limantour.

Favorite wildflower spot: The Yolanda Trail on the north side of Mt. Tamalpais. Runners-up are Chimney Rock, Kehoe headlands and Pierce Point, all in Point Reyes National Seashore.

Favorite place to take a motley crew of people of different ages, interests and hiking abilities for a picnic: Angel Island.

Favorite place to take young children: Tilden Park. The Little Farm, the Environmental Education Center, the Jewel Lake Trail, the pony ride, the merry-go-round, the steam trains . . . these should keep everyone busy for a day.

Place I would go to for one last hike if I knew for sure that the world was coming to an end tomorrow: The Rock Spring-Potrero Meadow-Laurel Dell loop on Mt. Tamalpais (#12 in this book).

Index

1992 Update Index

Outdoor Guide to the San Francisco Bay Area
1992 Update

p. 1, last paragraph: People for Open Space has changed its name to Greenbelt Alliance; phone 415-543-4291.

p. 3, paragraph 3: An unusually rainy March in 1992 granted a temporary respite from six years of drought.

p. 5, 6th line from bottom: As all inhabitants of the Global Village are surely well aware by now, on October 17, 1989, an earthquake measuring 7.1 on the Richter scale occurred on the San Andreas Fault. Its epicenter was about 60 miles southeast of San Francisco. The quake was christened "Loma Prieta" for a peak near the epicenter. In this Update I mention a few of the most noticeable effects the quake had on the areas described in this book.

p. 7, Organization: The new address of Save San Francisco Bay Association is 1736 Franklin Street, 3rd floor, Oakland 94612; phone 510-452-9261; FAX 510-452-9266.

p. 7, Recommended reading about the Bay: Mikiten, Erick, *A Wheelchair Rider's Guide to San Francisco Bay and Nearby Shorelines.* California State Coastal Conservancy, 1330 Broadway, Suite 1100, Oakland 94612-2530: 1990. Very detailed and helpful.

p. 8: The scientific name of poison oak has been changed from *Rhus diversiloba* to *Toxicodendron diversiloba.*

p. 10, bottom: On October 20, 1991, a wildfire raged through the Berkeley-Oakland hills, killing over 30 people and causing hundreds of millions of dollars in damage. Some eucalyptus haters blamed the plentiful trees for speeding the fire's spread.

p. 19, after 1988: 1989—On October 17 a 15-second earthquake measuring 7.1 on the Richter scale shakes up northern California, killing 60 persons and inflicting an estimated $10 billion worth of damage.

1991—On October 20 a wildfire rages over the Berkeley-Oakland hills; see note above for p. 10.

p. 20, Recommended reading: Hoover et al., *Historic Spots . . .* 4th ed., rev. by Douglas E. Kyle. Stanford: 1990.

p. 21, paragraph 2: In 1989 a federal commission included the San Francisco Presidio in a list of Army bases to be closed. The foresighted Phil Burton stipulated in the legislation establishing the GGNRA that if the Presidio ever closed, its land would be transferred to the park. On June 15, 1991, dignitaries including House Speaker Thomas Foley dedicated the Phillip Burton Memorial at

Fort Mason. The 10-foot-tall statue of Burton, sculpted by Wendy M. Ross of Maryland, now dominates the Great Meadow as Burton dominated the San Francisco political landscape in life.

The NPS is seeking ideas and advice from the public on future uses of this multimillion-dollar piece of real estate. For information, write Presidio Planning Team, Box 29022, Presidio of San Francisco, San Francisco 94129; phone 415-556-8600. The NPS has also established a Presidio Planning Information Center at GGNRA headquarters in Building 201, Fort Mason. This center will include copies of many technical analyses, maps, meeting summaries and other documents related to the Presidio conversion. Eventually the Center will relocate on the Presidio. Hours: 9–5 Monday through Friday, Saturday by appointment; phone 415-556-3111; FAX 415-556-3122.

The Golden Gate National Park Association has published an Official Map and Guide to the Presidio. It is available at park bookstores or from Mail Order—GGNPA, Fort Mason, Building 201, San Francisco 94123; phone 415-776-1607, ext. 242.

p. 22, Organization: The address of the Golden Gate National Park Association is Building 201, Fort Mason, San Francisco 94123-1308; phone 415-776-0693; FAX 415-776-2205.

The GGNPA has opened the National Park Store for books, maps and other merchandise on Pier 39; hours 10–8:30 daily; phone 415-433-7221.

p. 22, Recommended reading: Rubissow, Ariel, et al., *Golden Gate National Recreation Area Park Guide.* San Francisco: Golden Gate National Park Association, 1990. A pocket guide, plentifully and colorfully illustrated with photos and maps.

p. 27, bottom: The Loma Prieta earthquake of October 17, 1989, drastically affected the Bay Area's transportation scene. The greatest loss of life occurred during the collapse of a freeway, the Cypress section of I-880 in West Oakland, which may never be rebuilt. As everyone knows, a section fell out of the Bay Bridge. Miraculously enough, Caltrans managed to repair it in just a little over a month. Perhaps just as miraculously, our previously much-maligned BART saved the day for Bay Area transit: it went through the quake without damage, and while the bridge was closed BART carried unprecedented loads of people between San Francisco and the East Bay without major mishap. From a pre-quake ridership of about 218,000 per weekday it went to a high of over 350,000 on some days. One can hardly imagine how disastrous the post-quake Bay Area economic scene would have been without BART.

One interesting consequence of the Bay Bridge closure was the appearance of commute ferry service between San Francisco and the East Bay for the first time in a half-century. For a while ferries were running regularly to the Ferry Building from Vallejo, Richmond, Berkeley, Oakland and Alameda. The boats acquired enthusiastic bands of devotees, but, alas, not enough to make them self-supporting, and they had to be heavily subsidized by Caltrans. As this goes to press, some of them are still running, but PHONE FIRST to be sure: Red & White Fleet (San Francisco, Angel Island, Tiburon, Vallejo), 415-546-BOAT, 415-546-2815; Alameda-Oakland-San Francisco Ferry, 510-522-3300. A wheelchair-accessible ferry terminal is located at Clay Street in Oakland's Jack London Square.

Berkeley TRiP Commute Store is a good source of up-to-date information on ferries and all other transit. Its address is 2033 Center Street, Berkeley 94704; phone 510-644-POOL (510-644-7665); hours M–F 8:30–5:30. TRiP also sells tickets, passes and maps for the major Bay Area transit systems.

The Metropolitan Transportation Commission (MTC) issues an invaluable booklet called *Regional Transit Guide*. It is available for a moderate price from bookstores or from the Commission (510-464-7738).

p. 30, paragaph 2, Recommended reading: Drummond, Roger, *Ticks and What You Can Do About Them.* Berkeley: Wilderness Press, 1990.

p. 33, bottom: Discord continues between mountain bikers and other trail users, especially as regards single-track trails in the Marin Headlands and the Tamalpais area. At one point the Bicycle Trails Council of Marin threatened to sue the GGNRA over the perceived unfairness of its trail policy. If you want to ride a mountain bike—or if you want to *avoid* mountain bikes—it is essential to get up-to-date trail rules from the appropriate administering agency. In general, the speed limit is 15 miles per hour, and 5 m.p.h. when passing and on blind turns.

p. 34, paragraph 3: As a consequence of California's budget problems, the State Park System has raised its fees. Most campsites now start at $12, day-use parking at $5. Reservations are still made by phoning Mistix at 1-800-444-7275. Senior citizens (age 62+), the disabled, disabled veterans and former prisoners of war are entitled to special discounts and passes; for information write Department of Parks and Recreation, Box 942896, Sacramento 94296-0001.

p. 35, paragraph 2: Both the Bay Trail and Ridge Trail projects are progressing rapidly. For information about the Bay Trail, phone ABAG at 510-464-7961. The Ridge Trail Council now has an office at 311 California Street, Suite 300, San Francisco 94104; phone 415-391-0697.

p. 36, paragraph 3: The Redwood Empire Association is now located at 785 Market Street, 15th floor, San Francisco 94103; phone 415-543-8338.

p. 41, last paragraph: The correct phone number for the Angel Island-Tiburon Ferry is 415-435-2131.

GGT is talking about instituting a bus route between San Rafael and the Richmond BART station; if you are interested, phone 415-453-2100.

p. 42, Facility: Coastal Lodging of West Marin, Box 1162, Point Reyes Station 94956; phone 415-663-1351. An organization offering information about the ever-burgeoning supply of bed-and-breakfast places in the area.

p. 43, Address and phone: In 1990 the GGNRA moved its Marin Headlands Visitor Center to the old Fort Barry Chapel at Bunker and Field roads, near the junction with Conzelman. The building is wheelchair accessible. Hours: 8:30–4:30 every day except Christmas; phone 415-331-1540.

p. 43, How to get there by car: The 70-year-old tunnel leading to Fort Cronkhite was closed in the spring of 1989 because ominous cracks had appeared in its ceiling—even before the earthquake! The tunnel may be closed for years, but you can still reach the headlands via scenic Conzelman Road.

p. 46, Facilities: The visitor center has relocated to the Fort Barry Chapel, as noted above under p. 43.

p. 46, New facility: The Bay Area Discovery Museum, "a children's museum for ihe whole family," has opened in old Army buildings at 557 East Fort Baker Road. Hours 10–5 Wednesday through Sunday; moderate fee for adults, small fee for children; phone 415-332-7674. The museum is wheelchair accessible. Coming from the north on Highway 101, take the Sausalito exit; from the south, the Alexander exit; then look for the signs.

p. 47, Regulations: See note above for p. 33 on mountain bike rules; get up-to-date information from one of the visitor centers.

p. 48, Recommended reading: DeCoster, Miles, et al., *Headlands: The Marin Coast at the Golden Gate.* Albuquerque: Published for the Headlands Center for the Arts by the University of New Mexico Press, 1989. Many photos.

p. 52, Description: The visitor center has moved (see above, p. 43) but there is still a parking lot at the trailhead north of Building 1050.

p. 53, How to get there: The new visitor center is closer to the Bobcat trailhead than the old one.

p. 56, bottom: The phone number of the Golden Gate Raptor Observatory is 415-331-0730.

p. 57, paragraph 3: While the tunnel is closed, you must return via Bunker and McCullough roads.

p. 64, Facilities: In January 1990 a new visitor center opened at the entrance. The GGNPA raised the funds for it. Constructed of cedar, the hexagon-shaped building is designed to fit in with the CCC style used elsewhere on Tamalpais. It is wheelchair accessible. Hours: 9–4:30 Monday through Friday, 9–5 Saturday and Sunday; phone 415-388-2596.

p. 64, Recommended reading: Hart, John, *Muir Woods, Redwood Refuge*. San Francisco, GGNPA, 1991.

p. 69, line 5: Southside Road is now Pantoll Road.

p. 74, paragraph 1: See note above, p. 33.

p. 74, Organizations: Mt. Tamalpais Interpretive Association, 801 Panoramic Highway, Mill Valley 94941; phone 415-388-2070; leads hikes on weekends.

p. 74, Facilities: Because of storm damage, Lee Shansky Camp has been closed indefinitely.

RVs and other self-contained vehicles may stay in the "enroute campground" at Pan Toll for one night only, between 6 P.M. and 9 A.M. only. The "campground" is simply the lower parking lot—no facilities available.

Picnicking is available at Bootjack (groups may reserve by phoning 415-456-5218), Rock Spring and East Peak; not at Pan Toll.

p. 74, Regulations: The state park is collecting a moderate day-use parking fee at Pan Toll, Bootjack and East Peak.

p. 75, Nearby facilities: The phone number for the Mountain Home Inn is 415-381-9000.

p. 75, Recommended reading: Spitz, Barry, *Tamalpais Trails*. Potrero Meadow Publishing Co., Box 3007, San Anselmo 94960. Spitz has been hiking and running these trails for years.

p. 75, bottom. Recommended viewing: Chater, Cris, *Steaming Up Tamalpais*. This award-winning 25-minute film is now available on video for $30 (plus California sales tax) from Chater at 61 Matilda Avenue, Mill Valley 94941; phone 415-383-6138.

p. 77, Facilities: Lee Shansky Camp is closed indefinitely.

p. 77 and p. 84, maps: Southside Road is now Pantoll Road.

p. 85, Facilities: During periods of drought the water at Laurel Dell may not be potable.

p. 97, Regulations: Moderate parking fee; see note above for p. 74, Regulations.

p. 118, Facilities: A group picnic area in Miwok Meadows can be reserved by phoning 415-456-5218.

p. 118, Regulations:. The state is now charging a moderate parking fee.

p. 124: The Redwood Grove group picnic area can be reserved by phoning 415-456-5218.

p. 130, Facilities: An additional Seashore phone number, 415-663-9029, gives a recorded message about the day's weather, campsite availability and whale visibility. The Seashore broadcasts park information on AM1610; tune in your car radio when driving on Bear Valley Road or toward the lighthouse.

p. 132, Nearby facilities: Another organization providing lodging information is: Bed and Breakfast Cottages of Point Reyes, phone 415-927-9445. The National Seashore headquarters also issues a free list of nearby inns and motels.

Olema Ranch Campground accommodates RVs; phone 415-663-8001.

Trail Head Rentals, 88 Bear Valley Road (just off Highway 1) in Olema rents mountain bikes, tents, daypacks, binoculars and other gear; phone 415-663-1958.

Bear Valley Stables no longer rents horses, but Five Brooks Stables leads trail rides. Reservations are advisable for weekends; phone 415-663-1570.

Camelid Capers provides pack llamas for day trips into the National Seashore; phone 415-669-1523.

p. 132, Recommended reading: Evens, Jules G., *Natural History of the Point Reyes Peninsula.* Point Reyes: Point Reyes National Seashore Association, 1988.

p. 138: The phone number for Golden Gate Transit in Sonoma County is 707-544-1323.

p. 139, paragraph 2: The Wine Train is now running between Napa and St. Helena, currently two round trips every weekday and three on weekends and holidays. It features gourmet meals. The locals are still grumbling, but apparently many people who have ridden the train have found it a charming experience—though not an inexpensive one. For reservations and information phone 1-800-427-4124 or 707-253-2111.

p. 140, line 3: The current address of *Sonoma County Farm Trails* is Box 6032, Santa Rosa 95406.

p. 145, Facilities: Armstrong Woods Pack Station runs overnight pack trips into the Recreation Area seasonally; phone 707-887-2939.

p. 164: Bale Grist Mill open weekends; demonstrations at 1 and 4 P.M.; moderate parking fee; phone 707-963-2236.

pp. 165-240: The telephone area code for all numbers in Alameda and Contra Costa counties is now 510.

p. 168, paragraph 1: The new address of the EBRPD is 2950 Peralta Oaks Court, Box 5381, Oakland 94605-0381. The phone number for the administrative offices is 510-635-0135; for general information 510-562-PARK.

p. 168, Facilities: The EBRPD issues an annual pass entitling the cardholder to free parking, free swimming, camping discounts and a monthly newsletter. For information and rates, write EBRPD Public Affairs Dept.-Parks Pass, Box 5381, Oakland 94605-0381.

The EBRPD has a variety of camping facilities available to the public by reservation, notably at Anthony Chabot Park (see p. 207) and at Del Valle Park near Livermore. Reservations may be made Monday through Friday, from 8:30 to 4, by phoning one of four numbers in the 510 area code: from the Oakland area, 562-CAMP; from Contra Costa County, 676-0192; from the Livermore area, 373-0144; from the Hayward area, 538-6470.

p. 168, Regulations: The EBRPD has raised some of its fees.

p. 173, paragraph 5: New address and phone numbers for EBRPD, see note above for p. 168, para. 1.

p. 175: In 1992, financially troubled AC Transit is threatening to eliminate some of its routes; for up-to-date information, phone the system or Berkeley TRiP at 510-644-7665.

GGT is talking about running a bus between San Rafael and the Richmond BART station; for information phone 415-453-2100.

p. 176, Recommended reading: Mosier, Page, and Dan Mosier, *Alameda County Place Names.* Fremont: Mines Road Books, 1986.

Pitcher, Don, and Malcolm Margolin, *Berkeley Inside/Out.* Berkeley: Heyday Books, 1989.

p. 177, How to get there: AC Transit #78 is now running on Sundays; but see note for p. 175, above.

p. 180, How to get there: AC Transit #71 runs from the Richmond BART station to Clark Road.

p. 184 and p. 185, How to get there: The #7 is currently on AC Transit's tentative hit list.

p. 184, Facilities: Delete the archery range and the tennis courts. For new address and phone numbers of EBRPD, see note above for p. 168, para. 1.

p. 195, Features: The disastrous fire of October 20, 1991, began at a spot near this section of the trail.

p. 200, How to get there: AC Transit #46 runs from the Coliseum BART station to the former EBRPD headquarters at 11500 Skyline Blvd., whence trails lead into the park. On weekends #46 also runs to Roberts Recreation Area.

p. 203, Facilities: Roberts Recreation Area swimming pool is disabled-accessible. New phone numbers for EBRPD: see note above for p. 168, para. 1.

p. 207, Facilities: Ticketron has closed its California outlets. The campsites are now reservable by calling the numbers listed above for p. 168, Facilities.

p. 207–08, Lake Chabot Facilities: Fishing dock accessible by wheelchair.

p. 212, How to get there by car, paragraph 1: The west end begins at Coyote Hills Park: From Highway 880 (Nimitz Freeway) exit at Decoto Road/Highway 84, go west on Decoto to the Thornton Avenue/ Paseo Padre Parkway exit, north on Paseo Padre a mile to Patterson Ranch Road and west on it to its end. From the Dumbarton Bridge (Highway 84) go north on Paseo Padre and continue as above.

p. 215, Phone: 510-795-9385.

p. 216, Facilities: New phone numbers for EBRPD: see note above for p. 168, para. 1.

p. 223, Facilities: Ditto.

p. 236, paragraph 2: The EBRPD has succeeded in buying Las Trampas Peak and has constructed a trail to it.

p. 237, Facilities: See note above for p. 168, para. 1.

p. 245: The current address for the Santa Clara Valley Chapter of the Audubon Society is 22221 McClellan Road, Cupertino 95014; phone 408-252-3747. The current address of the Loma Prieta Chapter of the Sierra Club is 2448 Watson Court, Palo Alto 94303; phone 415-494-9901.

p. 247: SamTrans information number: 1-800-660-4BUS (660-4287).

p. 248, Recommended reading: Trail Center, *Peninsula Parklands: A Guide to Outdoor Recreation in Santa Clara, San Mateo,*

Santa Cruz and San Francisco Counties. Los Altos: Trail Center, 1989. An indispensable map and guide available from the Trail Center (see p. 245).

Coastside Harvest Trails available free with SASE from 765 Main Street, Half Moon Bay 94019.

Rusmore and Spangle, *South Bay Trails.* 2nd ed., 1991.

p. 248: Phone for campground: 408-438-2396.

p. 252, Maps: See note above, p. 248, about Trail Center's *Peninsula Parklands.* The *Skyline to the Sea* maps may also be obtained from the Trail Center.

p. 254, Facilities: Wheelchair-accessible nature trail.

p. 257, Maps: See note above for p. 252.

p. 257, How to get there by bus: These buses currently run on weekends only.

p. 259, end paragraph 2: After the Loma Prieta earthquake of October 17, 1989, the park had to close for almost two weeks because of damage to its water system. The quake also destroyed five stone chimneys and caused rockslides and cracks on the access road, Highway 236.

The epicenter of the quake was about 20 miles southeast of Big Basin in the Forest of Nisene Marks State Park. That hitherto not-very-popular park has now become a magnet for hikers eager to visit this geological phenomenon.

p. 259, bottom: Big Basin is experimenting with tent cabins, a bit like those in Yosemite, for those visitors who prefer something a little more luxurious than a regular campsite, or who don't want to buy or rent a tent. The fees are somewhat higher than regular state-park campsite fees. Reservations are available from Mistix.

p. 264–65, Facilities and Regulations: Delete phone number 879-0454; call 415-879-0227 for a recorded schedule. Reservations for guided tours, November through April, should now be made through Mistix, not Ticketron; tickets go on sale at the beginning of November.

p. 272, Facilities: Current museum hours are 10–5 Tuesday through Saturday, noon–5 Sunday.

p. 274, Additional walking tours:

Chinatown Discovery Tours, 415-982-8839;

Culinary Walktours of Chinatown and North Beach, 415-441-5637;

Helen's Walk Tours (various parts of San Francisco), 510-524-4544;

San Francisco Presidio, 415-923-WALK.

p. 275, paragraph 2: Muni issues an invaluable map and guide to its system, updated every year or so. It is available for a small price at drugstores, map stores and other outlets all over the City.

p. 275, Recommended reading: Bakalinsky, *Stairway Walks in San Francisco,* 2nd ed., 1992.

p. 278, Recommended reading: See note above for p. 22.

p. 279, paragraph 6: See note above for p. 21, paragraph 2.

p. 292, line 5: The #41 now runs only during weekday peak periods.

p. 298: The current address for the Sierra Club's Loma Prieta Chapter is 2448 Watson Court, Palo Alto 94303; phone 415-494-9901; for the San Francisco Bay Chapter, 5237 College Avenue, Oakland 94618; phone 510-653-6127. The current address for the Golden Gate Audubon Society is 2530 San Pablo Avenue, Suite G, Berkeley 94702; phone 510-843-2222.

p. 299, Facilities for the disabled:

Fishing pier: Lake Chabot, 207.

Museums, visitor centers: Bay Area Discovery Museum, see note above for p. 46; Muir Woods visitor center, see note above for p. 64.

Recommended reading: *Wheelchair Rider's Guide . . . ,* see note above for p. 7.

Swimming pool: Roberts Recreation Area, 203.